A KEEN SOLDIER

A KEEN SOLDIER

THE EXECUTION OF SECOND WORLD WAR
PRIVATE HAROLD PRINGLE

ANDREW CLARK

ALFRED A. KNOPF CANADA

PUBLISHED BY ALFRED A. KNOPF CANADA

Copyright © 2002 Andrew Clark

National Library of Canada Cataloguing in Publication Data

Clark, Andrew, 1966–
A keen soldier : the execution of Second World War Private
Harold Joseph Pringle.
/ Andrew Clark.

ISBN 0-676-97354-X

1. Pringle, Harold Joseph. 2. Military offenses—Canada—History.
3. Courts-martial and courts of inquiry—Canada—History.
4. Executions and executioners—Canada—History. 5. World War,
1939–1945—Canada. 6. Soldiers—Canada—Biography. I. Title.

KE7177.P75C53 2002   343.71'014   C2002-902094-8

First Edition

www.randomhouse.ca

Text design: Daniel Cullen

Page 324 constitutes a continuation of the copyright page.

Printed and bound in the United States of America

2 4 6 8 9 7 5 3 1

For my grandfather
Major Thomas Alexander Jamieson
and his son Thomas Meighen Jamieson.
"No more lamentations."

CONTENTS

1.

CASERTA

The sun was up over Avellino. Light filled the small valley and fired the branches of the pine and chestnut trees that sprang from the mountains surrounding the town. Vineyards stretched across the Italian countryside, and occasionally a bird broke the silence of the morning quiet with its call. In a ruined castle above Avellino by the main road to Naples, a young Canadian soldier named Harold Joseph Pringle slept in his tiny room on a hard cot. During the Second World War, Canadian soldiers had used the castle to watch for smugglers and black marketeers bringing illegal goods from one city to the next.

At one time, tens of thousands of Allied troops, most of them Canadian, had been stationed in Avellino. By July 5, 1945, however, the war was over and the armies that had raged over Italy were no longer necessary. The Canadians were all gone. In fact, there were only thirty-one Canadians in the entire country. But there was one more task to perform before the final residue of the Canadian army could go home.

Shoot Harold Pringle.

A mile from Pringle's cell, five Canadian privates dressed in pressed uniforms eyed their watches as they assembled outside their headquarters. It was fifteen minutes to six in the morning, but it was July, so the sun was already shining brightly. The brigadier appeared and gave a nod to a sergeant who was standing by. It was time to get going. The soldiers climbed into two jeeps and drove up the winding road.

The brigadier was a veteran of the First World War, and as they drove it occurred to him that the Canadian army had not executed a single soldier during this entire war. That was a change from the last one, in which 26 Canadian soldiers had been put to death. Over one million Canadians served in uniform during the Second World War, and 92,757 of these men had fought in Italy between 1943 and 1945. Of those, more than a quarter, 26,254, were killed or wounded. Canadians had fought in Japan, Burma, France, Germany, Sicily, Italy, Holland and Africa, and during this time some had fallen on the wrong side of military justice for crimes ranging from theft to rape to murder. Yet not one had been deemed to necessitate a military firing squad. It was, the brigadier thought, a situation that the Canadian brass in Ottawa and London could not abide. So, on July 5, 1945, he and thirty Canadians were to correct this imbalance by turning Harold Pringle into that singular casualty. Harold Pringle, whose name the brigadier had found so innocuous when he had first heard it, would be the only soldier executed by the Canadian army during the entire war. In fact, he would turn out to be the last soldier ever executed by the Canadian army.

The jeep rolled down the dry dirt road. One private whispered to his friend, "Do you suppose he will already be awake?"

Soon the brigadier's party pulled up beside the old castle and the soldiers dragged themselves out. The brigadier was now shaking. As he and his men approached the castle, the guards who had spent the night outside Harold's room stepped sheepishly aside. Inside, they found a chaplain from the British army who had been ministering to Harold. He had spent the night sleeping in the same quarters as the sentries. It was five minutes to six in the morning. The brigadier recognized the priest. "You know why we're here," he told him. "You can be on hand if you like."

The men then walked silently past the chaplain to the door of Harold's cell. The priest called out, "Harold, Harold, son. We are coming in."

Harold was lying on his cot, clothed, and he began to awaken. He thought, I must have finally fallen asleep. An officer Harold did not know began speaking.

"Private Harold Joseph Pringle, His Excellency the Governor General in council…"

The chaplain laid a hand on Harold's shoulder.

Harold felt a cold tingling buzz up the small of his back. He scanned the room nervously. "Harold, we received word from Ottawa," said the priest. "They found against you. Your appeal has been denied. So it will be today, this morning." Harold knew what "it" meant. By eight o'clock this morning it would all be over. Once he was dead, his guards and executioners could all go home. He would never go home.

As the words fell on Harold's ears, he felt the priest's hand on his shoulder. He heard the priest ask if he had any requests, any food he wanted.

"Do you want a bit of rum?"

"No, I never cared much for drinking," he said.

The priest handed Harold a cigarette, which he took and lit. Harold looked east out his barred window and saw the blue Italian sky hug the green banks of the mountains that surrounded Avellino. It was just an optical trick, but the mountains looked surprisingly close. Harold could see details, small trees and shrubs on their cliffs. One of the privates gave him a sheet of army paper and a pencil. Harold sat at a small table, on which lay three prayer books, one volume of the New Testament, and the book *True Devotion to the Blessed Virgin Mary*. His wallet was also there, in it a few snapshots of family and old girlfriends; there was a tin box with his rosary, two medals (which would later be confiscated) and a mirror, badly broken. Harold inhaled deeply and felt the tobacco burn.

He began:

July 5, 1945
C5292 Pte. Harold Pringle
My Darling Mother and Father and Brothers and Sisters,
Well Mother Darling this is going to be an awful surprise to you
all and I sure hope and pray that you dont take it too hard. But
the papers have just come back from Canada....[1]

FIFTY-FIVE YEARS LATER, in the Italian city of Caserta, I stood before Harold Pringle's grave and stared at an ash that was nestled on the wet, green grass before his gravestone. It was a cigarette ash, cylindrical and small and fresh-looking. It was curious. Curious because as far as I knew, I had been the only person to stand at Harold Pringle's grave since his burial. I had walked through the graveyard looking for Harold's plot. For a moment, I had thought it would never be found and was overcome with a kind of foolish despair. Then the cemetery's gardener had appeared. "*Dove* Harold Pringle?" I asked him in Italian: "Where is Harold Pringle?" He was obviously accustomed to this kind of enquiry. He tucked his hand under my arm the way Italians do, with a firm and friendly grip, and he guided me to Grave 11, plot 8. The walk seemed to take an eternity.

"Here," the gardener said in Italian. "Pringle is here."

When asked if Harold received many visitors, the gardener replied, "You are the first." He left and I was transfixed. Then I knelt down for a closer look, reading the inscription: "H. J. Pringle. Hastings and Prince Edward Regiment. Age 23. 5 July 1945." On a rose bush to the right of his marker, a single red bud prepared to bloom.

Seven hundred and seventy men lay in Caserta Cemetery, a large marble crucifix looming up before them like an officer inspecting troops. The men came from all over the Commonwealth. There were 498 from the United Kingdom, 98 from Canada, 6 from Australia, 49 from New Zealand, 54 from South Africa and 1 from the British West Indies. Most died young, in their early twenties, but occasionally there was an older soldier tucked in their midst, a sergeant aged thirty-eight or a thirty-four-year-old private. The scene reminded me of a passage written by a British soldier and published in the army newspaper *The Union Jack*. It described being under fire during a nighttime bombardment. The soldier looked up:

> I shivered—it was very cold and, even as I looked, it seemed to
> me that the moon was obscured, not by a cloud, but by a great
> array of marching men. They marched soundlessly, with set
> shoulders and unwavering mien. Unaccountably, I knew that here
> was a parade of the dead of all the wars of the world since time
> began…There were faces I recognized—God, so many faces.
> Young men, those of my own generation and, involuntarily, here

and there I called a name as some known and loved face passed me by.[2]

I LAID A BUNDLE of lilies on Harold's grave. The wind, cool and fresh with salt from the Mediterranean Sea, blew gently across my face. Looking down at the ground beneath me, I saw the ash and thought that it must have been left recently, since for the past four days it had rained steadily. Here was evidence that someone had stood where I was standing, perhaps only a few hours before. The gardener might have dropped it, but he wasn't smoking now. Was this evidence that I was not the first?

The idea was incomprehensible. It was impossible to imagine that anyone would have gone to the trouble of finding Harold Joseph Pringle. My own journey to him had begun as a preoccupation that had eventually consumed me. To learn his story I had quit a job that had taken ten years to gain, studied Italian, spent money that wasn't there, travelled fifty thousand kilometres in cars and planes, in trains and boats and by foot, and pored over countless dusty files in libraries in North America and Europe—all in an attempt to learn the story of a man whom the Canadian government and army had killed and then made every effort to erase. It became obvious that I was not writing this book—I was serving it. It would end when the book decided it was finished.

To some, my book was degenerate. "Three hundred and forty-four people in this regiment died in World War II and he's the least one to give any honours to," Don Kernaghan, an executive with the Hastings and Prince Edward Regiment Association, told me when I called him in March 2000 asking for permission to interview veterans from Pringle's outfit. "I'm not interested in seeing him made a hero and I don't think anybody else in this unit is. He is a slur on the whole name of the regiment."[3]

So, while standing at Harold Pringle's grave, at the moment Winston Churchill would have called "the end of the beginning," my thoughts ran back to the first time I heard his story.

It was Christmas Eve 1986, and my family was at my grandparents' house in Ottawa for the usual festivities. My maternal grandfather, Thomas Jamieson, was a veteran, a Canadian who had served as an officer with the British Eighth Army in Italy. Like many veterans, he found remembering his time spent overseas uncomfortable and he said little to his family about his experience fighting in Europe. The day the Second World War began, my grandfather and his friend Jack Bennett were painting my great-grandmother's house. They set down their brushes, walked to the nearest town and enlisted. Tom Jamieson signed on as a private and was quickly promoted to the rank of lieutenant. He was shipped out in 1942, a few months before his first son, Tommy, was born.

The war left those who fought it changed, superficially or otherwise. My grandfather, for instance, left with a full head of hair and returned almost completely bald. After the war, he displayed what is now called post-traumatic stress disorder. There were nightmares, a hatred of loud noises, occasional remoteness, a love of drinking. Whatever he was dealing with was a solitary concern. Grandpa's war experiences were not up for discussion.

We knew he had been in Italy and had fought at Monte Cassino. Later, while I researched this book, I discovered that he had worked as a British officer attached to the Polish Corps when it attacked Monte Cassino. He acted as a liaison officer and communicated with the British by radio while the attacks were prepared, then went up with them while the attacks were underway. On May 11, 1944, two Polish divisions were ordered to storm up the sheer cliffs across ground that had already claimed thousands of lives. They picked their way through gullies and brambles and debris and over corpses that had been rotting for months until they came into range of the German machine guns. The Poles fell in waves, but they pressed on and held through the night while the Germans pounded them with artillery. When the sun came up, the Germans began picking off the survivors. By midday, half the divisions were gone. The survivors retreated. On May 23, the Poles were at it again. This time they captured their objective. In all, the two weeks of attacks cost 281 officers and 3,503 men killed or wounded. Historians would later describe the Polish attacks as "selfless immolation." During the battle, as my grandfather burrowed for cover, he discovered a medieval tapestry of the Crucifixion of Christ stuck inside some rubble. When he and his fellow officers reached the rubble, he handed the tapestry to an

Italian priest. Then an army photographer snapped a picture. The black and white photograph shows a handful of exhausted men standing in ruins, all looking perplexed and despondent.

What little I knew I had learned from my grandmother, Marion. "He really didn't like talking about it," she said. "But every now and then he would say something, about being under fire or about the children in Naples starving. The soldiers looked at it as a horrible job but they had to do it."[4] But on this particular Christmas Eve, my grandfather broke his silence. Someone mentioned the Australian movie *Breaker Morant*, about Australian soldiers who were wrongly accused of murder and executed during the Boer War.

"Yes," my grandfather said. "Military justice. I know about military justice."

He told the family about a Canadian private named Pringle. This soldier, it seemed, had fought in Italy and then, for some unknown reason, had deserted. He made his way to Rome and then fell in with a gang of other deserters. These men made a living by hijacking trucks on the roads outside of Rome. My grandfather did not go into too many details. There had been a murder, and Pringle had been implicated. The army decided he would pay with his life and ordered the few remaining Canadians in Italy to carry out the sentence. There was almost no one left to kill him, and my grandfather was one of a handful of officers considered for running the execution. "We had to train the cooks how to fire rifles," he said, "because there were no Canadian combat troops left in Italy to do the job." Pringle, he recalled, "was a nice chap whom no one disliked." The loathsome chore of leading the firing squad had been tossed between the few Canadian officers left in the Italian sector. Ultimately, it fell on another "nice chap"—a captain from the Calgary Tanks. After my grandfather finished telling this story, I saw what I thought were one or two tears well up in his eyes. Later on, perhaps sensing my literary aspirations, he told me, "It would be best if those involved were dead when this story gets out."[5]

Years later, my grandmother told me that my grandfather had been terrified by the prospect of leading the firing squad. "The way he told it was, in a battle, you were part of a cast of thousands, so to speak, you did

what you had to in order to survive. It was kill or be killed. But killing a
Canadian in cold blood was something else entirely. I'm so grateful he
didn't have to do it, because I'm sure it would have destroyed him, he
would never have recovered."[6]

Harold Pringle's story put the hook in me, and I had a kindred spirit
in my grandfather's eldest son Tommy, who was three years old when my
grandfather returned from the war. Over time they forged a bond, but a
distance remained from that early separation. In Pringle, Tommy saw the
possibility of answers. Why, Tommy wondered, had his father been so
moved by the Pringle story? We all knew that Tom Jamieson had seen
and done things in Italy that had left scars, but he had never shown that
kind of emotion. Pringle was special. For some reason this doomed soldier's story encapsulated some cynical truth for my grandfather, a truth
only those who had lived through the war could understand.
Unfortunately, my uncle never got to figure it out. He died in 1991, and
for a few years Pringle's story drifted to the background. Every now and
then I would find myself thinking about it and wondering just what had
happened. For the most part, however, I left it alone.

It was on a trip to visit my grandfather at the Perley and Rideau
Veterans' Health Centre in Ottawa that my interest was rekindled.

It was Thanksgiving 1998, and as with all my other trips to visit
him, I walked past rooms full of quiet, frail men. Outside each living
quarter was a glass cabinet. These were decorated with pictures of soldiers, now old, in their prime—virile, smiling men. There were black
and white images of uniformed youngsters holding children they
would leave behind for war, and posed portraits, hat on, eyes right, sent
back from France or Italy or Holland to show a wife or mother that he
was all right.

On that day, I sat beside my grandfather, holding a box of choco-
lates, talking about other grandchildren. He had a habit of discussing
those who weren't present. Perhaps he felt more comfortable expressing
himself that way. What was Matthew doing? How was Amy? My grandmother sat on the other side of the hospital bed, smiling. Occasionally
she would ask, "Do you want some tea, Tom?" Outside, it was a crisp,
bright, cold Ottawa Valley October day. It was all very normal. My mind

wandered to the holiday food and wine that were waiting for me, perhaps drinks with old friends after the family gathering.

Then there was an interruption. From down the hall came a steady "Baaaa, baaaaa, baaaa." It sounded like an inhuman mixture of animal and man. My grandfather raised one of his broad hands and brushed it over his eyes, across his forehead and down past the back of his head. I recognized the gesture immediately. It was a family trait, a sign passed down through generations of Jamiesons that signifies utter irritation. I do it. My brother does it. My uncle Tommy did it. After completing the gesture, my grandfather exhaled an exasperated "Jesus Christ." In this succinct, old-fashioned curse, my grandfather could pack tons of unexpressed rage.

"Baaaaa, baaaaa, baaaaa."

"Oh, Jesus Christ."

The Sheep Man, as we nicknamed him, became a fixture in my visits. My brother Matthew and I joked about him. Regardless, his "baaaing" was accepted. When you visited Grandpa, you heard the Sheep Man, and that was that. Then, one morning, Matthew called from Ottawa.

"I was up at the Perley and that sheep guy was going at it," he told me. "He's going 'baaaaa' and it's driving Grandpa crazy, you know, he's saying 'Jesus Christ.'"

"Yeah."

"So, Granny says, 'Be nice Tom, it's just Doug.'" The "baaaaaaaing" then got louder, and Grandpa's hand was working like a windshield wiper on his forehead. "And I say, 'Who's Doug?' And Granny says, totally matter-of-fact, 'Oh, he was a machine gunner in the war.'" Matthew paused a moment. "He's not making *sheep* noises, man," he said, "he's making *machine gun* noises."

"A machine gunner?"

"Granny said he had a family and a good job after the war, and now his mind is gone and all that's left for him is making those machine gun noises."[7]

That is when I began to wonder if it really was the dead who made the supreme sacrifice. Maybe it was the soldiers who survived who, in the final tally, gave the most. They came home with memories and with, perhaps, the nagging question of whether it was all worth it. A researcher named Samuel A. Stouffer put the conundrum best in a 1949 book *The American Soldier: Combat and Its Aftermath.* "There is one great fear in the heart of every serviceman," he wrote, "and it is not that he will be killed or maimed, but that when he is finally allowed to go home and piece together what he can of life, that he will be made to feel that he has been a sucker for the sacrifices he has made."[8]

I KNEW HOW HAROLD PRINGLE would have answered that question, and as I stood before his grave, I thought of the letters he had written back home to his family. He had only a Grade 6 education and his writing was marred by spelling and grammatical errors, yet the sentiments were clear. "I sure will be awful glad when I see you all again," he wrote. "It sure has been a long time hasn't it. And how." "Well Mother Darling I haven't heard anything about my trial yet but I [don't] think it will much longer now. I wish I could tell you everything but the good Lord knows it all and knows I am not guilty of what they charged me with." Most of all, I recalled how he had longed for snow. Harold Pringle dreamt of snow as only a Canadian could, knowing the beauty and comfort its cool whiteness can provide: "Say you said they had lots of snow in the old road well we hardly ever see snow over here or in England. All the time I've been over seas I have never seen any more than an inch of snow. I sure will be glad when the day comes to get back where there is lots of snow. And how."[9]

I looked out toward Mount Vesuvius, which stretched twelve hundred metres upwards, its peak disappearing in cloud. The sky was a pale blue, tinted grey by petrol fumes. The landscape was brown and green, speckled with orange trees whose fruit clung to branches lush with dark green leaves. Palm trees rose above the cemetery walls, and the smooth green lawns and foliage reminded me of an English garden. The white marble markers were unscathed by weather and time. The rows were adorned with roses and other flowers, symbolizing youth and life. It was beautiful, but Harold would never see snow here.

I reached into my pocket and a retrieved a letter sent to Harold's mother by the Welsh priest who witnessed her son's execution.

My Dear Mrs. Pringle,

I have delayed in sending this letter of sympathy in order that I would not be the first to break to you the sad news of the death of your dear boy Harold. I am the Catholic Chaplain who attended him every day for the six weeks prior to his departure from this world of sorrow and tears and I have no doubt as to his eternal destiny. Every morning from the day I met him, he received Holy Communion and his spirit was indeed sublime. He never complained—was always cheerful and he won the hearts of all who came in contact with him. I assure you his death came as a blow to me personally, and the pain I felt at his untimely end makes me, to some extent, understand what you, his mother, must feel. I have prayed for you and will continue to do so.

May our Divine Lord be your consolation in this great trial which has fallen upon you. Ask the help of Our Lady of Sorrows— think of her there at the foot of the Cross as she received her Divine Son in her arms. She knows what you are going through, she knows it from her own experience, and she will know how to console you. Let your tears mingle with hers and they will lose all their bitterness. You have that great consolation that your dear boy had a saintly death, and you can look forward to the day when you will be reunited to him in the joys of heaven.

I would like to express my sympathy to your husband and all your family and believe me I share with you most intimately your great sorrow. Harold had a big place in my heart—we spent hours together every day and his passing grieved me more than I can say in words. I was with him to the end and immediately said mass for him. I can still see his smiling face before me and my only consolation, which must be yours too, is the thought that he is smiling down on me now from his place in heaven. I feel he is helping me in my work and above all I feel he is helping me to be a better and holier priest.

I would like to ask you a favour—could you possibly let me have a photograph of Harold. I want to have him always before me as a friend and a guide and a teacher—because he has taught me how to live and to die in the love of God.

Once again—accept my most heartfelt and sincere sympathy and may God bless you always.[10]

I FOLDED THE LETTER and placed it back in my pocket. Then I brought out another, different letter. After checking to make sure that the gardener was not watching, and for some reason being careful not to disturb the cigarette ash, I drove the letter deep into the dirt in front of Harold's tombstone. I had carried the letter from Canada. It was a message Harold Pringle had waited fifty-five years to receive.

2.

FLINTON

M y search for Harold Pringle began in Ottawa at the National Archives of Canada, where I placed an Access to Information Request for his military service record. A service record lists generic information, medical details and conduct reports, and each soldier who served during the war has one. My request took three months to process—the file had to be censored. When I finally got access, the archivist who handed me Pringle's file said it was the largest he had ever seen. But the file did not tell me much about his life before the military. There was nothing of the formative years that psychologists like to muse about. It gave his date of birth, February 16, 1920, and listed his parents' names, Mary Ellen and William Pringle. It listed his hometown as Flinton, Ontario. While factual, these figures told me nothing human about him. I requested a photocopy of the file. The woman who took the order asked me, "The entire file?" and looked askance at the seven-inch stack that sat between us on her desk. "Yes," I replied. "The entire file."

It was lucky I did because listed in bad handwriting on a form among the approximately one thousand pages of documentation were the names of three of Harold's siblings. I knew I now had a shot at finding Harold's family. I began combing through Canadian telephone books looking for Pringles, reminding myself that families back in the 1930s tended to be large and hoping that at least one Pringle sibling might still be in or around Flinton. With a sketchy list in hand, I mailed out bushels of form letters to small towns and cities such as Madoc and Belleville. The letters were brief and addressed to "Pringle Family Members." They asked the recipient if he or she was related to Harold Pringle or had any knowledge of him. After two months and no replies, I made cross-reference searches on the Internet and collected telephone numbers. I began making cold calls. Still there were no results. One morning I made a call to a woman named Veronica and went through what was becoming a pat speech: "Hi, my name is Andrew Clark. I am a journalist researching a book on a man named Harold Joseph Pringle. I was wondering, were you related to Harold Joseph Pringle or do you have any knowledge of him?"

A woman's voice answered, meekly, "No, never heard of him." She politely excused herself and hung up.

More weeks went by and hope began to fade. Tracking people down by last name is difficult, especially if they don't want to be found. It seemed likely that I might never see a photograph of Harold Pringle, never even get an accurate description of his personality. Without the words of those who knew him, the book I wanted to write would be nothing more than a collection of statistics and court records. After all, Harold Pringle was no master criminal. He was never immortalized in the newspapers, and following his execution, the Canadian government erased him as fast as it could. In fact, the Canadian military maintained that none of its soldiers were executed during the Second World War. Even the service record I had viewed had been sealed for forty years. If I could not contact a family member, I would be forced to piece Pringle's early years together from pure conjecture.

Then, in mid-May, a woman named Teresa telephoned, saying that Veronica, the woman I had called months before, was in fact Harold Pringle's sister and that she was willing to meet with me. There was a catch—I must come up immediately. I took down the address, walked out of my office and got on the highway. That afternoon, Veronica and Teresa, who turned out to be Harold's younger sisters, greeted me cordially. They were very gracious, but they were both, understandably, suspicious of my motives. "I don't know why you are doing this," Veronica said, running her fingers across the top of her sister's kitchen table. "It's going to cause an awful lot of pain for so many people. Just such an awful lot of pain."[1]

More than anything else, Veronica and Teresa feared publicity. After his execution Harold had become a shameful secret, and there were nephews and nieces who were unaware that he ever existed. He was mourned, but he was rarely mentioned. As the years passed, Harold's sisters and brothers began to hope that his sad story might be left in the past. Harold was dead and no amount of literary handwringing was going to bring him back. My book would broadcast the painful details and cast the spotlight on the remaining family. Veronica and Teresa worried that their neighbours might talk behind their backs and label them a disgrace. The Pringles had suffered enough. "Mother and Father never did recover from it," Teresa told me.[2] Now, thanks to my book, that loss would be rekindled and spread across more generations.

Veronica and Teresa's worry was based on personal experience. In 1985, Harold's fate had been dragged into public view when the Royal Canadian Legion's monthly, *Legion Magazine*, published a story entitled "Still on the Books." The article was based on Harold's military record and a number of interviews with veterans, none of whom knew him. It portrayed Harold as a cold-blooded killer. "The army should have straightened Harold Pringle out," it read, "but it failed to do so."[3] Flinton's local newspaper picked up "Still on the Books" and ran it as a novelty story. When Harold's mother, Mary Ellen Pringle, read the article she was devastated. Prior to seeing it, she had been a healthy eighty-year-old. For the next two weeks, Veronica, Teresa and the rest of the family watched as their mother sank into depression and illness. She died broken-hearted. You would never be able to prove it in a court of law, but as far as the sisters were concerned, there was no question: the public airing of her son's misfortune and the portrayal of him as a ruthless criminal killed Mary Ellen.

"I didn't want to have anything to do with you," Veronica told me. "But we were all talking, and we have been thinking, and I suppose if we don't have anything to do with you...." Here she let out a tired breath. "Well, where will that leave Harold?"

"Somebody has to speak for him," added Teresa. "Somebody has to tell the good things about him. That's why we called you. We saw that they were thinking of pardoning some soldiers who had been executed in the First World War. We thought maybe something could be done for Harold."

While I was pursuing Harold Pringle's story, the notion of courage would pop up again and again. But I never expected to find it in two ladies who served me tea and salmon sandwiches. I couldn't help marvelling at their guts. I met with Harold's sisters twice more after that. On the second visit they allowed me to copy the letters Harold had sent back to Canada while he was overseas.

Veronica and Teresa had been too young when Harold had left to have any adult understanding of his relationship with their parents. Veronica was seven and Teresa three when he went away to war. Teresa's only real memory was a domestic one. Harold was ironing his uniform and, as toddlers do, she was crawling beneath the ironing board, playing with the laundry. Harold stopped ironing, looked down at her and smiled.

Veronica and Teresa, however, knew someone who had been a contemporary of their brother's. It was their cousin, Betti Michael, who was the Pringle family's unofficial historian. Betti was the daughter of Harold's father's sister, and she had grown up in Flinton. She eventually left, had a family of her own and earned her living working for the post office. She was blessed with a quick mind and had an affection for the past. In her spare time she wrote books on local history. Betti was proud of her heritage; she had traced the Pringle family line and collected a scrapbook of photos and memorabilia. Betti had been only ten years old when Harold left for war, but by then she had enough memories to last her a lifetime. "You'll have a great time talking to her," Veronica told me. "She's got stories about everybody."

Betti, who was seven years Harold's junior, lived in Port Robinson, Ontario. Her memories were those of a young farm girl who looked up to Harold as a dashing older figure, and she kept that affection right into her adult life. She recalled that Harold was a very handsome young man, a superb singer and a champion yodeller. At night, on the way back from a friend's farm or from his grandmother's house, Harold would sing and yodel to let his mother know he was on his way home. Betti recalled being

Harold in Flinton before the war.

—

mesmerized by the haunting sound of Harold's songs, which echoed through the dark stillness of the countryside. To her young eyes, Harold was from another world. He had a power and charisma that promised great deeds in the future. She was not the only female in Flinton to sense this potential. "Women loved him. He had a lot of girlfriends. They were crazy for him. He had kind of laughing eyes, as I remember," Betti said. "He was extremely handsome, a very good-looking fellow."[4]

Harold came by his looks honestly. His mother, Mary Ellen Lessard, and his father, William Aubrey Pringle, were both good-looking. Both had been born and bred in Flinton. Betti remembered Harold's mother as a dark-haired, fair-featured woman who was an accomplished cook and homemaker. Mary Ellen prepared succulent jams and preserves; she could sew, clean, tend to farm animals and give medical aid when necessary. Life during the Great Depression was hard. "She had a big family during a tough time," Betti said, "but she always seemed ageless." Money was tight, but like so many of the generation raised on Canadian farms between the wars, the Pringle children "never knew we were poor."[5] According to Veronica, "We always had enough to eat and clothes to wear. There was a lot of love."[6] Harold, it seems, was his mother's favourite and a favourite of the extended family as well.

Harold's father, William Pringle, was born on December 30, 1896. At age nineteen, in 1915, he enlisted in the Canadian Expeditionary Force. William's military record describes him as 5 feet 6 inches with light brown hair and grey eyes. He listed his profession as "farmer," and an army doctor described him as an "excellent" specimen.[7] Yet Billy, as he was known in Flinton, was a gentle, good-hearted fellow, and most of those who knew him found it hard to think of him as a soldier. The transformation began on December 1, 1916, when he joined the 4th Canadian Mounted Rifles at the front. The Mounted Rifles were stationed in a series of trenches called the Labyrinth along the Vimy Front in France, looking out toward an entrenched position that the Germans considered invulnerable. The Labyrinth had been a killing field for the French, who had held the trenches during 1915. When the Canadians worked to rebuild the dugouts, they often unearthed bits of the grey and blue uniforms of the French army.

Before the war, Billy Pringle, who was an expert marksman, made an extra living as a hunter and guide. This skill made him ideally suited for a job as a sniper. Snipers were responsible for preventing the enemy from making observations. This meant hiding out beyond the Canadian trenches with an observer. When an enemy head popped up, it was the sniper's job to put it down. The job, wrote sniper Corporal R. N. Siddle in *Maclean's* magazine in 1917, required "a very cool nerve and unusual powers of endurance." William Pringle would creep out into no man's land before sunrise and spend days there, surrounded by decomposing bodies, rats and stranded wounded soldiers. He lived on tinned beef, methodically picking off German soldiers with his rifle. Sniping was exceedingly dangerous work: "A hand exposed, hasty movement would bring a bullet." If snipers were detected, the Germans would also drop mortar fire on them. A soldier could quickly be blown to pieces. Since snipers worked in pairs, those who were killed were seldom found. "He is recorded missing," wrote Siddle, "and another man sallies forth."[8]

William Pringle survived the winter of 1917 and fought in the taking of Vimy Ridge, at which 10,602 Canadians were killed or wounded. In early September, the 4th Mounted Rifles were stationed in trenches near the village of Vimy. Shortly after midnight on September 5, the Germans subjected the unit to heavy artillery bombardment. The Canadians could hear what sounded like duds dropped amid the explosions. These duds turned out to be canisters of mustard gas. The effects of the gas were not immediately felt: it had settled during the night in deep craters. When morning arrived, however, the noxious fumes vaporized and rose up to the Canadian trenches. The gas killed ten men and wounded one hundred.[9] William Pringle was among those struck down. He suffered burns to his hands, face, lips and lungs. Blisters blew up and his chest ached. William, however, managed to hold the line. He was admitted to hospital four days later, and on his medical record, under the heading "Conduct Afterward," the doctor wrote simply, "Carried on."[10]

After forty-five days recovering in an English hospital, he returned to his unit. He served throughout 1918 in some of the bloodiest fighting of the war. Then on September 9, he was shot through the hand while attacking the German defences near the French town of Arras. This wound finished William Pringle's war. He was sent to England, where he recuperated in a hospital in the southern town of Witley. In 1919, he returned to Canada. During the conflict's four years, 59,544 Canadians had died and 154,361 soldiers had been reported wounded (quite often more than once). William Pringle tried to leave that behind. He came home, married his childhood sweetheart, Mary Ellen Lessard, and looked to the future.

William and Mary Ellen settled in Flinton. Harold was born in the southern Ontario town of Port Colborne where his grandfather worked in a cement factory. He was the first son and the second eldest of what would be eight children.

TODAY, FLINTON HOLDS NO more than three hundred inhabitants. It is the only incorporated village north of the Trans-Canada Highway (in Lennox and Addington County, just north of Kaladar) that is surveyed on a gridded street system. In 1936, the Ontario government opened a large one-storey school in Flinton, in anticipation of the multitudes of children it expected to grow up in the area. Flinton Elementary was the first Art Deco building in rural central Ontario, and it remains the village's largest structure. But the school has been closed for decades and is boarded up, with graffiti marking its exterior. It is a melancholy reminder of a more bustling period in the hamlet's history. Many of Flinton's earliest buildings are still in use, though, including the post office, which sits in the same white house where it has operated for the last one hundred years. It also serves as a general store.

Flinton is like every rural community. On the surface there does not appear to be much history, just a peaceful and time-worn way of life. But closer inspection shows that Flinton's history is, in fact, a masterpiece of Gothic Canadiana. It was founded by Senator Billa Flint in 1855. Perched by the banks of the Skootamatta River, it was originally named Flint Mills, after his saw and gristmill business. Today it goes by the nickname the "Village by the Skoot." Flint dominated life in the hamlet much like a feudal lord, and many of Flinton's streets still bear Flint family names. Billa Flint was appointed to the first Canadian Senate in 1867. It was an ironic appointment, since Flint had voted against Confederation and believed that senators should be elected, not appointed.

Senator Flint would not tolerate booze in his town and he worked hard to keep Flinton a dry jurisdiction. Villagers who craved a drop of the devil's brew had to make their way to the Yanch Hotel, a public house that opened in 1870 just outside the hamlet's boundaries. Billa Flint's reign over Flinton did not last, however; his mill burned down in 1886, and he subsequently moved north to the town of York Mills, which he renamed Bancroft after his mother-in-law. He died in 1894 in Ottawa and is buried near the early Canadian writer Susannah Moodie.

By then, Flinton's course had changed dramatically. A Danish pioneer named Laurence Roluff, who was out deer hunting, discovered a white stone streaked with a bright yellow mineral. Roluff thought it would make a pretty ornament and brought the rock back to his cabin, where he set it on the front windowsill. A Welshman named Elias Lloyd noticed the stone one week later while visiting a neighbour of Roluff's.

Lloyd persuaded the old Dane to lend him the stone and sent the rock to England for examination. Two months later, Lloyd's suspicions were confirmed: the bright yellow mineral was gold. He brought Roluff the good news and suggested the two form a partnership and begin mining. Roluff, however, was not enamoured with Lloyd, who he thought was "possessed with supernatural powers." Instead, he chose to hand over any claim to the property, free of charge.

Meanwhile, news of the gold discovery drifted down to the United States, where, in Cripple Creek, Colorado, an Irish prospector named John Guina heard of the find. Guina had spent time in the Flinton area, and when he learned that Lloyd was applying for possession of the land he decided to foil the attempt. Guina returned to Flinton and quickly found out that Lloyd was making his application for ownership by mail. He rode all night to Toronto, a distance of 350 kilometres, to beat the post and applied in person for the title. Not surprisingly, Lloyd was enraged. Calling upon the same supernatural forces that had so frightened Roluff, Lloyd vowed that he would use a "psychic power within him to lay a curse on the gold mine so that only disappointment and woe would come to those who owned it." Needless to say, the threat had little effect on Guina, who immediately began prospecting. He formed the Golden Fleece Mining Syndicate with Flinton's more prominent citizens, among them a doctor, a lawyer, the school inspector and a Catholic priest. The syndicate drilled two holes, one fifty and one thirty feet deep, but found no gold. Years of mining turned up nothing, and in 1885 Guina left Flinton an utterly defeated man. He was never heard from again.

For the rest of the nineteenth century, Flinton's Golden Fleece Mine was run by a series of hapless investors. A South African named Von Skimpfer, an agent with an overseas mining firm, purchased the mine in 1887. He hired a large crew and made many exploratory digs, but they too proved fruitless. Von Skimpfer's money began to run out. He laid off his crew but stayed on in Flinton, certain that the Golden Fleece would eventually produce gold. Teetering on the edge of bankruptcy, Von Skimpfer rented a small room in a local boarding house. He spent days at the mine alone, searching. One morning, Von Skimpfer had breakfast and left for another day's work. He was never seen again and his body was never discovered.

In the 1890s, the Toronto mining company of Taylor and Son leased the property from the Golden Fleece syndicate. Taylor and Son succeeded in drawing gold out of the mine. In total, $10,000 worth of bullion was raised and Flinton was poised to become a boom town. Its city grid system would finally be filled in with new homes. Miners were making the rich salary of ten cents an hour. But the bubble burst. The syndicate refused to renew Taylor and Son's lease, for reasons that were never explained. The only profitable year in the mine's history would not be repeated. Though it changed hands many times over the next forty years, the Golden Fleece never again produced any significant gold deposits. It finally closed down in 1932. In the 1970s, there was talk of reopening the mine. The Sands Minerals Corporation gave elaborate presentations and drilled for diamonds. Nothing ever came of it.[11]

GROWING UP IN FLINTON during the Depression was a mixture of equal parts geography and imagination, and to a large degree that still holds true today. "When you go there it's almost like stepping back in time," Harold Pringle's cousin Betti Michael told me. "It's like going back to a time when values were important and there was a strong sense of family. You treasured your grandparents and aunts and uncles."[12] There were endless fields and woods to explore, and in the summer kids swam in the Skootamatta. There was a shallow area for the beginners and a deep end for the older children. A single teacher taught all grades, from one to eight, in a one-room schoolhouse. During the winter months, the teacher would boil a large pot of water on the wood stove that heated the classroom. Each student would bring a bit of food—some carrots, meat or beans—and place it in the pot in the morning. By lunchtime, a delicious pot of communal soup was ready. The swimming hole became an outdoor rink in winter. Most children wore skates fashioned out of old boots. Torches were lit in the evening, allowing for nighttime skating and dances by torchlight.

Harold Pringle's family lived in a small two-room farmhouse on a few acres of land within walking distance of the centre of Flinton.

Harold's father had a favourite rocking chair, where he would sing old tunes such as *Molly Malone* and *Johnny's So Long at the Fair*. The Pringles were poor, hard-working people who cherished the land and found meaning and fulfillment in their modest homes and pastoral pursuits. But they were also fiercely independent. Most of the Pringle men worked as trappers, hunters and fishermen. These pursuits were typical of Flinton's local economy, which was driven by subsistence farming, lumber, digging in mines that produced very little precious metal, and roadwork. During the summer, William worked on road crews and fished. He got about by bicycle, which he referred to as his "wheel." During the winter, he spent time at hunting camps out in the bush. The family ate what he caught, plenty of venison and rabbit.

During the Depression, William earned one dollar a day working for a childhood friend, Archie Meese, who was also a veteran and had served as an officer. Meese had been blinded in Belgium during the Battle of Passchendaele. He was a very large man, with broad shoulders and an imposing frame, but his blindness made this formidable figure seem like that of a gentle, vulnerable child. He was married, with three children and a sizeable income. William filled the unique position of "Archie's eyes." Meese would place his hands on William's shoulders and William would lead him around Flinton. Aside from the obvious—helping him cross the street and negotiate stairs—Billy would describe the scenery, read to him and point out unique sights. He took Archie hunting and fishing; the pair caught one of the biggest fish in the village's history, which hung in the Northbrook Hotel with a sign that read "Caught by Archie Meese. Assisted by Billy Pringle." "He never saw his children," Veronica said of Archie Meese. "No, he never saw them."[13]

Most families in Flinton kept a few head of cattle, a team of horses, chickens and a couple of pigs. Each farm had its own garden. Mothers worked hard making rolls of homemade butter, salt pork, sauerkraut and pickles. Eggs cost 10 cents per dozen, flour $2.50 per cwt. Flinton is berry country, and in June wild strawberries covered the fields and woods. In August blueberries grew in abundance; during the Depression, they were sold for 58 cents for an eight-quart pail. Manufactured goods were purchased at one of Flinton's two general stores. The largest, R. W. Kimberly

General Store, was run by Joe Demore. Hawley Stone ran a flour, feed and dry goods store from the back of his house. Stone also served as Flinton's undertaker. The children craved his wife's cookies, which he sold at inexpensive prices. The most costly sweet on offer was a choco-late-covered marshmallow with a raspberry jam centre. Men who wanted a professional haircut went to Flinton's barber, Mister Lowry, a black deaf-mute who operated a store not far from the post office. As a courtesy, a customer would wait outside in front of Lowry's window until Lowry spied him. This way, the barber would not be startled. Flinton's men could find cold beer at the Stewart House, which was run by the Yanch family. This bar was distinguished by its very high steps and was known as a place of action by all the village's residents. The Canadian Pacific Railroad connected Flinton to big cities such as Belleville, Ottawa and Toronto. Two trains stopped each day in nearby Kaladar, one at dawn and the other after midnight. Night passengers stopped the train by lighting a lantern that hung at the outdoor platform. "You'd have to wave it back and forth so that the conductor could see you," recalled Betti. "Then the train would stop and you'd put out the lantern and hang it back up and get on the train and be on your way. I remember waiting for that train at night—you got quite a lonely feeling."[14]

Dr. Thomas John Clayton Tindle looked after Flinton's medical con-cerns. The doctor was a dedicated man who made house calls in a horse-drawn carriage. Tindle bought the first car in Flinton, a 1933 Ford V8, and was often seen speeding along the hamlet's roads. Health prob-lems outside Tindle's area of expertise were attended to by a number of what we would now call alternative practitioners. Harold's grandmother Maggie Pringle, for instance, acted as both midwife and veterinarian. If a horse caught cold, Maggie was brought in to fix things. D. H. "Cat Skin" Fletcher, the brother of the manager of the Golden Fleece Mine, cured pneumonia. Fletcher would skin a cat and then apply the fresh skin, flesh side down, onto the chest of someone suffering from the deadly respira-tory disease. When the skin turned green, it was exchanged for another one. The cat-skin remedy was also used for infections and blood poison-ing. Doctor Tindle was philosophical about the use of folk medicine. Once he visited a mother who had been giving her son's infected foot the cat-skin cure. Worried that the doctor would not approve, she removed the feline bandage before he arrived. Tindle came in, took one look at the ailing foot, told her, "Well, the cat skins are fetching it" and left her to finish off the cure.

Harold attended school until Grade 6, typical for a rural kid growing up in the 1930s. Harold and his father were close; they spent plenty of time together hunting and fishing. When Harold was growing up, the kids would often walk down along the Skootamatta River and into the heart of Flinton. They would visit the war memorial and read the names. There were about a dozen, quite a high number for a town of two hundred; William Pringle's name was there plain and proud for everyone to see.

Harold left school at fourteen and went to work in a lumber camp. At age fifteen, he worked on highway road crews. He worked on farms and at the local hydroelectric plant. In the winter he acted as a chauffeur for the local police force. Harold gave almost all his money to his family. His sister recalls how he would hand over his earnings, keeping twenty-five cents for himself.

Like most young men in the Depression, Harold found himself without any real trade or career to pursue. He lived on a system of temporary solutions. He found short-term work and hoped that one day he would have a permanent job. But the Depression wound into the late 1930s, and Canadians watched nervously as matters in Europe worsened. By 1939, war seemed inevitable. On September 3, 1939, England declared war on Germany, and Canada followed suit one week later.

3.

OVERSEAS

~~~~~~~~~~~~~~~~~~~~

Canada declared war on Germany on September 10, 1939. The country was led by Prime Minister William Lyon Mackenzie King, a man with no military experience. In 1937, King had met Adolf Hitler and found the dictator's eyes to "indicate keen perception and profound sympathy." Two years later, writes historian Brian Nolan in *King's War*, the sixty-five-year-old prime minister believed he had been "anointed by the Almighty to save the world and rid it of evil." In a personal journal King declared himself "really in good shape to start the work of war."[1]

The same could not be said of his country. Canada had been crushed by the Great Depression and still reeled from the effects of the First World War. "Its consequences," write Desmond Morton and J. L. Granatstein in *Marching to Armageddon: Canadians and the Great War 1914–1919*, "remained in broken dreams, broken bodies and broken families."[2] In 1935, the Canadian government paid its one hundred thousand disabled and dependent veterans $41 million, a cost second only to the price of servicing the two-billion-dollar national debt. Amputees were a common sight in every Canadian city and town, and some veterans who appeared physically normal hid invisible psychological scars. Every community had at least one eccentric former soldier. In Carleton Place, Ontario, during the 1920s, one shell-shocked veteran who wanted a chocolate bar walked down to the grocery store and held it up at gunpoint.[3]

The rise of Fascism in Italy further demonstrated that the "War to End All Wars" had not done the job. There was a sense of cynical disappointment, and the young recruits of 1939, while filled with optimism and thrilled by the notion of heroic deeds in Europe, also felt a sense of disbelief. Across Canada people asked themselves, "Can we actually be doing this all over again?"

It is difficult to imagine what sort of conversations went on in the Pringle household during the fall of 1939. At forty-two years old, William Pringle was proud of his time in the army, and no one could accuse him of failing to live up to his obligations to his country. Harold, the eldest son, idolized his father's military record and was eager to prove himself. William Pringle was faced with a difficult decision.

He decided that his son would not go alone: he would be there to look after him. "This was a situation that demanded people take up arms and do it again," Betti Michael said of her uncle's decision to go to war a second time. "Uncle Billy was concerned for Harold. He was an important part of the family. This was the eldest son going off to war in his father's footsteps. He wanted to protect Harold from what he knew was coming."[4] On February 5, 1940, after the farm had been put in order and Christmas had passed, William and Harold took the train to Picton and enlisted. Harold, who was a few days shy of his seventeenth birthday, claimed he was born in 1920 instead of 1922.[5] The youngest Pringle son, one-year-old Cecil, cried for an entire day.

At the war's outbreak, the Canadian army boasted only 4,500 men and was outfitted with First World War equipment. Some regiments still used horses. Despite this, thousands of eager volunteers flocked to recruiting offices. Over 50,000 men enlisted in the fall of 1939. Harold and his father joined Flinton's local military outfit, the Hastings and Prince Edward Regiment, which had its peacetime armoury in nearby Picton. The Hasty Ps, as they were nicknamed, had a distinguished record. During the First World War the unit had fought with distinction and its men had won many medals. Being a Hasty P was a matter of pride, and men caught trains from all over the country in order to join the regiment. In Picton, as the recruits poured in, a festive atmosphere reigned. New soldiers tried their luck with local girls and drank their pay. Only two per cent of the men had reached Grade 6 and their average age was nineteen, the minimum required for active military service. Of those who signed on, quite a few were as young as seventeen. Farley Mowat, a recruit from Port Hope, Ontario, harboured literary aspirations, and after the war he chronicled the history of the Hasty Ps in his book *The Regiment*. He also wrote about his personal experiences in *And No Birds Sang* and *My Father's Son*. In *The Regiment*, Mowat artfully describes life as a recruit during the early months of the war:

> Why did they come? Not out of the empty patriotism of a bygone age—that much is certain. Perhaps some of them came simply to escape the insecurity of hard times. Perhaps some of them came to escape the consequences of failure. Perhaps some came only to escape from boredom, from ugliness, from misery at home. Yet these were the minority. Most of them came because they could not help the spirit that was in them; because the Regiment itself had meaning for them that few could have expressed in words. They came because it was the hour of their pride, the hour of need.[6]

By fighting for King and Country, William and Harold were also keeping Pringle family tradition. Though the Pringles were an ordinary hard-working Canadian family, they possessed an extraordinary amount of military intestinal fortitude. An earlier William Pringle, the first of the clan to arrive in North America, landed in Cape May, New Jersey, around 1650 and took an oath of fidelity to King James in April 1654. William moved north to New Haven, Connecticut, and settled into life as a colonist. He had a son: Joseph, born in 1663, who had a son, Joel, born in 1695. Joel moved north to Albany, New York, which at that time was a remote wilderness on the outskirts of British territory. During the Seven Years War his son Joel Jr. fought against the French, serving in the British militia. On July 8, 1758, he was one of 12,000 British soldiers led by General James Ambercrombie in an ill-fated attack against

Fort Ticonderoga. The stronghold on the shore of Lake Champlain was defended by 3,500 French troops. It was a key strategic target for the British, since its capture would open up an attack route into New France. Ambercrombie and his men unsuccessfully stormed its walls and suffered 1,964 casualties. Joel was not among them; he survived the war and became a successful farmer.

In 1776, however, the American Revolution disrupted business. Ever the loyal subjects, Joel Pringle's sons, Joel the Younger, Timothy, William, Joseph and Doctor, joined the Rogers' King's Rangers, a Loyalist regiment formed by a veteran of the Seven Years War, Robert Rogers. In 1769, Rogers had published a pamphlet on guerrilla tactics, which included suggestion such as "If you are obliged to receive the enemy's fire, fall or squat down till it is over, then rise and discharge at them."[7] By the time of the American Revolution, Rogers had become an alcoholic and was unfit for command, so his brother, James Rogers, led the regiment. The Rangers were feared for their stealth and their lack of mercy. They were the prototype for the modern British Commandos units and for the American Special Forces, and Robert Rogers' dictums on guerrilla warfare are still used today by the Green Berets.

While Joel Sr. and his sons were away fighting, American rebels victimized their families. Their land and property were confiscated, their houses burned and the women assaulted. Terrified, the Pringle women and children fled Albany and escaped to Fort Edward on Lake George. In 1781, they arrived in Quebec, at Fort St. Johns (now Saint-Jean-sur-Richelieu) on the Richelieu River. After the war ended, the Crown gave land to Rogers' King's Rangers veterans near the Bay of Quinte, on Lake Ontario. Each Ranger drew a lot from a surveyor's hat. These tickets entitled them to a plot in the northern wilderness. From this homestead, the entire Pringle clan fanned out across central Ontario. In 1794, Joel's son, Joseph, became the first non-native man to settle north of the Salmon River, the fringe of English Canadian settlement. His son, also Joseph Pringle, was the first non-native child born north of the Salmon.

By 1812, British North America was once again at war with the United States. Joseph Pringle, who was born in 1788, became an officer in the Lennox County militia. His six sons fought alongside him. On July

15, 1814 the Pringles fought at the Battle of Lundy's Lane, one of the most vicious melees of the conflict. During a five-hour struggle, 3,000 British and Canadian soldiers fought 2,600 Americans in a graveyard near what is now the city of Niagara Falls. The fighting was mostly hand to hand. It continued into the night, and at its finish 1,496 men were dead, wounded or missing. The Americans retreated and the British took 235 prisoners.

After the war ended, the Pringle family spread out. Joseph Pringle, Jr.'s son Abraham was born in 1825. Abraham and his wife settled in Flinton, a small hamlet in central Ontario, and had eight children. Dexter, the eldest son, married and had seven children, one of whom was William "Billy" Pringle, who fought during the First World War. When you included Billy Pringle's time during the First World War and Harold's in the Second, the Pringles spent a fair portion of their 346 years in North America fighting for the British monarchy.

Even from birth Harold Pringle seemed surrounded by the legacy of war. Harold was born in Port Colborne, a small southern Ontario town that sits on the Niagara Peninsula, which just happens to be the cradle of the War of 1812. Fifteen miles away at the Chippewa River, American and British soldiers had clashed on July 5, 1814. There, the American general Jacob Brown brought 1,300 troops, militia and Indians against the 1,500 British troops led by General Gordon Drummond. On that day the American general Winfield Scott led a fearsome bayonet charge against the British and won the field. All told, 137 British troops and 48 Americans died. At the battle of Queenston Heights, General Isaac Brock staved off an American invasion and died in the process; at Stoney Creek, 700 British troops defeated 2,000 American invaders; at the battle of Black Rock, the British beat 2,000 Indians under American general Phineas Riall; and at Fort Erie, 3,500 British troops besieged an American force of 2,000 for two months in 1814.[8]

Life as a new recruit in 1939 was an adventure. Harold was one of many young men getting paid to fool around with firearms. For most of the volunteers, army life was their first time away from home, and though the regime was tough and the officers, sergeants and corporals were intimidating, there was plenty of roughhousing and joking about.

Soldiers talked in heated tones about the Germans and what they would do with them once they got over there. This war, they vowed, would finish things once and for all. The first group of volunteers set sail for England in January 1940. Harold's unit was part of the second wave, which was to land in England by autumn. It moved from Picton to Camp Borden north of Toronto, and throughout this period the recruits engaged in basic training. In August 1940, Harold and the rest of his group from the Hastings and Prince Edward Regiment set sail. They arrived in September 1940.

But instead of being assigned to stay with the Hastings and Prince Edward Regiment, Harold and his father were sent to the 1st Canadian Infantry Holding Unit. This must have been a terrible disappointment to Harold, who aspired to be with the Hasty Ps. Conditions were spartan and the barracks in which the soldiers lived rough. Pipes froze and roofs leaked. Life as a soldier in a holding unit consisted of marching drill and warfare training. Canadian military historian Bill McAndrew describes them as "administrative catch-alls for lost troops."[9] Holding units were led by wealthy civilians who had bought their way into the army and secured a post far away from combat; they were run by non-commissioned officers, who were for the most part veterans of the First World War. These soldiers were obsessed with rules and regulations and with old-fashioned spit and polish. It was a toxic blend of leadership. A Canadian officer ordered to examine declining morale summed up holding units like this: "It is obvious to anyone who has had to spend any time in one of these organizations that they are in the true sense of the word the doldrums and a breeding place of poor morale."[10]

Harold's father saw to it that his son stayed out of trouble and learned how to keep his uniform and gear in top working order. Since Harold was already a fastidious dresser, he had no difficulty keeping up with military etiquette. Despite the gruelling monotony of life in a holding unit, there was a new country to explore, with cities larger than Harold could have ever imagined back home, not to mention English pub culture and its strange idiosyncrasies.

Harold Pringle maintained a clean record until April 1941. There were two minor infractions for brief Absent Without Official Leave

(AWOL) incidents while he was at Camp Borden, but these were hardly unique. Though this behaviour was not accepted, the military realized that soldiers were prone to overstaying their leaves. In London during the Blitz, two Hasty P non-commissioned officers ran into a burning building in a bid to rescue a child who was trapped inside. A British Civil Defence officer witnessed their bravery and asked the men for their names and unit numbers so that he could nominate them for a decoration. They declined the offer. They were not looking for attention—they were two days over their leave.[11]

Nonetheless, in April 1941, Harold's life took a wrong turn. Looking back, it is easy to see it as the critical first step downward. That month, Harold's father was discharged from the army and sent home. This by itself might not have been enough to set Harold on a bad course—at forty-two, the elder Pringle was no doubt too old for active service. But there seems to have been much more than age behind William Pringle's expulsion from the military. As a civilian, he had been able to put the memory of his time serving on the Western Front behind him. But when he returned to the army, those memories began to creep up on him. He found himself back in Aldershot, England, at the same camp he had been stationed in before going to France in 1915. Military training rattled his nerves. Firing guns, being on parade, bayonet drill—all these old habits worked together to bring Billy Pringle back to the trauma of the First World War. In April 1941, he seems to have experienced a nervous breakdown: he began to suffer the severe post-traumatic episodes that would plague him for the rest of his life. Back home in Flinton, he would sometimes freeze up at the dinner table, unable to swallow and having trouble with breathing. It would take him up to half an hour to snap out of this paralyzed terror. William Pringle was not the only older recruit to crack during training. A Canadian military physician attached to his holding unit recorded that "several men about age forty or over have come under my attention showing symptoms of anxiety following recent 'toughing' measures applied to the whole unit."[12]

For a proud warrior, it was a searing, and no doubt terrifying, humiliation. For the boy who idolized him it was crushing. Former Hasty Ps say that Harold fell into bad company after his father was shipped home. "The son, well, he didn't like the way the father was treated," one ex-soldier said in an interview with me. "And he was the first son, so he rebelled."

Harold rebelled by going AWOL. In May 1941, after a month-long stint assigned at the Provost Corps (the military police), he returned to his holding unit; he was given a week's leave on June 7. He didn't come back. Harold was absent for 21 days before he was picked up in July. He was sentenced to 7 days' field punishment and forfeited 11 days' pay. During the next two years, Harold was frequently AWOL. In November 1941, he was sentenced to 180 days in detention. In January 1942, he was given 14 days' field punishment, and that August he was given 7 days' more. On April 16, 1943, Harold and two other Canadian privates were reported missing.[13]

On this particular excursion, Harold was heading back to a woman. Her name was Esmee. She was English, lived in Portsmouth and had a husband serving overseas in the British army. Harold met Esmee in a café in March 1943 while on another AWOL spree. According to Esmee, Harold told her and other patrons at the café that he had been in an accident and was on convalescent leave. In the following weeks Harold and Esmee met frequently at the café and, in her words, she "became friendly towards him."[14]

"Friendliness" between British women and Canadian soldiers was a source of concern for the military. During the war years, Britain was a far more modern and permissive society than Canada, and English women were one of its most appealing fixtures. In 1940, the army had tried to stop the fraternization by warning its men of the dangers involved in amorous entanglements. One Roman Catholic priest lectured army reinforcements on the various types of English women. The worst of the lot were prostitutes, a "cold, calculating lot." Next came "working girls" who were employed in munitions plants, factories and the like; if these "have any morals, they have discarded them." The best were the "good girls," who lived at home. "Treat them as you would treat your best girl at home," the priest recommended.[15] It is hard to imagine a worse argument against cavorting with English women than telling legions of twenty-year-old men away from home for the first time that there were women of no virtue, women of easy virtue and women you were to "treat" as you would those at home. It was like telling a ten-year-old that he could have chocolate, strawberry *and* vanilla ice cream. If anything, the admonishment must have spurred the young Canadian recruits on their way.

The intermingling of British women and Canadian soldiers had two effects: it broke up Canadian marriages and it led to marriages abroad. By 1943, the Canadian headquarters was processing two divorces a week; army chaplains estimated that they spent half their time doing marriage counselling. Some of the romantic equations could be extremely complicated. In *The Half-Million*, an account of the Canadian army in the United Kingdom, historians C. P. Stacey and Barbara M. Wilson cite the case of the wife of a British soldier who sought child support from a Canadian who had fathered one of her three children; the Canadian had already asked permission to marry another British woman. In another case, a chaplain was compelled to tell a pregnant fiancée that her groom was already married and the father of three children. By 1946, 44,886 Canadians were married overseas, most to British women. These unions produced 21,358 children. Even today British missing person Web sites are filled with messages from British men and women looking for information about mysterious Canadian soldiers. Ten cases of bigamy were prosecuted in military courts and another twelve in civilian court.[16] Venereal disease was also a concern. By 1945, 33.8 soldiers out of every 1,000 suffered from syphilis or gonorrhea.[17] According to Canadian general Christopher Vokes, Canadian soldiers on leave had two interests: "to get drunk" and "to get laid."[18]

A poem published in the Canadian army newspaper, *The Maple Leaf*, celebrated the notorious reputation that Canadians earned while overseas. Written by "author unknown," it is entitled "Ode to a Canadian":

> He'll ruin your life, run off with your wife,
> And think he is doing no wrong.
> He'll take you around if you lend him a pound,
> And take all you have for a song.

He's forgotten his wife, he'll be single for life,
With the boys he's a regular guy.
And he's got a life story that's covered with glory,
But he's much too wicked to die.

He has personal charm that is meant to disarm
The unwary that gets in his way,
And, don't listen to him for he's only a whim,
And he'll surely lead you astray.

Though you know he's a liar your blood is on fire,
As he whispers "I love you so much."
You go weak at the knees as he whispers "Oh please!"
And you feel his experienced touch.

Though he makes you so mad and often quite sad
Still, you cannot send him away.
He's a real bad guy and a regular cad,
So why do you whisper "Please stay."

He'll wed you, of course, when he gets his divorce,
But, while waiting, "Oh, Honey, why not?"
So, just think of this when he begs for a kiss,
That a pram costs a helluva lot.[19]

To what degree Harold fit this profile is uncertain. He did, however, write his mother saying that he had "almost been married three times" during his time abroad.[20] Women had swooned for him in Canada, and there is no reason to believe that the English variety was any different.

In early April 1943, Harold told Esmee that his leave would end on April 19 but that he might be able to get an extension. Esmee offered to "assist him financially" if he would stay. "Thinking he was in desperate need of financial help," she later wrote, "I at various times at his request, drew from my Post Office Savings Bank the sum of twenty-one pounds and handed it to him."[21]

Pringle's version of events differs somewhat from Esmee's recollections. Later, in a legal brief, he admitted telling her he was on sick leave and "pretty near broke" but said that Esmee told him that "if he could get an extension of leave from my unit she would lend me some money on condition I would pay her back as soon as I returned to my unit."[22] They remained friends for two months. Harold took the money in chunks. First seven pounds, then three, and so on up to a total of twenty-one.

It seems pretty obvious that what went on between Esmee and Harold involved more than mere friendly feelings. A woman would not give a man twenty-one pounds—an enormous sum of money in 1943—simply because she thought he was an all right fellow. In fact, it seems to have been a fairly serious romance. During this time, Harold wrote his family saying that he had a girlfriend and wanted to marry her; he even sent a picture of her back to his family. On May 22, 1943, suffering from guilt over the money he owed, Harold surrendered himself to military police, telling them he wanted to arrange to pay Esmee back out of his deferred earnings.

To the army, Harold Pringle appeared to be a kid who was having trouble adjusting. At his court martial for being AWOL, Pringle's commanding officer reported on his military career. He "is capable of being a soldier if he sets his mind on it," he wrote. "Corrective punishment is the only thing that will bring him along." The commander of the detention barracks observed, "This man has lost his interest in the Army but I believe he can be made into a good soldier with the strict discipline he will receive here." "His trouble is almost purely AWOL," his captain wrote. "Nothing substantial offered in mitigation, other than fairly good character references. In view of which this may be considered a case for an early draft." Harold was sentenced to nine months in the Glass House.[23]

The Glass House was Headley Down, the Canadian army's military prison in England. The jail earned its nickname from the thick glass ceilings that covered part of its main hall. The Glass House was a cluster of concrete buildings that had previously been used as a pig farm; the man who owned the land said that while it made a poor prison, it would still make a fine pig farm after the war. Six months' hard time in such conditions did not appeal to Harold, and on June 3, at four thirty in the morning, he escaped from custody and went into hiding. On July 6 he surrendered himself to police in London. Four days later the Canadian authorities sentenced him to nine months. It seems as if each time Harold collided with military authority, it drove him further in the other direction. They would jail him, he would take off. It was a game of will.

Military prisons were designed to turn bad soldiers into good ones. The assumption was that those inside were not career felons but civilians who were experiencing difficulty adapting to the exacting discipline of military life. The Glass House turned prisoners into good soldiers by making life there so uncomfortable that life in their unit was preferable. Conditions were so severe, in fact, that they made even combat preferable. The Glass House's unofficial slogan was "They never return."

Discipline was stern and swift, and no deviation was tolerated. Prisoners chose to wet themselves rather than move a muscle while on parade. Men slept six to a room. Fighting was common and prisoners would often use handmade weapons, such as slivers of glass, to wound each other. In his history of the Military Provost Corps, veteran Robert Boyes quotes a soldier who spent time locked up:

> You were never still. Three drills a day with full kit and all your webbing had to be scrubbed white and your brasses polished back and front.... They used to throw all the dirty pans and mess tins from the cookhouse into the cages and all you had to clean them with were a bucket of sand, cold water and rags, and believe me those pans had to shine like silver. There had to be dead silence. If it was raining they used to throw all the tins outside and when they were rusty they used to give you them back and say you hadn't touched them. Some of the younger prisoners used to crack and cry. If you back answered a guard they had a favorite trick of making you run on the spot while you were having your meal, so just try having a plate of stew while you are running on the spot. It was the same on physical drill. You could always tell the weak from the strong. Some used to stagger and crawl after twenty minutes. There was no end to it, it was go, go, go. No, Major, you

can't buck the system, so you have just got to obey the rule of law. I saw things and did things that I thought weren't possible.[24]

Mental punishments were a specialty. Canadian military jailers looked upon "terrifying" their charges as a "pleasure," wrote the diarist for the 1st Canadian Infantry Division Field Punishment Camp. "Reports have it that the Sergeants furtively sneak to some dark corner periodically to dream up new ways in which to torment the unlucky soldier who dares to come to camp." Soldiers were ordered to hold the position "toes and nose" for hours. This meant standing with one's nose and toes pinned to the wall. Men were chained to trees and left for days. In his novel *Execution*, Canadian Second World War veteran Colin McDougall describes watching a soldier pulling a child's wagon full of bricks. He would travel back and forth, fifty feet, between two chairs. At each stop he would yell, "Unloading!" and then remove the bricks. Then he would yell, "Loading!" and put them back. This went on for hours.[25] Suicide attempts were not uncommon; they were recorded in the Prison War Diary with casual entries, such as "August 6, 1943, Private Gunn attempted self-injury by cutting his wrists."[26]

Although the army hoped to keep wayward soldiers from mingling with career criminals, many prisons housed inmates who were lawbreakers by profession. Organized gangs ruled cell blocks, just as they did in civilian prisons, and as a result, many men who had never before been on the wrong side of the law found themselves adopting criminal behaviour. Even the soldiers assigned to guard the prison had discipline problems. Some went AWOL themselves. In September 1943, while Harold was in the Glass House, the prison record reported five staff charged with minor offences and another three AWOL. Another was charged with molesting a local girl.[27]

Soldiers also had their pay docked while under sentence; penalties were so harsh that it was common for a private to leave the Glass House owing the government half a year's pay. The financial bite had an adverse effect on rehabilitation. Soldiers left broke and many decided to simply go AWOL again. Prison became a merry-go-round.

This cycle applied particularly well to Harold. As the eldest son of a father who, after his discharge from the army, was listed on his military forms as "veteran, invalid, unable to work,"[28] it was Harold's responsibility to support his family. Throughout his time in England, Harold seems to have earned extra money by going AWOL and working for local farmers and London shopkeepers. This money he sent home. Harold's soldier's pay was only forty dollars a month, twenty of which the government kept as enforced savings. Combined with pay penalties stemming from his time away from the army, this left Harold somewhere in the neighbourhood of three hundred dollars in debt to the Canadian government.

Canadian military psychiatrists assigned to investigate the causes of absenteeism determined that enormous debts led to recidivism. "I feel that one of the big factors in repeated absences is the pay-debit incurred during prison sentences," wrote Major A. E. Moll. "To a private five hundred or more in debt the prospect of becoming debt-free is rather hopeless. When this stage is reached the man is so far in debt and his future so hopeless that further increases in debt mean nothing to him."[29]

Another army psychologist, Major L. J. Loftus, cited the example of a private from Nova Scotia named L. G. Doiron. He was thirty-four and he had a fifth-grade education and a wife and five children back home. When interviewed, Doiron reported that while he was in England, his wife "had gotten mixed up with bad company." She died in 1941 after drinking bad liquor. One year later, Doiron's four-year-old son died of tuberculosis. Subsequently, Doiron was charged with drunkenness, as well as with the theft of a watch. In 1944, he was in prison and $296 in debt; he had not been paid for two years and had not gone on leave for one year. Loftus estimated that it would take fifteen months before Doiron would be out of debt. "Obviously, in some cases these figures have reached such an amount that it is practically impossible for the man to ever clear it up," wrote Loftus. "There is a rule that a man must have so much money paid before proceeding on leave. With a pay deficit these men returning to the detention barracks will almost never be eligible. I feel that many of these men will return to Detention."[30]

One month after Harold was sent to prison, Esmee began a letter-writing campaign demanding that the army repay her her twenty-one pounds. No doubt she wanted to replace the money before her husband returned home to find it missing. "I feel that Pringle's conduct is one of disgrace to his own countrymen," she wrote in a letter dated June 11,1943. "He has fraudulently obtained the sum of 21 pounds from me, which I can ill afford to lose, and I appeal to you for advice and assistance in the matter with a view to being reimbursed."

Esmee sent at least one letter every three months to Canadian headquarters, and as a result the officers there became well acquainted with name Harold Joseph Pringle. Not one to deal on the lower levels, Esmee went right to the top, to Major General Percival J. Montague. He was a veteran of the First World War and had won the Military Cross. He had spent much of the war assigned to headquarters, and in 1917 he took a seven-foot fall off a duckboard and broke his leg. In 1919, Montague returned to the legal profession; he eventually became a judge in Manitoba. At the beginning of the Second World War, he was appointed Chief of the Judge Advocate General, the legal branch of the Canadian army and later Chief of Staff. Montague's office responded to each of Esmee's letters and apologized for Pringle's conduct. Her complaint was a nagging and embarrassing problem but not a claim to be taken seriously.[31]

Montague had more pressing issues to pursue. As the man responsible for Canadian military law, he had the complicated and vexing problem of turning juridical concepts into a workable wartime administration. Canadian military law had its roots in the British system, which itself originated in the eleventh century, a time when there was little difference between military and civilian jurisdiction. William the Conqueror had introduced military justice when he brought courts of chivalry to England in 1066. By 1521, the responsibility for deciding military cases fell upon the Earl Marshal. It is from the Marshal's court that the term "court martial" eventually developed. By the seventeenth century, British military law was divided into two branches: naval and land. The English Military Code of 1666 defined three types of courts: General Court Martial, Regimental Court Martial and a Detachment with the power of a Regimental Court. The Mutiny Act of 1689 sought to balance the need for an army with the threat an army could pose to a government. It declared that no standing army could be kept in England without the approval of Parliament. The Mutiny Act also established, for the first time, one of the key differences between civilian and military law. It was essential "that an exact Discipline be observed and that Soldiers who shall Mutiny or Stirr up Sedition or shall Desert Their Majesties Service be brought to a more Exemplary and speedy Punishment then the usuall Formes of Law will allow."[32]

Military law evolved further during the eighteenth and nineteenth centuries. More power was given to commanding officers to hand out summary judgments for lesser crimes. In 1906, the army stopped "imprisoning" soldiers and began to officially "detain" them for long periods of time. During the First World War, Canadians fell under the authority of the British Army Act. Deserters were executed; 306 soldiers were shot by firing squad, 26 of them Canadians. Most were young and many suffered from shell shock; Manitoba-born private Stephen McDermott Fowles, for example, was only twenty-one years old when he was executed for desertion in 1916. In recent years activists, such as those in the Shot at Dawn Campaign in Britain, have lobbied for the pardoning of soldiers executed during the First World War. New Zealand posthumously pardoned their five executed soldiers. In 2001, the Canadian government announced that although it would not pardon those executed, it would include their names in the Book of Remembrance, a tome that is inscribed with the name of every soldier who fought and died during that conflict. The British government has steadfastly refused to re-examine its cases. In 1993 Prime Minister John Major said that it was wrong to rewrite history "by substituting our latter-day judgement for that of contemporaries, whatever we might think."[33]

It is a sentiment with which Major General P. J. Montague would have agreed. In the summer of 1943, he was staring down the questions of desertion and of capital punishment. The first Canadian troops had left for Sicily in April, and the military brass suspected that the Italian campaign would be long and bloody and that it would create an array of new disciplinary problems. Montague and the rest of the Canadian high command did not want to be caught unprepared. "Both Lieutenant-General McNaughton and myself feel that military circumstances and considerations might on occasion arise when it would be very undesirable for us not to have the power to deal with a death sentence as expeditiously as possible," Montague wrote the minister of defence on 7 August 1943.[34]

A week later, in a secret army memo, he elaborated: "Army personnel in close contact with civil population as advance progresses under circumstances which will render it of the utmost importance, especially in view of record of the enemy in respect of offences against civilians, that civil population be impressed with the speed and certainty of military justice and be made fully aware of the authority vested in military officers." Swift military action would

> satisfy the outraged sentiment of people who otherwise might
> take private vengeance with no proof resulting in reprisals,
> chaotic conditions and general unrest among those who have
> been led to expect a situation under Allied military force widely
> different from that which existed under the enemy.... From the
> standpoint of humanity it is most important that a soldier should
> not be kept in suspense any longer than absolutely necessary if in
> the end a sentence of death will be carried out. Offences in the
> face of the enemy may have an adverse effect on morale unless
> soldiers are aware that they will be completely dealt with by
> military authority without an undue lapse of time.[35]

IN DECEMBER 1943, HAROLD was released from prison early and given seventy-eight days' remission on his sentence. He had been released early because he volunteered for active service. Throughout his time in prison Harold had insisted that he wanted to be back with the Hasty Ps, and that once he was with the regiment he had signed up to fight with everything would be all right. For once, Harold Pringle and the army agreed. At the earliest possible opportunity he would be shipped over to Italy to join the Hastings and Prince Edward Regiment, which had been fighting in Sicily and Italy since July. The regiment had been involved in some heavy fighting and was badly in need of reinforcements. The men of the Hasty Ps did not realize it, but the worst was yet to come. Names such as Ortona, Tollo and Lamone were soon to become painful memories of the most severe action the Canadian army had yet faced.

Here there is some disparity between Pringle's official record and the recollections of those he fought beside. Harold's sergeant in Italy recalled that Pringle was with the Hasty Ps shortly after Ortona. So does Ivan Gunter, a Hasty P who was attached to battalion headquarters as an intelligence officer. But Pringle's record has him coming over later, in late January 1944. I was told by Harry Fox, who was the Hasty Ps' regimental sergeant major from 1944 to 1945, that military records are often far from accurate. It seems safer to balance first-hand and official sources. It is at least certain that Harold Pringle arrived in Italy sometime in December 1943 or January 1944.[36]

WHILE HAROLD PRINGLE'S CAREER in combat was just beginning, Lieutenant Hugh Ramsay Park's war was coming to a close.

It was mid-December 1943 and thirty-year-old Lieutenant Park was leading a company of Canadians toward Ortona, a small town on the Adriatic side of the Italian coast. Rain poured down, as it had for the previous month, and the Germans threw up a heavy artillery bombardment. Park's men, who were new recruits, were elated by their first taste of action and they began to cheer the enemy fire. Lieutenant Park, in contrast, was a seasoned soldier. He was a tall man who sported a moustache; in his time away from the front lines he wore his cap cocked on the side of his head. Park was every inch the capable soldier. After arriving in Sicily with the 4th Canadian Armoured Division, Park recalls being constantly in action. The ten days prior to the attack on Ortona saw him serving what seemed like twenty-four-hour duty, which meant being under steady bombardment. Park had grown accustomed to the deep drum roll of enemy shells, but the jubilation of the new recruits galled him. "You hated the new arrivals more than you did the Germans," he would later recall. "They were so happy and joyous on the surface because they were scared to death but they didn't know enough to shut up. When you have been shelled for a long time, you get so that you can tell within a few feet where a shell is going to land by the sound of it. But if everybody is yelling and screaming and making racket you can't hear it and you get mad."[37]

Lieutenant Park began to curse his men; he screamed and demanded complete silence. All his intellect focused on listening to the sharp whistle of the shells as they arched down. It was the one you didn't hear that got you, they always said. So Park listened with everything he had while the shells dropped. Park's men looked at him in bewilderment. They were not angry, they were perplexed. He continued to order silence. "You couldn't work with people because noise bothered you to the extent that you were ineffective," Park would later say. "Which is no good because you're supposed to be commanding."[38]

In the army, news travelled fast, particularly when an officer was concerned. A few days later, at a briefing at headquarters, Park's name came up for an assignment. "Park's had it," a snippy young staff officer piped up. "He's finished."

That was it.

Lieutenant Park was labelled a shell-shock case. He was ordered to the rear to a small town called Avellino, where the Canadian army had its reinforcement depot. "You might as well go right now," he was told. He would never see combat again, nor would he receive any medical treatment. "They thought that just being away from the shelling should do the trick," he recalled. Park was made a quartermaster and given the accompanying rank of captain. He would survive the war without sustaining a scratch. "I've always wondered how I escaped without getting hit," he said. "There were so many people around me that were slaughtered."[39]

I SHARED HIS SURPRISE. For some reason it had seemed impossible that I would ever meet the man who had led Harold Pringle's firing squad—I had always imagined that man to be dead. In the spring of 2000, however, we came face to face. The meeting would never have taken place except for his middle name, Ramsay. There are far too many Parks scattered around Canada, and without a middle initial I could never have narrowed it down. But when I searched his initials, I came up with "H. R. Park" and an address in London, Ontario. I sent him a letter and waited for a reply. One week later I received a telephone call from

Park telling me that yes, he was the Ramsay Park who had fought in Italy, and what was it I wanted to know about Pringle?

That weekend we met in London. It sounds crass, but whenever a veteran made contact I acted as quickly as possible. The reality was that they might not be there the next day. Each month the ranks thinned as the last living vestiges of the war passed on. To many, this melting away was an unremarkable phenomenon. To me, it was critical. They were my only real link, and Park was the most important link of all. He was my contact with Pringle's final moments on earth.

When I met Park, I brought my usual interview gift: chocolate. Knowing how much my grandfather liked sweets, it seemed logical to me that the principle must apply across the generation. So I drove down the 401, past green farmland that was gradually being swallowed up by suburbia. I knew London pretty well, having spent the years between my fifth and tenth birthdays there. Still, there were not too many memories, just the strange sort that stick in a kid's head. There was a river, which turned out to be the small creek dubbed the Thames. There was snow. And I remembered a tank that sat in London's Central Park as a memorial to the city's Second World War veterans. The tank was a popular spot for boys. My brother and I used to climb all over it, straddling the turret and sliding underneath its belly.

Ramsay Park lives in a retirement home in the west end of the city. Park has his own room, his own telephone and his own kitchenette. Prior to our meeting, he told me to come right up and knock. Park answered the door, and I saw a man who was stooped from old age and needed a walker to get around. He still had a moustache, though it was now pure white. His hair had thinned, and it was combed over right to left. He had blue eyes. He greeted me cordially and asked me in. I gave his room a quick look around and saw what I began to recognize, as my research continued, as the trappings of old age. There were bottles for medication. There were pictures of grandchildren and children and of a wife, who I later learned had passed on. There were books, a mixture of novels and histories. There was a picture of Park's law school graduation class, Osgoode 1939. There was a picture of his unit, the King's Own Regiment, known as the Calgary Tanks. Over the next two years, I would visit

Ramsay Park each season. We would chat and he would share memories from his life and his time in the Canadian army.

Hugh Ramsay Park was born in New York City in 1913. His father was a geological engineer who worked for a large mining firm. The family came north three months after Hugh was born. They settled in Cobalt, a small town in northern Ontario that boasted one of the country's largest silver mines. Life was good. The Parks had central heating, and all their groceries were paid for by the company. Their house was grand, big enough to entertain many visitors. "There was always some high mucky-muck coming up from southern Ontario to visit," he told me.[40] Park's youth was picture-postcard perfect. There were skating and skiing in the winter, fishing and swimming in the summer and hunting in the fall. Park received a top-notch education and went on to university after high school. University led to law school. He graduated from Osgoode in 1939 at the age of twenty-six. He was single, good-looking and eager for a little adventure. The day he and his friends were called to the bar, two weeks after war was declared, they trekked to Toronto's armoury and enlisted. "They laughed at us," Park remembered. "They told us they had no money, no supplies, no nothing, the best we could do was leave our names and information and decide which part of the services we wanted to be in."[41] Park chose the Armoured Corps.

When his parents learned that he had enlisted, they were furious. As an American, Park had no obligation to fight a war to defend Great Britain. The Parks wanted their son to retract his enlistment, if it could be arranged. Such manoeuvring, however, was impossible. Park was on the list. He returned to Timmins and started practising law. In July 1941 he received a telegram telling him to report for duty. Park was given the unofficial rank of acting sergeant. After twelve weeks of training at Camp Borden near Toronto, he was promoted to lieutenant. In 1942, Park was transferred to England and stationed in Seaforth on the coast east of London. He was transferred to the Calgary Tanks, who were also known as the Calgaries. The regiment had lost 29 tanks during the raid on Dieppe on August 16, 1943. Two officers and 11 men were killed, and 138 men were captured. With the regiment decimated, reinforcements were assigned, Ramsay Park one of them. He was given one month's training and was made a Troop commander. In battle, he would lead a section of three tanks.

Park landed in Sicily with the rest of the Eighth Army on July 10, 1943. The Canadians were expecting heavy resistance, and the army's generals made contingency plans—among them, how to cope if an entire battalion was lost before reaching the beach. Instead, the Italians came running from the brush with their hands up. Thousands of Italian conscripts clamoured to surrender. As the Allies pressed inland, the weather became ferociously hot and sunny. The fighting was light, mostly skirmishing, and for a while the Canadians made quick progress. Then, at the base of Mount Etna, the Canadians came up against what Park remembers as "our first taste of German efficiency. From then on it was Germans, Germans, Germans."[42]

The Nazis had superior weaponry and were dug into formidable fortifications. Bill Stewart, who in 1943 was a twenty-nine-year-old correspondent for the Canadian Press, covered the campaign. "Sicily was an astonishing place," he later recalled. "You would see towns cut right into the side of a cliff. You could barely distinguish them, because the earth and stone were the same colour. It was tough territory to take. There was very little cover, the Canadians were always finding themselves advancing several miles over open terrain against the German defences."[43] Pringle's unit, the Hastings and Prince Edward Regiment, was in the thick of the fighting. At Assoro, the Hasty Ps scaled a fortified mountain and surprised a heavily entrenched German force. The attack was considered a suicide mission. Brigadier General Howard Graham thought the likelihood of "losing the whole battalion was almost a dead certainty," wrote Farley Mowat in *And No Birds Sang*.[44] Advancing through artillery fire and assaulting an elite German unit, the Hasty Ps somehow managed to secure the mountain. Allied High Command was impressed by the Canadians' progress. So were the Germans. Major General Eberhard Rodt, the commander of the 15th Panzer Grenadier Division, noted, "In fieldcraft, superior to our own troops. Very mobile at night, surprise break-ins, clever infiltrations at night with small groups between our strong points."[45]

The Sicilian campaign was rough on armoured units. Sherman

tanks that had been considered indestructible proved to be death traps. German 88mm guns easily pierced their armour, and the shells would then ricochet through the tank's intestines, bouncing along the walls and shredding the men inside. Shermans also turned out to be extremely flammable; they would "brew" when set alight. So many tanks were torched in Sicily that the Canadian infantry nicknamed them "Ronsons" after a popular brand of cigarette lighter.

The Canadian Calgary Tanks hit the bottom of southern Italy in September 1943, landing at Reggio, in Calabria, in support of the 1st Canadian Division. Although the Allied command was not precisely sure how they were going to take Italy, they knew that they did not want to fight a prolonged campaign up its spine. Yet, in the autumn of 1943, that was exactly what the Eighth Army was doing. Led by the charismatic British general Bernard Montgomery, it was pressing up through southern Italy. On October 1, 1943, the Calgary Tanks met the Germans at battle of Mota; the fighting was the worst the Calgaries had seen since Dieppe. On October 15, they repulsed a German counterattack. In the beginning of November, the Calgaries supported the Indian Division. By mid-November, the Germans had begun a strategy of slow and deliberate retreat. German High Command decided to make a stand at the Sangro River.

IN NOVEMBER 1943, THE Sangro River, normally a small stream, gushed over its banks, flooding the fields beside it. Almost without pause, rain ripped down and pelted the ground, softening it with each drop. Bright orange flames made a fierce juxtaposition against the grey sky and the brown, green mud. The flames leapt up from what had once been Italian villages, while refugees staggered from the burning ruins trying to escape. Aside from the rain, these disasters were all man-made. The Germans destroyed the dams that once held the Sangro in, causing the river to flood. They torched the villages. They mined the roads. The land around the Sangro was being claimed by war. No one but soldiers could live there, and then only briefly. The soldiers brought war with them. They brought its sounds and its calamity. The Italian civilians were learning that war moved. It arrived one day. It covered the ground like rain.

By late November, Ramsay Park, who was now an intelligence officer with the 1st Canadian Armoured Brigade Headquarters, was on the lead of the Canadian advance. An army must know at all times where it is and what faces it, and that was where officers like Ramsay Park came in. Each day, Park was sent out to find the enemy. Sometimes he went alone, on foot, crawling out into unknown land, searching for a sign of the Germans. Sometimes he was driven miles toward enemy lines. Sometimes he was in a tank, leading a Troop of three Shermans, trying to get as close as possible. Park had been at it ten days straight. No break. No sleep. All the time under constant shelling. It did not matter if you were in a town square or an olive orchard. Night or day, it did not matter. The Germans would get their range and then pour it on, firing all night. "It drove you nuts," he would later say. "Of course, you did the same to them but that was different."[46] There were two or three officers at headquarters who had lived through the last war; they told the younger officers that there was no question that there was more shelling and noise and racket at the Sangro than there had been in any battle in the First World War.

Four days earlier, Park had lost an entire crew. A shell had torn into Park's Sherman tank and ripped through it, the shrapnel shredding the crew of five inside. The captain of a tank, however, stands and looks out the top with his legs extending a little into the turret; because of this Park made it out without a scratch. He returned to headquarters, a little rattled, and was out in combat again the following day.

Park was once again leading a tank. It crept cautiously down a village street toward a small piazza, a cobblestone square with a fountain that had been blown apart. It was time to reconnoitre, so Park and his crew disembarked from the tank and scanned the landscape. The Germans spotted them and unleashed their guns. Shells were lobbed into the town, crashing into buildings along the piazza. The crew scurried under the belly of the tank, desperate for cover. The shells continued landing, shrapnel skipping along the cobblestones, clinking and sparking on the stones as it began to skid in from both sides. The men curled up inside the underbelly of the tank. Park was in the middle.

Panic was setting in. Park's radio man was trying to raise help, trying to get a nearby artillery unit to call in a concentrated barrage, a "stonk," on the Germans. The radio man got someone on the line and called to Park. He held the telephone receiver out and Park reached for it. Park was looking at the soldier, trying to hear him over the deafening bombardment; he could see that the radio man was urging him to speak. Park's fingers touched the receiver. He saw the radio man's head move, just a few inches, maybe four. It slid over to the left and sat on his shoulder. Park heard nothing on the telephone. The head sat there and its eyes stared at Park for few seconds. Then it toppled over and hung from the radio man's torso by a strip of skin. Park called to his men but heard nothing. The tank's belly was pressing down on him. He was trapped underneath. He heard the sound of shrapnel breaking through fabric and lodging into skin. He heard the shells groan overhead and crash down. He called to his crew again, but they were all dead. Park crawled through the bodies and squeezed out through an opening made by their legs and arms. His crew had caught the shrapnel that could have killed him. He crawled out, covered in blood, and his shoe caught on a soldier's belt. He struggled to cut the strap. Park made it back to headquarters, but he would never remember how he made the trip. The next day he was out in action and feeling pretty good. He did not know it, but he had reached his limit. In a few days he was on the way back to Avellino. "That," he later recalled, "finished me off."

4.

ITALY

In September 2000, I received a short handwritten letter. "I had a stroke but I can write," it said. "I know a lot about Pringle. I was his sergeant in Italy." It was signed "Tony." This letter was the best response I had received to a classified advertisement that I had placed in the *Legion Magazine* calling for any information about Harold Pringle. Unfortunately, there was no last name and no telephone number. On the back, however, there was an address in Peterborough, Ontario, a city about two hours from Toronto. I immediately wrote back, addressing my reply to "Tony, a veteran." The following morning, I could barely function for thinking of the letter and what it might mean. Finally, unable to wait any longer, I got in my car, drove to Peterborough, found the address and knocked at the door. An elderly man with a perfectly groomed head of grey hair answered. He was wearing a white golf shirt and grey slacks. "I'm looking for a man named Tony," I told him. "He is a veteran of the Hastings and Prince Edward Regiment and fought in the Second World War."

The man smiled genially: "That would be me. We were just reading your letter." "We" turned out to be Tony Basciano and his wife Patricia. Tony, who was born in Italy but grew up in Peterborough, Ontario, had joined the army in 1939 at age seventeen and had quickly been promoted to corporal and, once in Italy, to sergeant. He led a platoon "D" Company from 1943 to 1945, fighting in Europe and Italy. Tony admitted to being "banged up" a bit while in Italy. When pressed for a little more detail, he said, "Shells." After only fifteen minutes talking with him I could easily see why he must have been an excellent sergeant. He had common sense and a quick sense of humour, and there was a motherly quality to him that demonstrated that he was a man who would not take unnecessary risks but was willing to take the right ones. In the Hastings and Prince Edward veterans' association, he had a sterling reputation. "If Tony tells you something, you can take it for fact," Major Robert Bradford told me.[1]

In a way, Tony had prepared his entire life to be a sergeant. He was the eldest child in a large Italian family; his mother had died when he was a toddler; years later his father was hospitalized for a very serious illness and the children were put in separate foster homes. That Christmas, young Tony went to the hospital and told his father that if he did not get better soon and come home the family would be permanently split up. Tony told him, "You have to get better. You have to come home." His father did. That, I suppose, was Tony's first order.

Tony heard about Harold's execution in 1945 while he was stationed in Holland. After he returned to Canada, he went to Flinton with the intention of visiting Harold's family: "I'd heard, you know, that the father had gone through the town holding the paper that told him Harold was dead and that he'd yelled at people, 'Look what they did to my boy.'" Tony spent two days in Flinton trying to work up the courage to see William Pringle, but he never managed it: "I went right to the house and stood outside but I never went in. I couldn't do it. I lost my nerve. I never met his dad and I am mad about that."[2]

In 1946, Tony returned to Peterborough, where he trained as a barber and eventually opened up his own shop. He married, and he and Pat became proud parents and then grandparents. Tony became a regular at his grandson's hockey games. Despite the passage of time, Tony never forgot Harold Pringle. His wife says that throughout their marriage, he would sometimes mention him, out of the blue: "We will be driving somewhere and Tony will say, 'I wonder why they killed him?'"[3]

In 1985, a reporter contacted Tony about Pringle, but Tony did not want to discuss it then. He was protective of those he had fought with, Pat said. Between men from the same regiment there were bonds that transcended time. "People aren't born to kill, but when the circumstances come up it's kill or be killed," she said. "That's why a lot of soldiers, when they came back, would never talk about the war to their families. It was such a horrible experience. A couple of the guys Tony knew were winos. But he would never think of them that way. He would think of them the way they were when they were fighting together overseas, the way they sacrificed for one another. When Tony saw them on the street he would walk right up to them and talk and shake their hand."

Time had changed Tony's mind. "There is no point keeping quiet about Harold now," Tony told me. "I'm the only one living, I think, who knew him. I always thought he was the only one in the family, the only one born to the family." Here Pat added, "Tony used to say he got mixed up with the wrong people in the army."[4]

Tony told me that being AWOL in 1942 was far from uncommon:

> They often did that, you know. I was at a camp at Rygate where, heck, the guys never slept in their own beds. They slept downtown in some girl's bedroom. Harold started to go bad in 1942. I can remember seeing him down at Rygate. Him and a guy, a corporal—heck, what was his name. The officers had him marked. We were told about certain guys and told to watch them. He was let out of prison to come and fight with us. None of us cared about his record.
>
> Harold was a brave bugger, you know. He was to be shot sitting in a chair and he had the choice of sitting facing away from the firing squad. But he chose to sit facing them and with no blindfold. He walked in and almost took over, you know. He told the squad, "Come on, do what you've got to do. Let's get it over with."[5]

Tony recalled first meeting Harold Pringle in December 1944, when the 1st Canadian Division found itself advancing toward Ortona. The Hasty Ps and the rest of the Eighth Army had been fighting since July 1943 in terrain that most military strategists believe is among the worst an army can try to take. Italy is a series of valleys, rivers and mountain

ranges from the end of the boot to the Alps, and the Allies never wanted
to attack it by land. The British High Command wanted to conquer it in
a series of amphibious landings, such as the ones the British and
Americans made at Anzio, a small beach town south of Rome. Anzio,
unfortunately, proved to be a disaster. Instead of breaking out and pushing
on to Rome, the Allies were pinned down for months, suffering high casualties. Consequently, the Italian campaign became an infantryman's war.

Harold Pringle had arrived in Italy from England by convoy on a
route that made many diversionary changes to fool the U-boats that
hunted Allied vessels. He disembarked at Naples, the Allies' main port.
The Americans had bombed Naples during the autumn of 1943, destroying the harbour and much of the city. Before retreating, the Germans had
finished the job, mining and demolishing anything that could be of
value. After capturing Naples, the Allies enlisted the help of the city's top
crime family, the Camorra, in order to fix it. The Camorra had a Robin
Hood image and were ferociously anti-Fascist during Mussolini's reign;
the people of Naples both feared and admired them. They were merciless
to their enemies, who could be roughly described as anyone who did not
do what the Camorra wanted them to do. In exchange for its help, the
crime syndicate received special favours from the occupational government. For the remainder of the war, the Camorra ran the black market
almost untouched.

After landing, Harold Pringle was sent to Avellino, a small city of
thirty thousand people located thirty-five miles east of Naples in the
province of Campania. Ramsay Park had been sent there in December.
Avellino was nestled in the Apennine mountains and was lush with pine
and chestnut trees. It was here that the Canadian commanders had
decided to set up their main reinforcement depot. The city was ideally
situated between four main strategic points: Rome and Naples on the
west side of Italy, Ortona and Foggia on the east. At Avellino, reinforcements were armed and outfitted and then shunted up to whatever
regiment needed bodies. The average Canadian army infantry battalion
had about nine hundred men and officers. There were four rifle companies, each consisting of three platoons that had three sections of ten men
each. These companies were named Able, Baker, Charlie and Dog.

Behind these rifle units were support companies that provided special arms fire, mortar companies, and pioneer companies that built roads and cleared mines. Each regiment had its own headquarters, with a medical attachment, intelligence officers and liaison officers. There were also various support troops who brought up supplies, food and armaments.

Avellino was a sort of unofficial court. A bad posting could be a death sentence. Michael Cloney, a lawyer from Toronto who had graduated from Osgoode in 1939 with Ramsay Park, found himself in Avellino in 1944. He was to be sent to the Hasty Ps as a reinforcement officer but at the last moment was kept back to act as a legal officer at staff headquarters. "That," says Cloney, "pretty much saved my life."[6] After the war Cloney went on to a distinguished career in the Judge Advocate General, and then became an Ontario Appeals Court judge. Cloney's pessimistic analysis is borne out by other veterans and by statistics. According to Canadian military historian Bill McAndrew, who along with historian Terry Copp wrote *Battle Exhaustion: Soldiers and Psychiatrists in the Canadian Army, 1939–1945*, few combat troops "managed to survive a year in action without being wounded."[7] During one of our interviews, I asked Tony Basciano about his responsibilities in the regiment. He told me he was a platoon commander. Wasn't that, I replied, the job of an officer? "Yes," he answered. "But they never lived long enough. They kept getting killed. So most of the time I did it." Tony remembers one comrade who returned from the hospital, his second trip in six months, to find only one man remaining from the original platoon of thirty-five. "Where is everyone?" he asked the last survivor. "Dead or probably better off that way and I'm not sticking around to join them," was the answer.[8] That night both soldiers deserted.

Harold Pringle was no law school graduate. Without a special skill set worth preserving behind the lines, he was sent up to the Hastings and Prince Edward Regiment, which was slogging its way past the Sangro River on the approach to Ortona.

Judging by the regiment's war diary, if Harold arrived in Italy that December, he arrived in Ortona early on the morning of Christmas Eve with 159 other young and poorly trained reinforcements who were brought up through the village of San Leonardo. In *The Regiment*, Farley

Mowat describes how these recruits passed the bodies of a full platoon of Canadian soldiers on their way up. They did not have to wait long for an initiation in combat. The Germans dropped a barrage on them as they moved forward and caused seven casualties.

The Eighth Army's commanders had not expected a fight at Ortona, a picturesque town nestled on the coast. They thought it had the potential to become a rest centre, so they had not subjected it to intense bombing. By December 1943, most of Ortona's ten thousand inhabitants had been cleared out—the Germans had shipped the town's young men off as slave labour. The two battalions of German paratroopers who held the town mined houses and streets, blocked streets with rubble, constructed machine-gun nests and camouflaged mortar and anti-tank guns. The result was the first street fighting seen by the Allies during the Second World War. The Canadians fought house to house, clearing tenacious German troops from the town. They developed techniques such as "mouse-holing," in which the troops would blow a hole through one wall to gain access into a new house. They threw grenades into second-storey windows in order to bring the ceiling down on defenders holding the ground floor. CBC Radio reporter Matthew Halton described Ortona as a "death frenzy." By the end of a week's fighting Ortona had been flattened. The drive to it, which had crossed the Sangro and Moro rivers, had cost 4,206 dead, wounded or sick Canadians. And for many soldiers the worst was yet to come. "Everything before Ortona," Canadian Major General Christopher Vokes later said, "was a nursery tale."[9]

The fighting claimed many riflemen and officers and left the Hastings and Prince Edward Regiment and other Canadian units in the Adriatic sector decimated. Vokes sent word to his British Corps commander that "in my opinion the infantry units of this division will not be in fit condition to undertake further offensive operations until they have had a period of rest, free of operational commitments, during which they can carry out intensive training."[10]

Yet training and rest, by which the army meant any activity that did not include fighting, were not on offer. Instead, the 1st Canadian Division lined up along the Riccio River, north of Ortona, and settled into five months of static warfare. The Canadians found themselves on the opposite side of a channel at the foot of the Arielli, a high ridge on which the Germans were entrenched. This position blocked any advance north, and a stalemate ensued. Conditions were reminiscent of the trench tactics of the First World War. Winter rain and snow came down relentlessly as the Germans and Allies traded shellfire almost continuously. The situation was worsened by the fact that in London Allied generals were preparing for a major offensive in northwest Europe; supplies and reinforcements to the Italian sector dried up.

The Canadians entrenched along the Gully found themselves to be a smaller force attacking a larger one. The Germans had twenty-seven divisions in Italy, the Allies seventeen. Canadian Corps commanders believed that if the Germans discovered they were facing a smaller force, they might counterattack and pierce the Canadian line; they were determined to convince the Germans that their forces were at full strength. To achieve this, they decided to send nightly patrols out to harass the enemy. These diversionary attacks, which ranged in size from two to a dozen men, would also keep the Germans on the defensive and prevent them from reinforcing the German units fighting at Cassino.

"A waste of time." That is how Harry Fox, who became the Hastings and Prince Edward Regiment's sergeant major in January 1944, recalls the raids across the Arielli Valley. Fox, a Torontonian who before the war worked at Eaton's, also remembers these patrols as exercises in terror. Patrolling meant crawling through freezing mud, negotiating tripwires rigged in vine fields and creeping along paths sown with land mines.[11] Major J. K. Rhodes of the West Nova Scotian Regiment wrote, "Patrols were sent out with orders to beat up the enemy, to the same place, by the same route, several nights in succession. It provided the enemy with excellent opportunities to inflict losses and to take prisoners, seriously lowering morale. Daylight patrols were often ordered over flat country without any cover where we could actually see the enemy from our positions. Patrolling for no good reason seems to be only of value to the enemy."[12] In one forty-day period, a Canadian regiment sent out forty fighting patrols and another twenty-four reconnaissance patrols, as well as a plethora of security patrols. The Germans, meanwhile, sent out patrols of their own. The situation inspired one Canadian officer to suggest that "the only thing needed up here is traffic lights in the gullies to keep Canadians and Germans from bumping into each other."[13] Throughout this period, the Canadian units were woefully under strength. "I was supposed to have thirty-five men in my company," Tony Basciano told me. "We never had more than seventeen."

"Day after day," one Canadian officer wrote, "you sit looking at a hillside and you go out on patrol and get shot at time and time again. After a while the hillside seems to become impregnable."[14]

On January 30, the Hasty Ps made an attack against the Germans entrenched on the Arielli Ridge. The assault's objective was the German soldiers who were holding the area around the Tollo River. The Hastings and Prince Edward Regiment advanced one mile in broad daylight across flat open ground while Shermans from the Calgary Tanks shelled the Germans. At four in the afternoon, two Canadian companies leading the assault came close to reaching their objective until they were hit with an enormous concentration of machine-gun fire. They fell back to a shallow gully, where they held on overnight. By morning, forty-eight men were down. Canadian brigadier Daniel Spry ordered a second attack over the same ground. In one hour, forty-three more men were killed or wounded. "It was," the First Brigade's war diary noted, "a very heavy price to pay for the knowledge that the enemy is holding the Tollo in strength."[15]

As the Canadians toiled away in the Gully, morale weakened. Canadian military psychiatrist A. M. Doyle reported to Canadian headquarters that neuropsychiatric cases, dubbed "shell shock" in the First World War and "battle exhaustion" in 1944, had reached thirty-five per cent of total casualties and fifty per cent of those wounded. He informed his superiors that when neuropsychiatric casualties reached twenty per cent it typically was an indication that a unit's morale and fighting capabilities were seriously in jeopardy.[16] Some soldiers found an indirect route out of combat. Between December 1943 and February 1944, there were sixty-seven cases of self-inflicted wounds in the Canadian army. A decorated platoon commander later wrote that "lying in a slit trench during a shelling, the thought would occur to you that putting one foot up in an exposed position might be a sensible thing to do."[17]

Some soldiers went AWOL or deserted entirely. Rumours began to circulate through the ranks about phantom gangs of deserters. One legend had it that a renegade Canadian captain had gone mad and taken his entire platoon AWOL. Soldiers said the rogue platoon was out there freelancing in the Italian countryside, living by their own rules. To accommodate offenders, the 1st Canadian Division created a Field Punishment Camp in the castle at Ortona. It opened in February 1944 with twenty soldiers under sentence. "And so things went on and on," the war diary for 1st Canadian Infantry Division Field Punishment Camp states. "And our little family grew and grew, and at the end of March our guests numbered more than two hundred."[18] By the end of April, the Hasty Ps, which never had more than six hundred men in the field, had suffered four hundred casualties. It was a time, Mowat later wrote, "when each man believed that he and his unit had utterly been abandoned and forgotten."[19]

For those who have never had to endure the effects of combat, a clear understanding can be found by perusing the Battle Experience Questionnaires the Canadian army had its officers complete following the end of the war. Captains and lieutenants with combat experience were asked to report on such topics as the types of weapons they used and the sorts of weapons that were used against them. "When moving forward," they were asked, "did you clear your own mines?" Today these questionnaires—thousands of them—are stored in the National Archives in Ottawa. To those who have the time, they provide an eerie glimpse into the practical application of military objectives. They demonstrate that soldiering may be a patriotic calling, but it is also a skill, a craft practised by professionals. During the Second World War, Farley Mowat wrote in *The Regiment*, a Canadian infantryman had "to be proficient in rifle and bayonet, Bren light machine gun, two-inch mortar, .55 inch anti-tank rifle, Thompson submachine gun, Sten gun and five varieties of hand grenade," as well as "elementary tactics, battle drills, map reading, field craft, cooperation with other arms, gas defence, military law, field hygiene, patrol techniques, enemy methods and equipment."[20]

The Battle Experience reports are especially telling because they were written by men who were about to leave the army and who therefore had no incentive to lie. As a result, they have a searing candour. Roy Stuffe, a major with the 4th Canadian Armoured Division, wrote, "Some men who had seen their buddies blown to pieces suffered a subsequent mental shock and had to be evacuated." Mortars, another officer wrote, were an infantryman's greatest fear, and different reasons for this, such as "Can come out of nowhere," were given. There were other morale busters. "Hearing noises and not knowing what makes the noise," wrote a captain in the Essex Scottish Regiment. Captain Gordon Crutchen, of the Carleton and York Regiment, cited "being 'buggered around' without reason. Allowing men to get sloppy in appearance and long periods of idleness." Another officer referred to "being shelled by own artillery (or aircraft)" and "an unsuccessful action that appeared to be due to poor planning on the part of a leader." Another lamented "being kept in the dark as to the Big Picture." The officers adopted a clinical tone when responding to questions about their own tactics. "Some men will not carry hand grenades because they fear a piece of shrapnel or a bullet hitting the grenade in their pocket," one officer wrote. "There have been some bad experiences." Their language is infused with military jargon but their manner of speaking remains civilian. They are like plumbers discussing a faucet. "It is very handy to have a Tommy gun and some hand grenades on the turret of the tank," one officer wrote, "in case one encounters a slit trench." The use of "handy" and "machine gun" makes for a strange juxtaposition. One captain summed up fighting spirit: "Canadians must be led—they will not be whipped." Another officer complained, "Physical and mental fatigue under battle conditions was highest in new recruits who were too often brought to a company one night and participated in an attack the next day without a period of adjustment to battle conditions." Words were not always necessary to get a point across—one officer simply wrote his name, rank and serial number and left his questionnaire blank.[21]

By April 1944, Harold Pringle was no longer a new recruit. He had become a full-fledged member of the Hastings and Prince Edward Regiment. Tony Basciano remembers him as "the nicest guy, a good-looking young fellow. He was always perfect. His dress was just perfect. We used to wish we could dress like him. He was a likeable guy. Always trying to get along. Just A-1."

Tony made particular note of Harold's disposition: "Pringle always smiled—he was always smiling. Pringle, when he was fighting, he'd be there smiling." He also recalled a capable soldier, one who kept his cool under fire:

> He was an A-1 soldier. He was a good soldier. He was a brave bugger, you know. You had to have a man like that with you in action. 'Cause there is no limit to what you can do with him. When we were on parade we used to call each other by rank. But when we got into action, it was call us anything. If you had a parade at three in the morning, you'd tell him and he'd get his gear ready. All the sergeants liked him but he had a hell of a temper. God, he had an awful temper. He would have made sergeant easy, if he wanted to, if he didn't have that temper. He took orders but he didn't like it.[22]

ON APRIL 11, 1944, Harold was ordered out on patrol. Activities for that night were to be laid on fairly heavily. The Hasty Ps were dug in near San Tommaso and shells roared down, as they had all day. So far, however, there had been no casualties. The previous day, a soldier who had just arrived had been killed. The patrol for April 11 would send men from "D" Company, led by Captain Beauclerk, out to a fortified house on the German lines that the officers had nicknamed "Daisy." A fighting patrol from "B" Company would go to "Petunia," and a recce patrol from "C" Company would go to "Cornflower." Once darkness fell, Harold and the others would go. As he waited, Harold ate and thought of the patrol. Now that spring had arrived, the nights were shorter and that left less time. The patrols had to go out and get in. If dawn came and you were still out there—well, that would not be a good place to be.[23]

Harold Pringle sat in his slit trench and polished his belt buckle methodically, something he would do for hours before going on patrol. Harold worked that buckle until it shone, but he would leave it back at camp since its glimmer would draw fire on patrol. Harold also had other, more practical pre-patrol rituals. If there were any extra grenades lying around, he would shove some into his tunic: he had come to consider them a good means of introduction. In fact, he would not enter a house without first chucking one in. Harold polished his belt buckle and thought about Flinton and how good it would be to see the kids skating on the Skootamatta River. Then his thoughts returned to the evening's patrol. Captain Beauclerk, whom he liked, would be leading it. Captain Beauclerk was a good officer. And how.

As afternoon closed out, the heat subsided. It had been a very warm April, a nice contrast to the cold of the past three months. The evening promised to be fresh and cool, just like the evenings back home in Canada. Sometimes that was how the soldiers thought of patrolling, trying to convince themselves that it was just a hunting trip, an excursion out into the bush. Of course, there was an important difference: the deer didn't shoot back. The Germans did. One second a man was crawling along, and the next he was in the middle of a fight. Mortars were coming down, ripping everything to shreds, and there was screaming and darkness and nobody knew what the hell was going on.

Just after dark, Captain Beauclerk's patrol slipped out and began to make its way to "Daisy." Slow and sure was the way there, Harold reminded himself; advance on your belly or with at least one knee on the ground at all times. Keep low. Listen. The night sky always looked low in Italy. It wasn't big the way it was back home. And the birds, they were noisy. The slow push out went on for hours. Darkness. Silence. Breathing. Hand signals. Captain Beauclerk guided them closer and closer to the enemy. This was a fighting patrol, and that meant finding the enemy and engaging him. On a reconnaissance patrol, you just tried to spot him and track his whereabouts, gathering information. Harold pushed his nerves down. Remember: Beauclerk's a good officer. He knows what he is doing. It did not take much to be a veteran here. There were only two hundred of the original Hasty Ps, the ones who came over to England in 1940, left in the regiment. Harold Pringle crawled along, his rifle snug in his hands and his grenades well out of harm's way.

The patrol moved toward "Daisy," and as "D" Company came close to its objective, the Germans opened up, unleashing heavy machine-gun fire and grenades. The Canadians returned fire with their rifles, but the Germans began to bring more on. Captain Beauclerk was hit badly; tracer fire streaked through the bush, lighting the darkness. The bullets buzzed by. Two privates were wounded and it became obvious that "D" Company was in trouble. Harold and the remaining members of the patrol gathered up the wounded. It was tough work. Men screamed when they were hit. If they were really badly off they sank into a state of silent shock; in some ways that far-away look was more disturbing than the shrieking. The eyes drained and took on a dreamy glaze. With the wounded assembled, "D" Company moved out. Harold and another private gave covering fire as the patrol withdrew, blasting bullets into the darkness. Harold relieved himself of his extra hand grenades; they exploded in the bush, creating a bright orange glow that illuminated the blackness like a light going on in a darkened room. He could not be sure how many, if any, Germans were killed, but that was not the main goal. The important thing was to cause as much destruction as possible so that the Germans who were attacking became occupied with the business of defence. So Harold poured it on. One of his patrol caught a glimpse of him in the darkness. He was smiling.

The patrol made it back. Captain Beauclerk was still alive; he was sent to the hospital but there was no guarantee he would be alive for long. The two privates were dead. Harold and the survivors settled in. There was tea and a little bread for breakfast. Most of the men who went into combat would tell you that you did not always feel scared when you were in the middle of it. The head had to remain clear: you had a job to do. But when you got back and you felt a little safe, then the stress worked its way out. "You start to shake or cry or just come apart," one Hasty P later recalled. "It creeps up on you. When you're back, that is when you feel it."[24]

Unable to sleep, Harold wrote a letter home. Perhaps not surprisingly, the question of health was uppermost in his mind.

Somewhere in Italy

April 11, 1944

My Dear Dad, + Mother + all,

Just a few lines again to say I am Well and in the very best of
health. I sure hope this few lines find yous all in the very best of
health. Well Dad I had a nice letter from Aunt Ida last night and I
sure was glad to hear from them. Also to hear they where all quite
well. So when you see them give them all my best regards. How
are all the folks around Flinton. I sure hope they are all in the
very best of health. And also give them all my best regards. Well
Dad I was out on a fighting patrol the other night and was it ever
hot. But we all came back. One of hour officers got hit this morning But I think he will be OK I hope. As he sure was good. *And
how*. I sure hope you can read this awful writing as it is rather
hard to write as we have to keep hour heads down. And how.

But I dont think it will last much longer now at least we all
hope not anyway. Say Dear Dad how are all Grandmas. I sure
hope they are all well and in the best of health. I havent run into
Earl Pringle yet. But maybe he is still in England. I sure would like
to see him. Say Dad how are all my Sweet Brothers + Sisters +
Dear Mother. I sure hope they are all well and in the very best of
health. Well Dad I guess I will have to ring off for now. But I will
write again real soon. So I will say cheerio for now with lots of
love and the very best of luck to everyone + all to My Darling
Dad + Mother And My Sweet Brother + Sisters please write
real soon.

From your lonesome son

Harold

Answer Real Soon.

XXXxxxxxxxx[25]

The following day, there were no fighting patrols. The Canadians set
up forward ambush patrols in the hope of catching Germans, but the
enemy did not take the bait. Canadian artillery and mortars threw down
fire on suspected German positions and there was some success. An

ambulance was seen racing to where the Canadians had directed their barrage. On April 13, a patrol went out at ten thirty in the evening. After it crossed the first river opposite Canadian lines, the patrol heard movement. The Canadians open up with grenades and Tommy guns. They heard a yell but found nobody. At three in the morning, a strong German patrol attacked "A" Company. A heavy firefight ensued. No casualties were reported.[26]

That night Harold wrote his mother. He was worried about the family finances and promised her that "you will soon get that Money again so please let me no just as soon as you get it." Harold was concerned about the farm. With his father an invalid, Harold's younger brothers and sisters were helping out and he complimented them for their effort. As the eldest, and the one who would naturally take over the farm, Harold promised to treat Charlie well: "He sure is a wonderful worker and a good boy isnt he and I sure wont forget him when the war is over. And give him my advice and tell him never to start smoking or drinking."[27]

The rest of April was spent patrolling, crawling out along the same routes that the Hasty Ps and other regiments in 1st Canadian Division had been tracking since Ortona. On April 14, the Germans unleashed a large-scale bombardment on the entire Canadian front. On April 15, the shelling was again heavier than usual. The Germans dropped propaganda leaflets, which the Canadians found amusing. They contained advice on surrendering and a fairly explicit description of what the men at home were doing to the girlfriends of the men overseas. The Hasty Ps' mortars caught a dozen Germans moving forward and killed at least three. A patrol from "B" Company fought a German patrol. On April 18, a fighting patrol was sent to the caves outside a key point called "Johnnie." The patrol discovered that the caves were occupied by Germans; they threw in hand grenades. After that there was no movement from inside the caves. The weather each day was warm and bright.[28]

The nightly patrols seemed interminable, but the Hastings and Prince Edward Regiment would shortly move away from the trenches along the Arielli to the Apennine Mountains in the province of Lazio, the region beneath Rome. There they would see the Liri Valley, a flat and fertile stretch of land that ran up from the southern province of

Campania to Rome. To Pringle, to the Germans, to the Allies, to the Italian peasants, this valley would become *Valle di Morte*, the Valley of Death. The English and the Americans had already lost thousands there in futile attacks up Monte Cassino. Thousands more would be buried there. Olive trees, planted after the war, would nourish themselves on the undiscovered bodies of Allied and German soldiers, and for decades afterward farmers would believe that their blood fertilized the soil and fed bumper crops. The Allies had levelled the Benedictine Monastery on top of Monte Cassino in February 1944. At the foot of the mountain, in the town of Cassino, Italian parents had scrambled through the rubble, trying desperately to find dead children. Then more shells rained down and killed them.

5.

THE HITLER LINE

It was raining steadily. To the men in the Hasty Ps, however, it must have seemed like the sunniest day of the year. The regiment was pulling out after four gruelling months on the Arielli Front, and that meant there would be no more trench warfare, at least for a while. Only the officers knew why they were being sent to the town of Termoli and then south inland, but to Harold Pringle and the other privates, details like those were not especially significant. The Hasty Ps were getting out and that was all that mattered. There would be Italian villages to visit, complete with Italian women and "bottled sunshine," the Italian red wine that was popular with the troops.

At one thirty in the afternoon on April 20, 1944, the Hasty Ps' convoy of trucks pushed off and the rumble of artillery slowly faded into the distance. The convoy passed through Lanciano and swung south and crossed the Sangro, the river that the Canadians had battled for so bitterly in December 1943. By five thirty they were in Termoli. The kitchen staff unloaded their cookers and the Hasty Ps prepared to bivouac for the night. Before they could begin, orders came down from Brigadier General Spry to move three miles farther south to Campobasso. There the battalion bedded down for the night in a grassy field by the road. The rain stopped.[1]

The following day, the Hastings and Prince Edward Regiment was moving again. It became mixed up with an Indian convoy going the same way and a little negotiation was necessary to get the troops sorted. The Canadians travelled another thirty miles to the village of Montagano and camped in a lightly wooded area not far from the town. Sentries were posted, tents were raised and the weather was warm and clear. The next day, Italian civilians started turning up, looking for food and clothes. Extra sentries were posted to keep them out and the pioneer platoon (a kind of military construction unit) was ordered to erect signs in Italian telling civilians to stay away. The commanding officer, Lieutenant Colonel Donald C. Cameron, went to Avellino to arrange for reinforcements to be sent up.

Over the next week, the Hasty Ps were sent into Campobasso for baths and for recreation. Trucks left at four thirty in the afternoon and returned at eleven thirty at night. The regiment rested, but it also participated in what the officers called "toughening up exercises." These consisted of long marches and mountain climbing. "The troops slowly began coming back into a good physical shape after the rather idle period during the last three months," the Hasty Ps' war diarist wrote on April 28. On May 8, the Hasty Ps reached their final destination, the village of Limatola. Here the entire 1st Canadian Division was assembled in preparation for a major offensive. The regiment built a baseball diamond; Support Company won a close game against "A" Company. The regiment practised river crossings; a few lucky personnel were sent on leave to Naples; and church services were held for those Protestants and Roman Catholics still in camp. On May 12, Lieutenant Colonel Cameron briefed the Hastings and Prince Edward Regiment on the Cassino Front. He told them how the offensive had been going and about the job expected of the Canadian Corps and the Eighth Army. Put bluntly, he said, pretty much every unit in the Eighth Army had made a crack at Cassino and the casualties had been horrendous. The Canadians could expect a similar reception. "It proved," wrote the company diarist, "to be a very interesting talk." By May 15, the Hasty Ps were ready to head up the line to the Liri Valley and to the front at Cassino. The men could hear the guns, and smoke was so thick from the battle that it was impossible for the Hasty Ps' reconnaissance patrol to see the ground it was supposed to be occupying. Yet spirits were high, and the Hasty Ps whistled on their way to the front.

Their objective, the Liri Valley, was a stretch of land ten kilometres wide that ran between two mountain ranges. On its north side sat the Apennine Mountains, the side the Germans occupied in 1944, and on the south lay the Arunci range. The lowest peak held by the Germans was 300 metres and the highest, Monte Cairo, was 1,700 metres. Despite such daunting natural defences, the Liri was a key strategic goal. Straight up the valley, the Via Casilina, Route 6, ran to Rome—the only road to Rome suitable for motorized vehicles.

The most commanding peak held by the Germans was the 516-metre-high Monte Cassino, which dominates the entire valley. Thousands of years earlier Mark Antony had built his villa nearby in order to control the road from Naples to Rome. In AD 529, St. Benedict founded the first organized monastery in Italy on Monte Cassino, creating the Benedictine order. In the following centuries, the monastery was sacked many times and came to resemble a fortress. The Lombards seized it in 569; the Saracens plundered it in 883; in 1349, it was almost destroyed by an earthquake; and in 1799, it was overrun by the French under Napoleon. In 1944, when they found the Germans were dug in on the Apennines and on Monte Cassino, it was the Allies' turn.

On February 13, scores of Allied bombers blasted the monastery into a pile of rubble. To this day there is disagreement as to the usefulness of the attack. Italians resent the destruction and are highly critical of the Allies. After all, they say, the monastery was a holy, priceless piece of architecture and history that had withstood thousands of years and that contained many riches. The Germans and Italians both maintain that no German troops were in the monastery and that it was never used as a strategic location. Allied generals, however, believed that the Germans were using the monastery, which had a clear view of the entire Liri Valley, to direct artillery fire. It was also necessary to destroy the monastery for morale purposes. Even if there were no Germans in it, the Eighth Army's soldiers were convinced that there were, and that belief was crushing the army's fighting spirit. In his book *Rome '44*, British author and veteran Raleigh Trevelyan quotes a sergeant from the 2nd Battalion of the London Irish; "It just had to be bombed. Oh, it was malignant. It was evil somehow. I don't know how a monastery can be evil, but it was looking at you. It was all-devouring if you like—sun-bleached colour, grim. It had a terrible hold on us soldiers....We thought it had to be destroyed. We just didn't know how the place could be taken otherwise."[2] Lieutenant Bruce Foster of the 60th Rifles told Trevelyan,

> CAN YOU IMAGINE what it is like to see a person's head explode in a great splash of grey brains and red hair, and have all the muck all over you, in your mouth, eyes and ears? And can you imagine what it is like when that head belongs to your sister's fiancée? I knew why it happened, I was positive, it was because some bloody fucking Jerry was up there in that fucking bloody Monastery directing the fire that killed Dickie, and I know that still; to hell with all those Pontius Pilates who pretend they were so bloody innocent and had nothing to do with the bombing. Christ, Dickie was the finest, most upright man you or I would ever meet. I am just glad that he died quickly, which is more than a lot of other poor fuckers did up there.[3]

BEFORE THE WAR, the Liri Valley had been covered in orchards, olive groves and vineyards. There were dense woods of spruce and oak trees and fields of wild poppies. A little river called the Rapido snaked through the valley and met a small creek called the Liri. At the foot of the mountain stood the town of Cassino, with twenty-two thousand inhabitants, and beyond the town lay a number of small villages, such as Pontecorvo and Piedimonte. Each had suffered in its own way. Cassino had been utterly destroyed by bombardment: not a single building was left standing. Trevelyan describes how, in the town of San Michele, French Algerian troops dragged women and girls from their houses and raped them. One widow was raped thirteen times. In early 1944, after the Germans cleared the Cassino area of thousands of Italians, a grim stalemate ensued. The British, American, Polish, New Zealand, South African and Indian battalions slammed away at German defences and suffered devastating casualties.[4]

Cassino was like something dragged from Dante, a mountain "once glad," now barren "like some worn thing by time decayed...dripping

COURTESY OF MARION JAMIESON

Lt. Tom Jamieson, grandfather of author, far right, and fellow
soldiers inspect ruins of monastery at Monte Cassino, May 1944.

—

tears that collect and force their passage down the cavern from rock to
rock into this valley's depth."[5] The shelling was incessant. Soldiers
stormed up steep cliffs and were slain wholesale. The next day the attacks
were repeated. Corpses were left to rot for months in the rain. Supplies
were brought to the front lines by mule along trails on which the
Germans had fixed their artillery. Whole regiments melted away on
Cassino's slopes. The bodies of mules and men were everywhere.

This was my grandfather's battlefield, a place in which the boom and
whistle of explosives were as inescapable as the sun. After the war, Tom
Jamieson hated noise. He could not abide racket, sudden crashes or
radios turned too loud. This was a souvenir of his time at Cassino and
later up north in Ravenna. Much later, when he was in his eighties and
nearing death, he began recalling details and sharing them. His mind
would wander, sometimes to Italy, and he would believe he was back
there and would start giving orders. Cassino was the place he learned
that "your beard grows after you die," an observation he made to my
Uncle Bruce at one family gathering. "Your beard grows after you die,"
my grandfather told him. "The German boys would be laid out by the

side of the road and you would see their blond beards growing. They wore horn-rimmed glasses. Like you." Then there was the time he told my cousin Alexander, "After a while you don't bleed blood. Just clear liquid. I remember pulling this chap out from under a jeep and all this clear stuff was coming out of him and I was covered in it. The front of my shirt was soaking." This was the strange enlightenment of war.

Harold Pringle and the rest of the Hasty Ps were not yet familiar with the attractions of Cassino. As first-time tourists they would experience the Liri Valley's charms without preconceptions. Besides, there was a feeling among the ranks that the big push they were about to make could break things wide open and that the war might be drawing to a close. Once they smashed through, the Eighth Army could take Rome; that thought alone bolstered their morale. The Canadian troops dreamt of the pleasures they would enjoy once they liberated that city. Rome, with all its mystery, would open up for them. These fantasies sustained the men as they marched forward.

Somewhere not far from Harold and the Hasty Ps, a Canadian captain was preparing his men for the assault. His name was Colin McDougall. He was a Montrealer by birth and he had been fighting with the Princess Patricia's Light Infantry since 1943. "Oh to be in any other place than these bloody hills," McDougall wrote while directing artillery fire from an observation post in Sicily. "The sun gets hotter and the guns get louder. I wonder if we'll be here all day?"[6] McDougall had literary aspirations; before the war these might have manifested themselves in a coming-of-age novel or a romance. Now, in 1944, the war had twisted his psyche like a wet towel in need of drying, and like those of so many others who would experience war, it would never recapture its original shape. In the 1950s, McDougall would find himself living in Montreal, married and working at McGill University. He would also be consumed with the idea of, as he wrote in 1956, "purging the whole war experience."[7] McDougall would find that release in the story of the execution of Harold Joseph Pringle.

Colin McDougall was born on 13 July 1917. His father, Errol McDougall, was a respected Quebec judge, and his mother, Mary Wynifred McDougall, was a noted Montreal socialite. Colin attended

Lower Canada College, Quebec's prestigious English-language private school, and followed that with a BA from McGill University, graduating in 1940. He immediately enlisted in the army. McDougall married in 1941, shortly before being sent overseas to a reinforcement unit. After officers' school, he was attached to the Princess Patricia's Light Infantry, a regiment raised in Alberta with a long and esteemed record. The Princess Pats, as they were known, had served with distinction during the Boer War and the First World War.

Some soldiers, experts estimate between ten and fifteen per cent, enjoy the experience of combat. The risks and the adrenaline thrill them. McDougall, however, fell into the larger category of men—he was not fond of war. Nevertheless he did it effectively. He served in Italy from July 1943 until 1945, surviving some horrific fighting, including a day in which only seventy-eight of his unit's men returned from battle. McDougall's first glimpse of war left him spending its remainder searching for purpose and meaning, until he returned to Canada in 1946.

McDougall made several attempts at writing over the next five years but nothing stuck. In 1952, he visited Colonel James Gavin of the 82nd Airborne Division in South Africa and then visited a veteran from the 505 Combat Team. The story he heard left him inspired. In 1953, McDougall began work on the novel *Execution*. It would be a fictionalization of the execution of Harold Pringle.

Execution is a compelling depiction both of the war and of capital punishment. The answer to how much of McDougall's novel is real and how much imagined lies in the McGill University Rare Book Library in Montreal, to which McDougall bequeathed his papers and original manuscripts. The entire collection fits in two file boxes. There is a folder of clippings and reviews, including a letter from Saul Bellow, who tells McDougall that *Execution* poses the question, "How much cruelty puts out the human light?"[8] For the most part, McDougall's papers are handwritten notes on characters and plot. There are many entries in which he chastises himself for not writing more and for failing a project that was his life's passion. "The novel has become necessary to me as my own salvation," he wrote in 1955, "the only way I can reach contentment with myself. I have reached the point of no return."[9]

Harold Pringle's story was an ideal fit for McDougall because he believed the entire war had been one "continual execution."[10] McDougall was particularly disgusted by the connection between free will and capital punishment. Death in combat could be construed as fate. An execution, in contrast, was the pure exertion of free will. Execution was "the degradation of man, it is the injustice on man.... Is it enough," he wondered, "to say that execution is evil and that man is right when he struggles against it?"[11]

McDougall posed this question in *Execution* by changing the facts and by creating new "facts" of his own. Going through his papers, one can surmise what facts he kept and which he threw away. His finished text is filled with clues: "To get the story I want it may be necessary to make a catalogue of incidents (especially imaginary ones) and moods and feelings and then select these and fuse them together."[12] By connecting the dots, so to speak, one can determine what is factual and what is Colin McDougall's.

McDougall's biggest step was to split his Harold Pringle figure into two characters. Thus, in *Execution*, we have Rifleman Jonesy, a simple-minded farm boy, and Frazer, a cool and fearless soldier with a history of disciplinary trouble. Jonesy is an innocent, a Christ figure sacrificed at the end of the war by the army as a means of symbolically purging all the sins committed during the hostilities. He is young, twenty or twenty-one, and the picture of fresh youth. He is trusting and passive, incapable of fighting, a soldier who is relegated to acting as a servant to his regiment's company chaplain. Jonesy, McDougall wrote in his notes, is "always smiling, a permanent smile grown upon his face. His smile was a perennial, grown from seed upon his face."[13] Jonesy is also fastidious. He is an immaculate dresser and never looks anything but perfect. Yet Jonesy is mentally stunted. He is simple, almost borderline handicapped, and has only the barest concept of the events that swirl around him.

Frazer, in contrast, is a "baby-faced man who for two years in England spent most of his time in arrest or detention—but perhaps the only man Mitchell [one of the novel's central characters] had ever met who really merited the term 'fearless.' Frazer maintained that he never entered a Wop house, anywhere, without throwing a grenade in first."[14]

He does not shrink from combat—but he is changed by it. When Frazer finds his best friend dead on the battlefield, he feels "cut loose from his familiar anchors. He felt giddy and light-headed. He became aware of his utter loneliness up here: he had never felt like this before."[15]

McDougall must have decided to break Pringle into two characters because he believed that readers would not be able to empathize with a deserter. Jonesy would represent the pure and non-violent human spirit, while Frazer would represent the chaotic but powerful force to live, even if that meant killing. His decision paid off. *Execution* became a hit, selling many copies and winning the 1958 Governor General's Award for fiction. It was sold around the world. It is impossible to know whether *Execution* purged McDougall's war experience. One thing is certain, though: McDougall, who died in 1984, never wrote another book.

ON MAY 15, THE HASTINGS and Prince Edward Regiment came under increased shelling as it entered the Cassino area.[16] Traffic was heavy on the road into the valley, and their progress was slowed. The Canadians moved through the ruins of the Gustav Line, which the 8th Indian Division had broken the week earlier, and noticed a large amount of discarded German equipment, evidence of retreat. The following day the Hasty Ps were sent to the town of Pignataro to relieve the Indians. The Canadians liked the soldiers from the Far East, who were renowned as tough fighters who showed little mercy. It was because of the Indian troops that Canadian soldiers had to be careful how they tied their boots. Allied soldiers, by official regulation, were supposed to lace their boots crosswise. The Germans had them in straight lines. When the Gurkhas went on night patrol they would identify the enemy by creeping up to him and running a hand over his shoelaces. If they identified a German, they slit his throat. Norm Quick, a cameraman with the Royal Canadian Cinema Unit, remembers an Indian officer telling him, with much glee, an apocryphal story of how he and his patrol had discovered three Germans sleeping in a row at a forward observation post. The Indians decapitated the middle German and set his head on the chest of one of his still-sleeping comrades. Then they crept away. The Indian officer convulsed with laughter as he recounted the incident. Years later, in the

1980s, Sikh Mounties won the right to wear turbans while in uniform. Some Canadians were outraged. The reaction from those who had served alongside the Gurkhas, one veteran told me, was, "They can wear whatever the fuck they want."

The roads were now unmanageable for trucks, so the regiment proceeded by foot. Indian officers told the Hasty Ps' commander, Lieutenant Colonel Donald C. Cameron, that he would encounter some resistance just in front of Pignataro. As the regiment drew closer, it came under mortar fire and four men were killed. The Canadians discovered that the Indians were still clearing Germans from Pignataro, rooting them out of houses and foxholes. It had obviously been a tough scrap. The town was completely wrecked, and there were German bodies in abundance to indicate the beating the Indians had given them. The Canadians moved through the Indian Battalion and took over the pursuit of the Germans. The Hasty Ps occupied high ground facing the enemy. The Germans seemed to have an unlimited amount of artillery shells and mortar bombs, and heavy fighting ensued. The Hasty Ps captured two prisoners.

On the morning of May 17, the 1st Canadian Division was back on the move. At four in the morning, the troops were ordered to head toward the German right flank. Harold's unit, "D" Company, led the manoeuvre. At seven forty-five, they came under heavy machine-gun fire. Bullets riddled the air; Harold could hear the dull thwacking they made when they hit trees. The field became smoky and it was difficult to discern the enemy. To make matters worse, the maps that the Canadians had been issued were less than helpful. Lines identified as roads on a map turned out to be winding cow trails or open fields. During the melee, "D" Company was cut off from the rest of the regiment. Headquarters could not be raised on the radio, and at times both the Canadians and the Germans were trying to use the same frequency.

Nevertheless, "D" Company continued to fight its way forward. The Canadians were advancing through a dense wood where they could not rely on tank support. Harold and his comrades would clear out a patch of brush, fight until they gained the high ground, whether it was a small hill or a grove, pause to regroup and then push on. "It was an infantryman's battle," Cameron later wrote. "Best results were obtained by

Companies driving forward on a narrow front to the dominating ground, consolidating, fighting and moving up."[17] During the attack, "D" Company bumped into the 48th Highlanders, a Toronto regiment known as the "Glamour Boys," which was advancing up the road to Pontecorvo. The Glamour Boys joined in the advance.

Waiting down the road were fresh German troops from the 190th Panzer Reconnaissance Battalion. The Germans dug themselves into the dense woods and rained machine-gun fire down on the Canadians. German mortars were firing sporadically, ripping into the Canadian advance and causing confusion. When veterans talk of being in action they will often describe the speed at which events take place. At the same time, perception of events can slow down. The soldier feels bullets screeching by him, hears shells crashing down, wounded men screaming and the urgency of orders barked out in the frenzy of the fight, yet his sense of reality slows. There is a mute order. He sees the obstacle he must take, whether it is a machine-gun nest or half a dozen foes in a slit trench. He makes a decision. He executes it. The grenade is pulled and thrown, and if it makes contact, the problem may be solved. In real time this may last only a few seconds, but in the soldier's mind there is an objective system of cause and effect.

The German Panzer Battalion launched a final counterattack as darkness fell. Thirty German infantry and three self-propelled guns raced down the road from Pontecorvo. Bob Shaw, one of the 48th Highlanders' anti-tank platoon, was manning a 6-pound anti-tank gun, known to the troops as a "popcorn shooter" since it was rarely effective in combat. As the Germans attacked, a mortar gunner shot up a flare and Shaw saw the Germans attempting to cross a bridge over a small stream. One of the German guns was on the bridge, with another behind it and one on the ground on the Canadian side. Shaw fired his gun at the bridge; the shell collided with the self-propelled gun's gas tank and there was a fantastic explosion. The flames from the gun lit up the ground like an enormous bonfire. The illumination was a gift for the 48th Highlanders' Bren gunners. They methodically picked off the German soldiers as they scrambled around the flames. Meanwhile, Shaw hit another of the remaining German guns. The few surviving Germans fled.[18]

The "Battle of the Woods" was over. The last firefight had cost the
48th Highlanders nineteen casualties. "D" Company, which had taken
twenty-five German prisoners, rejoined the Hastings and Prince
Edwards Regiment. Seven men had been killed and thirty wounded,
"most of them seriously." Cameron noted that "our infantrymen when
fired on, particularly by a machine gun, tend to lie down and do nothing
about it and for some time Jerry happens to have the initiative. Such fire
must be returned with interest—and promptly....36 and 77 grenades
were found to be very useful in this type of fighting. Picks and shovels
were invaluable. Men needed no prompting or encouragement to dig.
'Thinning out' averted many casualties."[19]

On May 18, the Hasty Ps pushed forward. Harold's company was
held in reserve in a gully in the early morning, but by eleven they were
on the march again. As the Canadians moved through the remnants of
the German defences, they saw wrecked equipment everywhere. There
was also a German cemetery, a testament to the accuracy of the Allied
guns. That evening Lieutenant James Fraser led a fighting patrol out
toward the enemy, but the night became foggy and the patrol was stalled.
Then the Canadian artillery opened up and the patrol was forced to hide
out in a ruined house to avoid being hit by friendly fire. The following
day, the Germans shelled the Hasty Ps continuously with artillery and
mortars. Fraser led another patrol out and managed to gain information
about the German fortifications, killing one German and wounding
another in the process. Word came down the following day that a large-
scale assault against the Hitler Line was in the works. The German
bombardment continued unabated. The Hasty Ps sent out pioneer platoons to cut barbed wire and clear mines so that Canadian tanks could
use these routes in the upcoming assault. Then a Hasty P patrol came in
contact with the outskirts of the infamous Hitler Line.

Over the next five days the intelligence officers in 1st Canadian
Division learned quite a bit about the Hitler Line. What they discovered,
however, was by no means encouraging. The German army's top tacti-
cians, the Todt Organization, had designed the Hitler Line, and Nazi
High Command considered the fortification impregnable. It extended
across the Liri Valley from the town of Piedimonte south through the

towns of Aquino and Pontecorvo to the mountains on the other side of
the Liri River. The valley was an alluvial plain with sections of rolling
hills and fast-running streams. Some of these streams could be crossed
on foot, but most required bridging.

In early 1944, the Germans used forced labour recruited from the
surrounding area to complete the Adolf Hitler Line. It was 5,300 yards
long. Forests were cleared in front of it to allow for easy strafing by
machine gun. Earthworks were dug. Concrete, steel and reinforced concrete were used to construct pillboxes topped by German Panzer tank
turrets. Bunkers were tunnelled deep underground to enable German
troops to withstand shelling. Anti-tank ditches were scooped into the
earth. The longest stretched two thousand yards. For one thousand yards
in front of the Hitler Line the ground had been mined with every type of
explosive available to the Nazis. There were anti-tank Teller mines and
"S" mines. When detonated, these sprang five feet in the air and then shot
350 ball bearings through the surrounding area. Schu mines were hidden
in wooden boxes. These contained piric acid and were intended to blow
a man's foot off. The entire line was strung with acres of barbed wire and
with tripwires designed to detonate more mines. The Hitler Line's final
defence was the fields of tall crops the Germans had allowed to grow in
front of the line and even on it. These would absorb fire and hinder an
infantryman's ability to aim at the German defences. This was the Adolf
Hitler Line.[20]

The Canadians intended to break it.

IN THE EARLY MORNING HOURS of May 23, 1944, eight hundred Allied
guns opened fire on the Germans massed on the Hitler Line. The glare
from the explosives was so bright, Canadian poet and veteran Douglas Le
Pan later remembered, that "the birds thought it was dawn and started
singing."[21] Mortar shells burst above the Hastings and Prince Edward
Regiment as it waited behind the starting line. Beyond the men lay open
ground blanketed with poppies and yellow daisies; the ground was covered with shell craters so close together that one began where another
ended. It was a hazy morning and smoke was already clouding the battlefield. Swathes of dust rose from behind the German lines. The Hasty

1st Canadian Division soldiers prepare to storm the Hitler Line.

—

Ps were being held as the second wave. The 2nd Brigade, consisting of the Princess Patricia's Light Infantry and the Seaforth Highlanders, would make the first attack, supported by the Carleton and York Regiment. Once the initial assault had pierced the Hitler Line, the Hasty Ps would push through the ground captured by the 2nd Brigade and tear into the German defences. At least that was the plan. Unfortunately, someone forgot to tell the Germans.[22]

The 2nd Brigade jumped off at eight in the morning and almost immediately the situation worsened. The Canadian infantrymen were held up on uncut barbed wire, while mines stalled their tank support. German soldiers riddled the Canadians from fixed machine-gun positions. The

Canadians suffered terribly. Before the attack, Princess Pats major Bucko Watson told his men, "See you on the objective." By the afternoon, they were all dead. Tanks were hit by enemy shells and they "brewed" on the battlefield; the men inside were burned alive. Medics covered those Canadian tank gunners unlucky enough to survive with wet blankets and gave them morphine. No more could be done for them. The battlefield became obscured by smoke so that it was impossible for the Canadians to offer artillery support. Amid the chaos a creeping realization spread at headquarters: the 2nd Brigade was in danger of being wiped out. An officer from the Princess Pats described the situation:

> Liaison officers and runners go forward and do not return. There is nothing to see; walking wounded bring back black tidings but only in vague terms—map locations, enemy dispositions, everything definite—has escaped them. Everyone knows the attack has failed; no one is prepared to accept the failure as final. Reinforcements are moving up, new fire programmes are in course of organization, calls for help are being sorted out and accorded proper priorities. Fresh units of the Eighth Army are being deployed for a new blow. That three battalions have been dispersed, are pinned down and perhaps destroyed, is regrettable. But they no longer count—the battle belongs to others.[23]

By the end of the day, the Princess Pats had a fighting strength of 77 men. They had suffered 162 dead and 306 wounded, and 75 men had been taken prisoner. Among the survivors was Captain Colin McDougall.

To break the German resistance, the Canadian generals ordered a simultaneous artillery barrage of all guns in range. At one o'clock, 668 guns shot 3,509 shells totalling 92 tons of explosives down on Aquino— all within thirty seconds. It was the largest concentration of fire used by Canadians during the Second World War up to that point, and it succeeded in thinning out the ranks of the German defenders.

Harold Pringle and the other members of "D" Company spent the early part of the afternoon ducking artillery and mortar fire. "You didn't know what was to the left of you and what was to the right of you," recalled one veteran who had arrived in Italy in March 1944. This vet remembers the shelling vividly, as well as "trying to dig your way into the earth, but you couldn't dig deep enough." "During battle, you felt big," he recalled. "You stuck out. You were exposed. But we didn't know enough to be frightened. We were only kids."[24]

Harold, however, knew enough to be frightened. His time patrolling the Arielli and participating in the ill-fated assault at the Tollo River had shown him the true face of war. Every man, in the back of his mind, had some idea about the amount of luck he could count on. By surviving five months in almost continuous combat, Harold Pringle had beaten plenty of odds. A look at the casualty roll showed that. In the week leading up to the attack on the Hitler Line, Corporal Pyette and privates Chapman, Blemkie, Graves, Munro, Kirkey and Bibby had been killed. Harold may have asked himself how much more luck could he count on. As an anonymous soldier had written in the *Union Jack* in March 1944,

> It seems unreasonable of me to have expected any sort of protection when all around me people who probably have a much better entitlement to life than I are meeting with adversity and death. It is the most haphazard circumstances that strike down one man and not the next, the most entangled chain of events that decided the time and place when one shall escape and the other be killed. It would be wrong—illogical—of me to suppose that, because my parents and wife, and possibly one or two other people happen to like me, because I'm kind to animals, that there is a special reason why I should be preserved.[25]

Harold might have asked himself this as well: if he lived, which Harold would go home? The Harold who loved snow and cooked strawberries on the stove and who skated by torchlight was gone. Since leaving Canada he had spent six months in a military prison and had contemplated marriage to a young Englishwoman. He had killed his first man and had most likely gone on to kill more. He had watched other men, men he had never met or said a nasty word to, try to kill him. He had seen men die, horribly. He had seen men vanish in the blast of an artillery shell. He had thrown hand grenades into houses because he thought Germans were inside. He had followed orders. It was all becoming normal. As Ramsay Park would later remark, "You get used to killing, you know."[26]

As the German shells screeched over head, it is possible that Harold wondered seriously about whether this might be his last battle. It is also possible that this thought, on a certain level, may have comforted him. If he were hit, there would be no more wondering. Farther along the attack, Canadians were being slain. They were slaying Germans too. An unreal orgy of killing was spiralling across the Liri Valley. Blood was seeping into the grain field in front of the German defences and the sky was clogged with smoke and shells. A Canadian corporal, just back from the fighting, would later tell CBC Radio reporter Peter Stursberg, "I thought it couldn't be worse than the Moro River, but it was." Stursberg would report the horribly surreal scene to listeners in Canada. He would describe a Canadian soldier sticking a poppy in his helmet while a line of infantry snaked its way toward the front. In Pontecorvo, he would notice the remains of the town's First World War memorial blown to bits. He would see a cat squeeze through a ruined house, oblivious to the noise of the artillery.[27]

By 12:40, the Canadian brigade commander, Brigadier General Daniel C. Spry, told his officers he was convinced that the 48th Highlanders were "fairly cut-up" and that it was vital that they be supported. In fact, the 48th were taking fire from "more Spandaus [machine guns] than we'd ever seen congregated," one veteran recalled. "More mortars too."[28] It was decided that Harold's company would move forward and help out. Because "D" company would be moving into an area containing Canadian troops, no artillery, mortar or tank support would be available. The Hasty Ps' commanding officer "impressed on all that it was vital that we contact the 48th on our left and that although the opposition would be strong, it was understood that it would be taken."[29]

At two o'clock in the afternoon, "D" Company made for its first objective, the wire just in front of a heavily fortified German position. One platoon held the wire and gave covering fire while another dashed forward and occupied the ground. These attacks were made over open ground against machine guns and artillery. They were, in fact, virtual suicide missions. But somehow, the Hasty Ps managed to break into the Hitler Line. To their left, the 48th Highlanders were pinned down. In order to reach them, "D" Company would need to charge up a slope covered with waving grass and take a group of fortified farmhouses surrounded by steel machine-gun turrets in dug-out entrenchments. Harold's platoon of seventeen men, led by Lieutenant Don Kennedy, stormed forward. They were ahead of German barbed wire with nowhere to go but forward. With Bren guns, rifles and Tommy guns blasting from their hips, they made a mad charge that the Hastings and Prince Edward regimental diary would later call an "outstanding display of initiative and courage."[30]

Thanks to Colin McDougall we have a clear description of how Harold Pringle may have performed on that day. In *Execution*, McDougall describes Frazer (one of the characters based on Harold) attacking the Hitler Line. McDougall places Frazer in the Princess Pats and not the Hasty Ps, but his description meshes perfectly with how Harold's comrades described him, "A-1" and a "cool customer, especially in combat."

Wrote McDougall, "Little Frazer ran with a quick, chopping step, head up, rifle held across his chest, ready in an instant to sprint ahead or go to ground. Each motion was controlled. He moved over the field expertly: if there had been such a profession as crossing a steel-swept, mine-exploding field, Frazer would be its master professional. He hummed to himself as he ran; his darting glance at the same time locating the chief originating points of fire and calculated the distance to each available piece of cover."

Frazer finds himself in a shell hole with a badly shaken soldier named Russo, who prays while he presses forward. "Why don't you learn how to relax, sport?" Frazer tells him as he locks on to a machine gun firing from a tank turret and, "estimating the moment the belt would have to be changed," decides to make a break. "Hey," he says, slapping Russo. "It's time to git a-going." As Frazer advances toward the Hitler Line, he finds the body of his best friend, Simpson, and pauses for a few seconds to mourn.

Then he takes Simpson's machine gun and fills his pockets with Simpson's cartridges. He returns to Russo, whose eyes are "glassy," and tells him, "We're going again." His friend dead, Frazer finds himself feeling stranded on the battlefield. Meanwhile, McDougall has Russo nearly consumed with fear. Russo continues praying; "Hail, Mary, full of Grace." Frazer finds himself roaring with laughter: "Oh Christ, if only Sim could be here now."

He tells Russo, "We're going in behind that tank turret. Get it?" The two dart forward. A machine gun cuts in on them and Frazer almost trips over Russo's body as it tumbles at his feet. "Poor Russo," Frazer thinks. "Scared shitless but he still kept going." A German tank rolls toward Frazer. He hits the ground and digs his machine-gun tripod into the earth. A German officer appears. He is trying to take another Canadian, about twenty yards away, prisoner. Frazer opens up on the German and the fire from his machine gun decapitates him. He scurries forward and hides underneath the tank, waiting. Two German gunners climb from the tank. Frazer pauses a second and then fires. The two Germans go "crashing down together." "Now," Frazer thinks. "If I can only get over there and roll some grenades down....".[31]

By three o'clock in the afternoon, the Hasty Ps had reached their objective. They had saved the 48th Highlanders and the Hitler Line was broken. In fact, Canadians were busting through all along the Hitler Line. Canadian soldiers were mopping up the remnants, shooting Germans and taking hundreds of prisoners. Tanks were rolling through in hot pursuit of the retreating Germans. The Canadians were capturing so many of "Hitler's pets" that there were not enough men to escort them back to detention. The Canadians had broken the impregnable Hitler Line. It would be one of the most decisive victories in the army's history. But it had been costly. Between May 16 and May 23, 970 Canadians had been wounded. There were 303 sick, 7 suffering from burns, 16 accidental injuries, 8 cases of self-inflicted wounds and 237 cases of battle exhaustion. In the three weeks of operations in the Liri Valley, 789 Canadian soldiers had been killed and 2,500 wounded. A total of 400 had been sent back for mental stress. In Harold's regiment, 23.4 per cent of casualties were suffering from battle exhaustion.

But Harold was not one of them.

He was still alive. He was still breathing. The battlefield smelled of smoke and burning corpses, but he was not among them. Bullets had flown by his head. Mortars had shredded others around him, but he was untouched. Harold was still in "D" Company. He was there, and he was smiling.

6.

THE WHOLE WAY

The Germans were fleeing Rome. The Liri Valley was crammed full of mangled trucks, bombed-out Panzers, rifles and machine guns strewn around bodies. A German soldier lay alongside the road with his legs stretched out straight, his right foot hooked in under his left ankle. His left arm extended from his body, its hand palm-down on the ground with its fingers seeming to scratch at the dirt. The right arm was crooked up, the hand resting on the body's thigh. A rifle was slung around the right shoulder. You saw a neck and the beginning of a chin, but everything from there up was missing; traces of brain and skull had been spread out along the track of a troop carrier. A Canadian war photographer snapped a picture. Behind the Canadian army lay Cassino, "the most shell-torn and war-wrecked town the battalion has ever seen," according to the Hasty Ps' war diarist. Smoke swirled from burning tanks, and somewhere by the Hitler Line German prisoners were being made to clear Nazi minefields. About a dozen would be blown to pieces.

Rome was falling and would soon be liberated. For the first time in 1,500 years, Rome was being conquered from the south.

Brigadier General Robert T. Frederick, the commander of the Canadian-American Special Forces Brigade—the "Devils' Brigade"—suggested that the unit print up stickers with the words "The Worst Is Yet

To Come" written in German. These could be stuck to the foreheads of dead German soldiers killed on patrol.[1]

BBC correspondent Eric Sevareid met two GIs standing by the splayed body of a German. "Oh him?" they told him. "Son of a bitch kept lagging behind the others when we brought them in. We got tired of hurrying him up all the time."[2] The Americans remembered, perhaps, how the Germans had stacked American wounded before them while advancing during the battle of Anzio, using them as living human shields. Meanwhile, in various military theatres across Europe, the Germans had shot thousands of soldiers for desertion, a figure that was up exponentially from the First World War, in which they had shot 48.[3]

Pioneer battalions were digging graves and building wooden crosses near Cassino; soldiers were cataloguing the bodies, running their dirty fingers down lists of names and making marks with stubby pencils. In the valley below, the 1st Canadian Division was kept in reserve and the men of the Hastings and Prince Edward Regiment tried to recuperate. "We had a rule: for twenty-four hours after a fight a fellow could do anything," Tony Basciano recalled. "Get drunk, sit around, whatever he wanted."[4] The Canadians were elated by their victory, and reports from other units in the Eighth Army brought morale to a high. On May 27, the men camped down by a stream near Pontecorvo and went swimming. The next day a church service was held in honour of those who had died during the campaign. The freshly dead were still living memories, and Harold Pringle might have expected to see Lieutenant McGovern, who had been killed on the assault to relieve the 48th Highlanders, and to listen to him lay out the orders for another patrol. On May 28, the army put on a show that starred four members of the Canadian Women's Army Corps. The sight of Canadian femininity had a palpable effect on the troops.[5] Their attraction was not likely to be lost on Harold Pringle.

The Canadians expected that Rome would be their next stop. After fighting for almost a year with little let-up, they would liberate the Eternal City and enjoy its sights. And this time, unlike most of the other cities the Eighth Army had taken, there would actually be a city standing to liberate. Mindful of Rome's archaeological and cultural riches, the Allies and the Germans had agreed that Rome was too valuable to destroy and had declared it an "open city." That meant that neither side would bomb it or fight inside it. The Germans had pulled out on June 3. All the Canadians had to do was proceed up Route 6, the Via Casilina, and stride through the gates.

On May 31, however, the Canadians found themselves going backwards to the small town of Ferentino. Military ego was taking over. After being trapped on the beach at Anzio for three months and suffering thirty thousand casualties, the US army, said American commander General Mark Clark, wanted to be granted the honour of taking Rome. The decision was not only a snub of the Canadians, it was a strategic blunder. Many military historians believe that if Clark had chosen to move above the city instead of into it, he would have been able to trap much of the retreating German army. Instead, Clark went into Rome and prolonged the war in Italy. It was a decision that would cost quite a few Allied soldiers their lives.

Headlines such as "Americans Liberate Rome" outraged Canadian soldiers. Their discontent was exacerbated by the decision of Canadian upper echelons to place all Italian towns off limits as a way of preventing the spread of venereal disease. Canadian psychiatrists examining soldiers serving sentences for being AWOL and for desertion noted that after the Hitler Line, "disappointment in not being able to follow the Hun" had contributed to a rash of absenteeism.[6] The barring of Italian towns incensed the Canadians, who had been praised both in the press and by high military authorities. Even Stalin had praised the Canadian effort on the Hitler Line, calling the Canadians the best soldiers in the Eighth Army. "In many cases it happened that soldiers were ready with their packs on to go on leave when orders came through that they were not to go on leave. Many went anyway and later got into prison for going AWOL."[7] By June 10, the Canadian troops were stationed in Anagni, a town on the side of a hill near the Liri Valley. Over the next few weeks, absenteeism became a problem for the Hasty Ps as for the Canadian army in general. On June 25, the Hasty Ps were stationed in Alfie, a town in the hills above the Volturno Valley, fifty miles north of Naples. It was a hot, dusty place with no other towns nearby for recreation. A new Canadian commander was trying to instill "discipline" into the

Canadians, and that meant drills, parades, spit and polish. To troops who had been engaged in a year of heavy fighting, it seemed a pointless exercise. Farley Mowat wrote to his father describing the Canadians' base as "our concentration camp in the hills."[8]

It was not just diplomatic disrespect that was eating away at Canadian morale. Soldiers were very much aware of the conscription debate that was boiling in Canada. Today when English Canadians remember the war, they picture it as one unified and steady patriotic effort. Every man was dying to do "his duty"; those who were turned down for service cried outside enlistment stations. Meanwhile, women worked happily in the factories. In reality, however, after the casualty reports started coming back, enlistment dried up. In Quebec, where many considered the conflict to be "England's War," it was tough to fill regiments. Resistance to the war effort came from the top down. The mayor of Montreal, for instance, was jailed for advising his citizens not to enlist. In the rest of the country as well, fewer and fewer men were signing on. The governments of Britain and the United States implemented conscription, but Canada is a land of compromise, and Liberal prime minister William Lyon Mackenzie King tried to find a politically profitable solution. He instituted conscription but only for home service. Only those who volunteered would actually be shipped overseas; conscripts would remain in Canada and do make-work projects, such as guarding Hudson Bay. In this way, King thought he could placate anti-war sentiment in Quebec and elsewhere in the country while paying lip service to those actually doing the fighting. Thus was born his triumph of rhetoric over reason: "Conscription if necessary—but not necessarily conscription." The Canadians fighting in Italy were not impressed; they labelled these conscript non-combatants "Zombies."[9]

Mackenzie King's blatant political opportunism left a legacy of resentment. My grandfather, for example, loathed King until his dying day. This animosity extended to the "goddamn" Liberal Party in general. The Jamiesons were Tories who had voted conservative since the days of John A. Macdonald. In fact, it was only when I reached my seventh birthday that I realized that the Liberals were actually called the Liberal Party and not "the goddamn Liberal Party." This was the animosity left decades later—at the peak of the war hatred for King was red hot. On June 10, 1944, the conscription crisis led Mowat, stationed at Anagni, to write to his father, "A guy I know just got turned down for a compassionate leave to Canada to help his mother and sisters deal with a dying father and a family business that will also die without a man around. This soldier hero has been overseas a full three years, has been wounded but has survived eight months in action. Maybe when, and if, we do go home, it should be with fixed bayonets."[10]

Militarily, Mackenzie King's decision meant that the Canadian troops in Italy received almost no reinforcements. In September 1944, a soldier named Conn Smythe, who had already founded the Toronto Maple Leafs, wrote a scathing article for *The Globe and Mail* on the effects of King's compromise. Smythe had won the Military Cross in the First World War and had volunteered in the Second. After being wounded in France, he began to investigate casualty figures and discovered that companies were woefully understrength and that new recruits were badly trained. Canadian divisions were being decimated because of the lack of men. The article caused so much controversy in Canada that King sent his minister of defence to France and Italy to investigate. One Canadian commander, Major General Christopher Vokes, confirmed Smythe's allegations, saying that sending undertrained recruits into combat was "an act of murder."[11] "Please do not send any more reinforcements," one Canadian officer had written sarcastically back to headquarters during the spring offensive, "as we do not have time to bury them."[12]

A Canadian officer Joe Pigott later said, "We had only feelings of disgust, of contempt for the Prime Minister and the politicians who were not facing the realities of the crisis, and most of all we felt anger. The feeling was becoming very deep-seated in all the troops that they were being used and sacrificed by their government in order not to face public opinion."[13]

This reality made twenty-two-year-old Harold Pringle a seasoned veteran. There were others who had served longer and seen more action, but their numbers were ever shrinking. In the month of December 1943, 253 officers and 3,703 men of other ranks had been casualties, most of them from rifle companies.[14]

Those who survived learned a cold truth: there was dying, and then there was *dying*. Death in the infantry was, even by the standards of war, an ugly fate. Wrote William Connor, a writer for the *Union Jack*, "There are plenty of ways to kill a man in this war. All of them are costly. Most of them are uncertain. You can drill holes in him with bullets, blow him up with high explosives, knock lumps off with shrapnel or simply dump him in the sea.... The best brains all over the world are devoted to these lethal matters.... Such an array of perfected illwill could surely have only one result: to hasten humanity on its reluctant way to early extinction."[15] A man might be blown into a thousand pieces and the parts deposited in a sack. At the Canadian Reinforcement Depot in Avellino, Italian children entertained themselves by peering through a fence at the Allied cemetery and watching these packages arrive. Recalled one of those children, who was now in her eighties, "They would drop a head, or some legs, or just a torso, into the ground and then put a marker on it."[16] These pieces were later transplanted to permanent military cemeteries.

Soldiers also feared living. Medicine had made great leaps, and more and more severely wounded soldiers were surviving. But they pulled through only to anticipate a life without legs or arms or a face.

The mental wounds were harder to identify, but the more severe cases of battle exhaustion manifested themselves in acute symptoms. In *Battle Exhaustion*, Copp and McAndrew note that during the First World War the Canadian army admitted to 15,500 "neuropsychiatric disabilities"; of those, 9,000 had been classified as shell shock. In Italy, Canadian army psychiatrist Major Arthur Manning Doyle was diagnosing "gross hysteria with mutism, paralysis, aphonia. Gross ticquers were common and the range went from these to the poor inadequate personality who showed little outward evidence of anxiety but simply said 'I can't take it.'" About twenty-eight per cent of the Hastings and Prince Edward Regiment's casualties between November 28, 1943, and February 12, 1944, were classified as neuropsychiatric. War also played tricks with established notions of sanity: the rationality of a soldier's behaviour was gauged by its relationship to military objectives. An officer who exposed himself to enormous danger in the field and who volunteered for high-risk missions was considered an effective, sane and exemplary soldier. The fellow who said "I can't take it" was a candidate for the mental hospital or military prison.[17]

Then there was the able soldier who finally reached his limit. Opinion at headquarters was split on what his fate should be. "Should some demoralized malingering cases cropping up while in action be shot on the spot as an example?" wondered a general at the 5th Canadian Armoured Division.[18] Colonel Jim Stone was less critical: "Persons who are not exposed to the bullets and shells in a slit trench situation or having to advance over open ground against a determined enemy should be careful of using the words 'cowardice,' 'yellow' and 'malingerer.' Sooner or later, in those circumstances, we would all break down, some sooner than others."[19]

Battle exhaustion concerned the army because it was as detrimental to its fighting capabilities as physical wounds. A soldier who was shell-shocked was of no more use than a soldier without a leg: neither man could fight. So in late 1944, Canadian military psychiatrists began studying the phenomenon of battle exhaustion. They asked soldiers who had cracked up during or after action to write down their experiences. Military psychiatrist A. E. Moll met a thirty-year-old corporal from the Hastings and Prince Edward Regiment who had arrived in Italy in May 1944 and had fought at all actions since, including the Hitler Line. He had had a normal childhood and had no history of mental illness. By December 1944, he suffered from a slight paralysis in his right arm and acute anxiety. Moll had the soldier describe the events leading to his breakdown. His plain-spoken talking description provides one of the most chilling and accurate portraits of combat available:

> We sat there on the bank waiting, then all at once, we heard the
> guns start and the shelling started. The first few went over the
> bank then it broke loose, and one landed right behind my section
> about 50 yards, but it had hit right in a section of C Company
> and killed six outright, but we didn't know that at the time. Then
> the shells were lighting all around us, so I yelled to my section to
> follow me. I didn't know where we were going so long as I got

them away from the bank, but we ran about 100 yards and came
to a little ditch, and it was impossible to get any further so I gave
the order to stay in the ditch which they did.

The barrage lasted 12 minutes by my watch, and I made a
reccy or took a look, so to speak, and I could see the house. So I
said, is everyone ready and they were so I said the house is right
there, about 50 yards on our left, and when we start we will keep
going and bring all weapons.

I started and all the men followed and when we got to the
building I discovered I had more than my section, and I said we
are making a dash for the house. I knew where the door was, so I
showed them all, and at that time Jerry was sending back some
shells but they were going on over our heads, so I started and just
as the last man in my section came through the door 2 shells
landed right in the yard, and the 3 that had come with me was
still in the yard. I heard one of them yell for help but I didn't
know who it was at the time but I ran out and one of the boys
was coming on his hands and knees so I got him up and gave
him a hand to the house. Then I ran out and I had to pick up
the other one up and carry him. Those two were L/Cpl. L. and
Pte. B. one from 12 platoon, B Company, the other from support
attached to B Company. By the time I got out to the other chap
he was all on fire, and the acting C. S. M., Sgt. S. was there trying
to get the web off him, for the fire was coming from the 77
Grenade he was carrying in his pocket, so I ran over and gave
him a hand. I said boy am I glad to see you, and he replied how
are you feeling. I said not bad, but really didn't know how I felt.

I wanted to get him inside but he said he was dead so when
we got the web off the chap, we threw it in the mud. The C. S. M.
said to me "I guess its you and I for it, Mitch, there is a lot of
wounded out here, let's go." So we run around the house and
there was a chap there with his guts all hanging out. He was from
Company H. Q., Mac, a runner. He wanted us to get him in the
house but we couldn't move him as he was, so I ran in to find a
stretcher bearer and I saw one in the corner and asked him to

come and bring a stretcher but he said, "I'm hit Mitch." I asked him if it was bad and he said "Let's go," so I said "Get your stretcher." He said "It's right there" so I brought it and he started to work on the lad but only being a stretcher bearer for a short time he didn't know just what to do but was doing the best he could so the lad just relaxed. The C. S. M. said "I guess he's gone," and the lad tenses right up again and shouted "No I'm not S., I'm O.K., get me to the house" but that was too much for me and I took right out and I wasn't just sure which way I was going either.

I had only taken a few steps and I heard some more shells come and I shouted a warning to the rest to take cover so they put the lad on the stretcher and made for the house. The shells lit close but done no damage but I heard another cry over by some hay stacks and I run over and there was another wounded man. I didn't ask any questions, I just picked him up and made for the house and laid him on the table. That was Pte. H. He was dead in about 5 minutes and so was Mac.

The C. S. M. asked for someone to go with him up to the river to see if there was anymore up there that needed help. There was seven up there but were all dead. We lit some matches to see if there was anyone there we knew, and the first one I saw was a good friend of mine and the family and his newly married wife's family, lying there all in little pieces, so I said "I can't stand anymore, I will have to go some place S.," so he said "that's all anyway" and we came back to the house and the wounded had all gone.

The next thing was to make out a guard for the rest of the night because the order had come through that we wouldn't be going over that night, so I walked around and done guard the rest of the night.

At six in the morning, we got the order we were going over the river and a thousand yards inland, so when we were ready to take off I didn't feel too bad. We went across and started for our objective, but we only got about half-way when we met the enemy. We lost one man there and had to withdraw to the houses at the river bank. We were just there about 20 minutes and Jerry started to shell the house so then we got the order to come back across the river which we did. Just as we got back Jerry started to shell the road which he knew we would take and we had 6 more men wounded, 2 of which were killed. It was the rear platoon and the rest took out for the house which we had left in the morning, and as we only had 2 stretchers left I took Pte. M. on my back to the house. I am a small man but I didn't have any trouble making it and I guess most of my strength came from the excitement.

That evening we were moved out and back across highway 10, and took over a house from 5th Div[ision] which we stayed in for 3 days. It was very good there, not much shelling. It came time for us to take our turn to go back up to the houses along the river to do guard and run patrols. The patrols were to go up the river about a mile to contact the R. C. R. [Royal Canadian Regiment]

On the night I was to take the patrol, on the 11th about 2:30 in the morning, Jerry started mortaring the bank on our side, and I lost 2 men in the patrol. There was only 4 of us altogether, so I went to the R. C. R. and sent the other man back for help, so we got them out without anything worse happening.

At 12 o'clock we got the order that the C & Y [Carleton and York] Regiment had made their crossing and we were going through them, so we started and got on our first objective just at dark. At 12 o'clock that night, we got another order that we were going to cross the second river and we would have to wade it, so we did and we got on our objective and stayed there till the morning of the 13th. We were then told that the C & Y Regiment had gone across the river but it was a dry one and they had very little trouble so at 1 o'clock we started out and D company came back to take over our house and came under mortar and 88 shell fire and lost 6 men and 2 killed. There was no one to take the wounded back so our Coy 2 i/c [second-in-command] of ours asked for volunteers to go get the wounded back but there were only 2 men in the platoon of Don Coy which would go, so I went with him and we got the men in the house.

We then started out to go through the C & Y Regiment and we got through them O. K. Jerry let us right in once he seen what our plan was. We were about 25 yards from our objective when a patrol of Jerries came between us and the house so the order came back from the front of the Coy to lay low and not have any trouble till we got dug in. We did and while we were there a fighting patrol came up behind us and opened fire on me and my section. I never seen them till they started to shoot. Finally he found his mark and two slugs hit me and I thought I was finished so I jumped up and started firing back and one of the cpls [corporals] in another section threw a hand grenade which killed 3 of them and I had killed one with my mad try. The other 2 started to crawl away and I could see men take after them so I did. Someone took after me and turned me the other way.

I came right back to my section and someone said "Get away Mitch you're hit." So I didn't know which way to go. I guess I was shouting or something. Anyway, one of the boys was crying there in the ditch and I thought he was hit but he wasn't. He wanted to come out with me but I guess I wouldn't let him.

Then the section started to move off so I took off and the next thing I remember was being challenged and I couldn't think of the pass-word but I do remember saying "Don't shoot for I have plenty of holes in me now." Then I heard another fellow coming and more guns started to go and someone said "Get in that ditch, here comes Jerry." So I fell in the ditch. By this time Jerry had seen me and they were all shooting at me but didn't hit me but our boys of C Coy had drove them off.

Then a Sgt. came out and gave me a hand back to the house where one of the coy's were, and they dressed my back there. I wanted to go back but they wouldn't let me and they said there was a counter-attack coming. Just then I heard on the 19 set that my Company was cut off and would have to give up if they didn't get any help right away.

I don't remember much from then on. I do remember a sergeant handling me a little rough but I guess I must have had it

coming for I had a pistol and I wanted to shoot 2 Jerry wounded
there in the shed. Then a jeep came in with the ammo and I
wanted to go out with that but they said it wasn't very safe, it just
had a 50-50 chance of getting through but I got in it and they
made the 2 Jerrys get in too and we started out. I guess I had a
few words on the way out with the C. S. M. in the jeep about the
Jerrys but when I got to the ADS or whatever it was they gave me
a needle or something and I felt a little better. I was still talking
about my company but I got back to the four CCS right away and
was put to sleep. When I woke up I had been talking a lot but
they wouldn't tell me what about.

But I'm out of it and I don't ever want to go back because I just
never could be responsible in a tight place again and I know it.[20]

What could the army say about such a man? He was a distinguished
soldier with a perfect record. His instincts were always for the benefit of
his company and his men. He believed in the cause and had risked his life
countless times. This was a soldier who when he realized he had been
shot, decided, "I was finished" and went on a "mad try" so that his dying
moments would benefit his company. And despite all these qualities he
had reached his breaking point.

It is difficult to decide what category Harold Pringle fit into. The
first fact I had learned about him was that he had deserted. Was he a
good soldier who burnt out? Was he an opportunist who ran off at his
first chance? After volunteering to join the Hasty Ps, the regiment he so
dearly wanted to be a part of, why take off? Maybe Pringle had no stomach for combat. Maybe he just couldn't stand the fighting. Perhaps he
was like one twenty-five-year-old private whom Doyle described examining in 1944. The soldier had been sent back by his unit's medical officer
with this report: "This man has been seen by me on several occasions,
always crying and sobbing and saying he cannot go on. I have seen him
break down when a shell lands 1,000 yards away. According to his company Commander he has not seen any close action and has never done
his job. I feel he is absolutely useless as a soldier." The private told Doyle,
"I couldn't stand the shelling. It was too much. I never had too much

before. I was alright until they hit the house. I tried four times to go back but I couldn't take it."[21]

When, however, I considered the "A-1 soldier" and "brave bugger" described by Tony Basciano, the soldier who carried extra grenades in his belt and grinned during combat, and when I combined it with McDougall's description of Frazer, the soldier who wouldn't enter a "Wop house without throwing a grenade in first," the truth became clear. There was no way Harold Pringle was unfit for combat, and he was no shrinking violet when it came to the nasty business of war. But he had a hell of a temper. Perhaps that was what triggered his decision to leave the employ of the Canadian government. Harold Pringle reacted to his father's dismissal from the Canadian army by falling in with a rough crowd and going AWOL. In Italy he obeyed orders, Basciano said, but if he felt slighted or cheated, "he would fight anyone, he didn't care how big they were."

Those who knew him could not believe he would desert. "I could never see him doing that," said Basciano. "He must have had some reason. I always wondered, 'How come he deserted?' I think Harold just got sick of it all."[22] At our first meeting, Basciano told me there was one other Hasty P veteran remaining who had known Harold, and this man might have an answer. His name was Ivan Gunter; he lived in the small town of Bancroft, Ontario, not far from Peterborough. And as luck had it, he was a friend of Tony's. We arranged for me to visit Peterborough again, and Tony invited Ivan Gunter and his wife, Irene, down to join us.

Ivan had enlisted as a private with the Hastings and Prince Edward Regiment in 1940 and was later moved to the intelligence section of the unit. He had a distinguished service record. On July 18, 1943, on the Grammichele plain in Sicily, Gunter drove a motorcycle past the Canadian forward force, through a hail of German mortar and artillery fire and out into no man's land to spot for the Canadian artillery. When the motorcycle was shot out from under him, he continued on foot. He spent the rest of the day directing Canadian artillery fire. This effort helped the Canadians dislodge German resistance. It also won Gunter the Military Medal for bravery.

Gunter had a story that filled in the gap between Harold Pringle the keen soldier and Harold Pringle the deserter.

Since Harold had arrived in Italy, his record had been clean and, as Basciano says, he was well loved by the sergeants. Sometime in February 1944, Gunter said, Harold had been granted a forty-eight-hour leave and had gone off to Naples, or maybe Avellino. Harold enjoyed his rest and then caught his transport back to the Hasty Ps. Somewhere along the way the truck broke down and Harold was held up, for maybe three or four hours. When he finally made the regiment, he was immediately charged for being AWOL. That night, the regiment's sergeant major had Harold confined in a small villa beyond Canadian lines, close to the Germans. Private Ivan Gunter was sent to guard him.

The villa was a dangerous place to take shelter, and this was no accident; it had been selected to intimidate Harold Pringle. An evening bombardment was underway, with the villa smack in the middle of it. Shells had ripped the villa's walls, and the house was deserted. There were a few broken chairs and a table. No candles were lit because they would draw attention from enemy artillery. The barrage tore fiery streaks in the dark sky and the ground trembled from its concussions as the glare from distant explosions periodically illuminated the villa. Gunter and Harold Pringle spent the night waiting it out.

Harold Pringle sat silently, calmly. "They were shelling the hell out of us," remembered Gunter, "but he wasn't scared. I would duck. He just stood there." Though calm, Pringle was incensed: "He told me, 'I am not guilty.' He said the truck he was supposed to be on broke down. Something beyond his control happened."

Harold Pringle had been fighting Germans since his arrival in Italy. Now there was a different sort of enemy in his mind. Harold began to see himself pinned between two opposing forces, each one interested in his demise: the Germans were trying to kill him, and his Canadian commanders were trying to accommodate them. Basciano recalled being told to watch Harold when the boy from Flinton joined the battalion, and Gunter maintains that the regimental sergeant, major Angus Duffy, who left the Hasty Ps in January 1944, "had it out" for Pringle and wanted to keep him under his thumb. "To his dying day, Duffy thought Pringle was a bad character," Gunter said. Money was also an ever-present concern. Since volunteering to rejoin his regiment in action, Harold Pringle had been paying off a monetary debt to the Canadian government. This was the money he had been docked for his time spent in jail. Then there was the twenty-one pounds he owed his ex-girlfriend Esmee. Being charged again was too much. Harold was convinced he would never be given a clean slate.

The shells crashed down and light cracked the darkness. Harold stared out toward German lines.

"Do you know how much I make?" he asked Gunter.

The report of machine-gun fire echoed from somewhere down the line.

"I make ten cents a day. That's how much I get."

For a man who was in confinement and who earned ten cents a day, Harold's tone was unnaturally placid. "He didn't seem like he had a chip on his shoulder or anything like that," says Gunter. "My recollection is that he understood why they put him in jail. He was absolutely lucid." The conversation swung to the future. Harold spelled it out "matter-of-factly."

"I'll never make it out of the war," he said, looking out the window to where the shells were impacting in the distance. Gunter stared into Harold's brown eyes; they looked normal, if somewhat glassy. "They are going to shove me out right on up to the front trenches. I'll never make it out of the war and I'll be damned if I'm going to die for ten cents a day."

Gunter was stunned. "Harold, don't be a fool," he said. "You're gonna pay for it after the war. The war won't last forever."

"I'll never make it out of the war."

"You're a damn fool to do that. The war is not going to last forever and they'll get you after the war."

"I don't give a damn. They are going to kill me anyway. And I'm not going to risk my life for ten cents a day."

Gunter recalled that Harold told him he needed a seven-day leave in order to get organized, and then "that will be the last you ever see of me." He "made up his mind what he was going to do. There was no way they were going to kill him. Pringle was a cold guy—you didn't get lovable guys who were good soldiers." Gunter regarded him with a strange wonder. Harold repeated his intentions, with a tone of conversational resignation. For someone so determined to live, he seemed like a man who "didn't care about the future."

"It didn't matter," Gunter remembered. "As far as he was concerned, he was already dead."[23]

Gunter's story makes perfect sense. This kind of resentment was evident in many soldiers who, like Harold, had been incarcerated in England. Wrote Doyle, "There were a notable number of youths who had enlisted underage and whose bad behaviour appears to have commenced while being held in Holding Units undergoing a boring existence." When these boys were returned to their original units as reinforcements, they were labelled problem soldiers. Instead of binding to their regiment, something essential to the creation of a good solider, some men with AWOL records remained aloof. "The longer a well motivated soldier is kept in prison the less likelihood there is of his being rehabilitated," observed Doyle.[24] A British army psychiatrist observed, "The excellent Army tradition that 'once a man has served his sentence he starts afresh with a clean slate' is not observed as faithfully as might be desired. Men have declared, at interview, that after being in detention some of their unit Officers and N. C. O.'s have regarded them with suspicion and mistrust, have given them a conviction that it is impossible to 'start afresh' and that no amount of effort can win them complete approval."[25]

On June 7, 1944, two days after the liberation of Rome, Harold Pringle was listed as absent without leave from the Hastings and Prince Edward Regiment. It may be that he went to Rome with other Hasty Ps to have a bit of fun. Once there, he could not—or would not—find his way back. He was picked up on June 28 and placed under arrest.[26] Given his track record, Pringle was facing three to five years' hard time in a military prison. And given his experience in the Glass House, Harold may have decided that Rome was a much more attractive proposition. In *Execution*, Colin McDougall's Frazer deserts, and his story parallels the information in Pringle's service record: "After the Hitler Line, apparently, Frazer went AWOL from hospital in Caserta, got drunk and piled up a lot of charges. That wouldn't have been too bad by itself, but he skipped again—in a stolen sergeant's uniform, and this time he was tagged as a deserter. Then he must have figured out he'd have to sit out the rest of the war in Detention Camp and he went the whole way."[27]

7.

ROME

When Harold arrived in Rome, he found a city engrossed in an endless party that had begun minutes after its liberation. American troops poured into the city, as did some Canadian troops who went AWOL from their units and drove into the Eternal City. The soldiers enjoyed everything Rome offered; parties and dances roared all night. "Amorous women and cheap vino were in abundant supply," observed one British war diarist.[1] "The signorinas of the south don't hold a Roman candle to their sisters of the capital," wrote Sergeant George Powell, a correspondent for the Canadian army newspaper *The Maple Leaf.* "There's no question about it—the girls of Rome are beautiful. Nor are they all these black-haired, dark-skinned beauties that are supposedly so typical. There are blondes, natural or not so natural, and red heads that are fugitives from Hollywood. Their clothes are smart, they look clean and neat, they are not stand-offish when addressed politely and they don't come running at a whistle. And they wear shoes. They're a sight for war-sore eyes."[2] Venereal disease rates quadrupled. Rome swooned in a fever of absolute joy.

The Romans were ecstatic because the German occupation had been brutal; despite the initial jubilation at liberation, the occupation's scars would span generations. As was the case in so many other cities, torture, murder, starvation and disease were the hallmarks of the Nazi stay. At an

apartment on Via Tasso, the Gestapo tortured many Italians to death. At
Forte Bravetta, a military prison in the city's west end, they conducted
routine executions. On one day alone, 350 Italian civilians were shot. The
Germans did not act unassisted. The Italian Fascists were instrumental in
the cruelty; using the city's police force, they rounded up suspects and
handed them over to the Nazis. Men were incarcerated and then sent to
work as forced labour on the Hitler Line. The Roman police preferred to
use refugees rather than native Romans; they scoured the streets looking
for candidates. One of those destined for the front was a sixteen-year-old
refugee from Naples named Oreste Schiano di Zenise, whose mother had
sent him out to buy food. On the way back from his errand, he was
picked up by police and put in prison with other conscripts awaiting
transfer to the front. His family tried to buy his freedom, but the guards
were low on their daily quota of prisoners and would not let him go.
Finally a family friend, a woman who was the lover of a German officer,
used her influence to get Oreste out. "It saved my life," Schiano would
later say. "The men who worked on the front, many of them died."[3]

During the Nazi occupation, Jews were rounded up and sent to concentration camps, and informing became a cottage industry for Romans
with Fascist leanings. In *Rome '44*, Trevelyan describes Celeste Di Porto,
a Jewish prostitute dubbed the "Black Panther" because of her dark hair
and eyes, who turned in fellow Jews for fifty thousand lire a head.
Rumours circulated that the Black Panther liked to accompany former
clients to Gestapo Headquarters where she would pull down their
trousers to prove they were circumcised.

The Gestapo did not confine itself to Jews. Its agents ruthlessly
hunted down suspected Communists and Resistance workers. They
brought their unlucky quarry to the Gestapo interrogation centre, prison
and barracks located at 155 Via Tasso, a street named after Torquato
Tasso, one of Italy's greatest poets. Here Colonel Herbert Kappler, the
Gestapo chief, interviewed suspects. Kappler and his men employed
techniques that would become Gestapo trademarks. General Simone
Simoni, a sixty-four-year-old Resistance leader, was beaten with spiked
mallets and the soles of his feet were burned with gas jets. A woman
searching for her husband arrived at Via Tasso to find him being beaten

by the Gestapo. In order to prevent herself from being discovered and arrested, she was forced to watch the beating with apparent disinterest and to pretend he was a stranger. The Gestapo broke Resistance leader Giuseppe Montezemolo's jaw and beat his face so severely that his eyes were black and swollen shut. The Nazis tortured him with such regularity that in a moment of twisted hospitality they provided him with a folding deck chair in which he could rest between beatings. When guests at Via Tasso ceased to be valuable, they were conducted to Forte Bravetta and shot. On February 10, 1944, an average day, ten Italians were executed there.[4]

Collaborators such as Pietro Koch, an ex-wine merchant from Benevento, led a band of men who swept the city rooting out anti-Fascists. Scalding showers, bright lights and pins through the penis were Koch specialties. His two mistresses, Tamara Sangilli and Desy Totolli, acted as his helpers. These women, who before the war had performed in cabaret, mocked Koch's victims as he tortured them. They would describe, in minute detail, the torments that would befall the victim's families—the treats the Gestapo had in store for their wives, husbands and children—after Koch was finished with them.

In March 1944, thirty-seven-year-old Teresa Gullace, a pregnant mother of five, was shot. Gullace's husband had been one of those rounded up by the Germans for forced labour. On the day Teresa was killed, wives, mothers and sisters had assembled at the barracks where the men were being held. Communist leader Laura Lombardo Radice stirred up a demonstration, and as the protest gathered pitch, Gullace saw her husband through the wire fence and rushed toward him. Someone opened fire, either an SS soldier or an Italian fascist militiaman, killing her. Over fifty years later her death remains a symbol of the Nazi oppression.

Later that month, the anti-Fascist Partisan resistance exploded a bomb on the Via Rasella, killing 32 German soldiers. The bomb also killed a child and 6 other civilians. The German High Command called it a terrorist act and decided retribution was in order, decreeing that for every German soldier, 10 Italians would die. The executions would be held within twenty-four hours. Responsibility for the executions fell on

Colonel Kappler, who stayed up all night writing a list. By dawn he had 223 names. It was not enough. So, he would later recall, "I decided to add fifty-seven Jews."[5] Still he did not have enough names; more were scratched together. He was still short. The Black Panther hit the streets and managed to find Lazzaro Anticoli, a Jewish boxer, among others. Finally, Kappler hit his goal of 320.

Kappler was also short of men to carry out the killings. He asked the German army for help, but the German regular army officers wanted nothing to do with the endeavour and refused. This, they told Kappler, was Gestapo business. Exasperated, he gathered his staff and instructed them on their mission. As in all Nazi operations, there would be order. The Italians would be shot in batches of 5, with a single bullet to the back of the head. One of Kappler's underlings raised a question. At 10 Italians for every dead German, there would be 320 corpses. Disposal of bodies would be a problem. Kappler decided that the executions would take place at the Fosse Ardeatine, some caves off the old Ardea road that led into Rome. Once the killings were complete, the caves could be mined and sealed shut.

On a whim, Kappler increased the quota to 330.

On March 24 at eight in the morning, the prisoners were brought by truck to the caves. Guards were posted to keep civilians away and the prisoners were led in groups into the caves, bound to one another, just as Kappler had ordered. As the executions progressed, discipline among the Gestapo weakened. One officer refused to shoot, despite the threat of execution for disobeying an order. Another arrived and, upon learning two hundred prisoners had been executed, fainted. The German soldiers, Kappler would later remember, were "becoming spiritually depressed" and began to drink cognac. The alcohol made them messy marksmen. Some prisoners did not die instantly and had to be finished off with rifle butts. As the afternoon sun moved slowly across the sky, the bodies piled up and it became necessary to force prisoners to climb the mound of legs, arms and torsos before kneeling for execution. By eight in the evening, the killings were over. In all, 335 Italians had been killed. The man responsible would live, after a period in prison, to die of old age in Germany. Thirty years later, on German television, Kappler wept and said, "I did not create those conditions. I carried out orders, and it was very hard."[6]

During the Nazi occupation, while killings like these were carried out, a Roman Catholic Rosminian priest named Tom Lenane was living in Rome. He was young and from South Wales, and he had a finely honed sense of humour. Father Tom, as he was called, liked to laugh. He had been educated in top schools, among them Rugby and Oxford, and in 1939, Lenane had been studying at the Rosminian Chapel in southeast Rome. When war was declared, the Italian government expelled all British citizens. Father Lenane's superior, Father Hugh O'Flaherty, asked him to apply for an Irish passport (Ireland remained neutral in the war). Armed with these credentials, he could remain in Rome.

Father Lenane spent the years between 1939 and 1944 working against the Fascists. He and his fellow Rosminian brothers hid escaped Allied prisoners of war in the Rosminian school at Porta di Latina. It was a dangerous undertaking. If he had been caught, Father Tom would have been treated to a stay in Via Tasso and then killed. There were many close calls, but somehow Father Tom managed to avoid detection. He was lucky, and much of his luck could be attributed to his street smarts.

During the occupation, food and other necessities were scarce. Citizens ate bread made with flour ground from bone buttons. They ate rats, dogs, cats. The underground economy flourished. The streets of the Roman neighbourhood of Cinquecentro were lined with black-market stalls. Even after the Allied liberation in June 1944, staple foods cost small fortunes. A loaf of bread cost 100 lire, 100 grams of macaroni 225, flour 135, four eggs 30 lire each. In July, a pair of shoes fetched 4,500 to 5,500 lire. Shops sold kerosene for 150 lire a litre. Beef was 350, cheese 550, oil 500, sugar 400.[7] These were enormous sums for the average Italian. Father Tom became an adept black marketeer; he would venture to the outskirts of Rome and the black-market neighbourhood near the Via Appia Nuova and barter. He became somewhat of an alchemist; under his sly direction, shoe heels became blankets, a piece of art became food and wine, books became sugar, gasoline became flour. Father Tom took his illicit booty and distributed it among his escapees and the needy, at no personal profit. He epitomized the Christian spirit. He was a fearless man who was driven, he said, by a compulsion to "put on the light wherever he found darkness."[8]

Once Rome was liberated, Father Lenane enlisted and became a British army chaplain. In early July 1944, he drove out to meet the army near Florence. He would serve with the British Eighth Army during the very bloody autumn of 1944 and winter of 1945. The abject misery he witnessed in Rome would be replaced by combat, the orchestrated ritual of mechanized death.

He may have passed Harold Pringle on his way to the front.

HAROLD, AT THAT TIME, was making his way back to Rome after breaking out of a Canadian Field Punishment Camp. It is most likely that he slept in the open, posing as a soldier on leave returning to his unit. Harold was in the region south of Rome called Lazio. Its roads were full of wanderers. Wives walked highways, moving from camp to camp looking for lost husbands who had been interned by the Allies. Refugees streamed north looking for food. Children looked for parents. Soldier stragglers milled about cafés, drinking. The Italian sky shone like a plate of light blue glass, unbroken by the deprivation beneath it. Pringle adopted his middle name, Joseph, and began introducing himself as Joe.

In the summer of 1944, the road into Rome was constantly busy. Trucks, troop carriers, tanks, jeeps, mule-drawn carts and refugees on foot streamed toward the only functional city in southern Italy. The refugees came from places like Campania and Calabria, and most had nothing. During the German occupation, Rome had absorbed immigrants fleeing the fighting at Cassino and Anzio. Now, with the Germans retreating north, the city was swarmed by Italians looking for work, food and lodging. In a few months, Rome's population swelled by over one million people. It became an ideal place in which to disappear.

Harold made his way to the Via Appia, known to the Allied troops as Route 6, and hitchhiked up to Rome, driving up the Liri Valley past such familiar landmarks as Cassino and Pignataro. Hitching was a principal mode of transportation for soldiers—all you needed to win a free seat was a uniform. Nonetheless, Harold was running loose in a war zone in a foreign country, and he was striking out alone. He did not speak

Italian and probably knew only the few words necessary for a Canadian soldier: *dove* (where), *ragazza* (girl), *ragazze* (girls), *mangia* (eat). Still, what he could not say with words he could communicate with his uniform and his gun. By late June, the weather was bright and warm. Starvation was giving way to plenty. Potatoes were in abundant supply. Usually the crop would have been shipped out from Naples for export, but because that city's harbour had been destroyed, the food was landlocked. Olive orchards blown to pieces by artillery began to produce fruit on what few trees remained. Wildflowers sprang up in the roadsides. The war rolled north of Rome, toward Florence. Southern Italy began to shake itself to its senses.

Harold had made a habit of going absent in England, but his decision to run in Italy was a far bolder move. By cutting loose from the Hasty Ps, he was severing the last tether that linked him to his life back in Canada. It had been four years since he had been home, and during that time his quiet life in Flinton became more and more of a faint memory. He left a town of just two hundred and became a speck swirling around in the biggest event in history. He had been imprisoned. He had seen action. Judging by the night Ivan Gunter described, something in Harold Pringle's mind had broken. He was paranoid and was convinced that his officers wanted him killed. He would, in his own words, "never make it out." He was a mental burnout, suffering from what an army psychiatrist might have called battle exhaustion. Faced with jail or death, he decided to take evasive action. No doubt he felt like the only Allied soldier in Italy going on the lam.

In reality, however, he was far from alone.

"Throughout the campaign," a post-war British army report states, "the rate of desertion and absence without leave was continually a source of anxiety."[9] It is important here to distinguish between a soldier who is AWOL and one who is considered a deserter. The AWOL soldier is assumed to have plans to rejoin his unit; he is temporarily on the loose. If after twenty-one days the soldier has not returned, he is listed as a deserter. The deserter has taken a final exit. He is like the errant husband who goes off to pick up a pack of cigarettes and never returns.

Absenteeism and desertion were both particularly troubling

between the late summer of 1944 and the spring of 1945. The Canadian army conducted 2,088 field general courts martial in Italy in 1944, and 936 in early 1945. In March 1945, Canadian army psychiatrist A. M. Doyle produced a survey of soldiers under sentence (SUS) in Italy. He found 1,033 Canadians in detention, 100 awaiting trial and at least another 500 deserters at large. Doyle assembled a profile of the average soldier serving a sentence: he was 24.7 years old, had served 44 months, had seen an average of 5.7 months in the field and had a Grade 7 education. Eighty-four per cent were in detention for being AWOL or deserting. Another 16 per cent were in prison for crimes ranging from civil offences to military violations such as refusing to obey an order. Eighty-two per cent of those in detention were from "those elements that bear the brunt of hardship and fighting, namely the infantry."[10] Doyle believed 38 per cent of those serving sentences to be "reclaimable." These men could be returned to their regiments and would become good soldiers. He found 28 per cent to be career offenders and unsuitable for military service. Thirty-two per cent, he noted, were suffering from combat-related neuropsychiatric disorders. Some of these soldiers had been wounded, treated for battle exhaustion and then returned to their units for active duty. Desertion and absenteeism were not exclusive to the Canadian army. Between October 1943 and June 1945, there were 5,694 convictions for desertion in the British army in Italy. About 1,000 British soldiers deserted each month during the winter of 1944–45. By 1945, British military prisons in Italy housed more than 5,000 soldiers. American prisons incarcerated another 5,000.

Allied military leaders were puzzled by desertion: it was not restricted to what they referred to as "problem soldiers." The British report on desertion admitted that while some deserters were

> genuine cowards—men who deliberately set out to avoid
> action—their number, however, was probably no greater relatively
> than in any other campaign. The most serious aspect of the prob-
> lem in Italy was the number of soldiers with good records who
> eventually broke down under the strain of prolonged action. One
> of the principal causes of such collapse was the need to return

men again and again to the line after evacuation for wounds or exhaustion. Men felt that they would go on being sent back into the line until they were killed, totally incapacitated by wounds, or broke down and deserted.[11]

Desertion was caused, in part, by the nature of the Italian campaign itself. By its conclusion in May 1945, the Italian campaign had run twenty-two months, making it the single longest sustained action of the entire war, in any military theatre. Strategically, the Italian offensive was intended to force the Nazi High Command to keep German troops in Italy, and thereby to prevent them from reinforcing the Normandy Front. Tactically, however, Allied field commanders were trying to drive the Germans out of Italy. It is no surprise that Joseph Heller's notion of a "Catch-22"—a dilemma with no solution because of mutually conflicting conditions—originated on the Italian battlefield. The Allies would spend the rest of 1944 and much of 1945 attacking German forces in order to keep them in Italy.

In late August 1944, the Allies assaulted the Gothic Line, a system of German defences crossing northern Italy. Allied generals were initially optimistic. Unlike the hilly ground south of Rome, the fields of Romagna beyond the Apennine Mountains were flat and ideal for swift tank attacks. Allied commander Harold Alexander decided to launch a two-pronged strike that would start at the town of Ancona, a seaport on the Adriatic side of Italy. The Eighth Army would strike up the flatlands through the Rimini Gap, around the shoulder of the Apennines and on to the Po Valley. The American 5th Army would swing down through Florence and Bologna. Unfortunately, the Allied generals did not take into account the terrain's other predominant features: canals and rivers. These would impede vehicle movement. The attacks exacted a high toll. In September alone, the Canadians suffered 4,000 casualties in battles at such places as Rimini, San Martino, Lamone and Ravenna. During the Gothic Line assault, Major A. E. Moll, a Canadian military psychiatrist, saw about five hundred battle exhaustion cases. These soldiers were sent back from their units with notes from field medical officers such as, "He was sent out of action by his officer because he became completely demoralized and was unable to do anything except shake and cry," or "Evacuated from the front line by his company commander as useless and demoralizing to other men. Became so confused that he didn't know what he was doing."[12] Soldiers did not spend much time recuperating. Those deemed salvageable were sedated for two or three days, given a shower, a shave and food, and then shipped back to the front. Soldiers who were thought to be unfit for further action would be transferred to Special Employment Companies. These were non-combatant units that worked at manual labour. Meanwhile, the fighting continued. In the month of December the Canadians lost another 2,500 men.

By taking off, Harold Pringle thought he would avoid that fate.

He arrived in Rome, and soon he began living with a woman. Whether Harold had met her on his first trip to Rome is uncertain. It is clear that Harold was romantically entangled. Betti Michael, his cousin, was sure that Harold had left the army for passion. "I think there was a girl involved," she said. "He fell in love."[13] Harold's girl might have been Roman, or she might have been a refugee. She was probably young, a brunette and, given Harold's track record, pretty. She would likely have worn her hair in the style of the day, shoulder length with a wave. Roman women often wore floral skirts and high heels. She lived with a girlfriend in an apartment in the southeast section of the city, near the Via Appia Nuova. This neighbourhood sat just outside the city's ancient walls, close to San Giovanni di Laterano, a lavish structure that was once the Pope's official residence. It was known for the statue that stood in its local park: Re di Roma (King of Italy). The Via Appia's buildings dated back only to the nineteenth century, and there was plenty of Fascist architecture. Mussolini had invested great effort into Re di Roma and other similar neighbourhoods because he wanted them to become symbols of middle-class affluence and security in the new Fascist Italy. Ironically, in 1944, after Rome was occupied by the Allies, Re di Roma became a centre for absentees. The Via Appia Nuova, which soldiers called the Via Appia, ran straight through it, and once deserters reached Re di Roma they settled into its restaurants and cafés. It was just off the radar for military police. A deserter could hide out in one of the many apartments that lined its streets and venture into the heart of the city at night looking for entertainment.

In the early days of his time in Rome, Harold did not socialize. Instead, he stayed with his girlfriend and began to learn a little Italian. Harold clearly had a soft spot for women and judging by his previous affairs, this one must also have been passionate and impetuous. Perhaps because he was so close to his mother, he developed a trust and affinity for women and he found comfort and safety in romantic love.

In the summer of 1944, Harold was not the only Canadian falling for an Italian. The Canadians appear to have been universally awestruck. G. H. Adlam, a Canadian recruit, penned a poem in their honour for the army newspaper *The Maple Leaf*:

Raven-black tresses, perfumed and sweet,
Beckoning sloe-eyes, alive yet asleep;
Free-flowing hips with serpentuous sway,
Thighs framed by shadows forever at play;
Beauties unequalled 'neath Heaven's blue dome,
You gladdening, maddening, women of Rome.[14]

As the summer passed golden and warm, Harold settled into life away from the front with his sweetheart. Rome was bustling and full of luxuries. Food became plentiful, and parties and music were the order of the day. Slowly, as he became more secure, Harold began to stroll around Re di Roma. At times he would dress in the civilian clothes that his girlfriend had scrounged for him and sit in the park watching the street life. His adventure had begun as a bid to save democracy and follow in his father's footsteps. Now he was in Rome, trying to overcome shell shock, eating pasta and living with an Italian girl who barely spoke English and who affectionately called him "Giuseppe." If Pringle had kept up this regime, he would eventually have been picked up, court-martialled and sent to prison. Harold Pringle would have been another misfit who, in the words of one Canadian officer, never returned the money and effort invested in his training.

In late August 1944, however, Harold Pringle met another deserter, an American, and the course of his life changed once again.

Pringle met Bobbie Williams, a tall Nebraskan soldier from the 4th

Ranger Infantry Battalion with the nickname "the C Ration Kid." C Ration was a staff sergeant. He wore paratrooper's boots and had a scar running down his face and across his upper lip. It was a memento from his time at the Anzio beachhead.

The Rangers were an elite American force modelled on the British commando units. By 1944, they had fought fierce battles in North Africa, Sicily and Italy. At their Sicily landing, at the town of Gela, the Rangers executed a perfect landing. They used hand grenades and machine guns to take out tanks, completely destroying an Italian force. Their landing at Salerno in September 1943 had been worse. German guns caused high casualties. From that point on, the Rangers had been in action continuously. They fought up through central Italy and were then shipped up to take part in the landing at Anzio.[15]

Anzio would prove to be the undoing of the Rangers in Italy.

In January 1944, 767 Rangers, led by Colonel William Darby, were stationed at Anzio. On January 28, they were given orders to take the small village of Cisterna. The 1st and 3rd battalions set out that night. The weather was freezing, and the men wore scarves and gloves to fight off the cold. The Rangers crawled through the mud toward their objective. When they were eight hundred yards from Cisterna, a force of Germans opened up ferocious machine-gun fire on them. The Rangers were surrounded. They tried to shelter themselves by crouching in shallow ditches in an open field, but as dawn broke, their situation worsened. Officers were picked off. The Rangers fought tenaciously, knocking out seventeen German tanks. The Germans, in turn, bayoneted and machine-gunned American prisoners. They piled wounded Rangers up in stacks to serve as living barricades. They forced American prisoners to walk in front of them as they advanced, forming a moving, living wall. Years after the battle, Rangers veterans recalled how they killed their own men while returning German fire.

Only six men came back from the 1st and 3rd battalions. Bobbie Williams' 4th battalion lost fifty per cent of its men. Several hundred had been taken prisoner. After the battle, Colonel Darby was told by an observer, "Hollywood would have paid five million dollars to have that on film."[16] Ten years later, Hollywood recreated the ill-fated attack in the film *Anzio*, starring Robert Mitchum. Darby never saw it. He was killed by an 88mm shell a year after the Cisterna debacle.

Following Cisterna, the Rangers were attached to the 504 Parachute Battalion back on the Anzio beachhead. The fighting was stagnant and defensive, and the Germans conducted bombardments with regularity. Any movement on the American side would bring down a flurry of German shells. In March, the 4th Rangers were taken out of the line and separated into two groups. A total of 19 officers and 134 men were to be returned to the United States. The rest would be transferred to the 1st Special Service Force.

At some point, Bobbie Williams, the C Ration Kid, decided that he was done fighting. Perhaps he was picked to go home but decided he wanted to stay in Italy. Perhaps he was sent to Special Force but was loyal to his regiment and was angry not to be kept a Ranger. Either way, he deserted, and like so many deserters he found his way to Rome.

It is likely that Harold met the C Ration Kid at a café on Via Taranto, a street that ran off the Via Appia. At first, the two men must have eyed each other carefully. The C Ration Kid was in uniform, while Harold would have been in civilian clothes, a light blue blazer and green pants but it did not take the C Ration Kid long to identify Harold as an absentee—he was too quiet for an Italian. After a few muffled hellos, they took a table in the corner, and over coffee and spaghetti the pair discussed their mutual interests: staying alive, which meant staying in Rome—both of which meant staying the hell out of the army.

There were plenty of guys in Rome now, the C Ration Kid told Harold. They were posing as American soldiers and walking freely around the city. So far, Harold had been lucky, but if he did not find a way to blend in and survive, he would sooner or later be caught by the military police. Every day, truckloads of absentees were being carted back to detention barracks. The army was sending some back to combat and others to detention. The thought of a military prison sent Harold into a sweat. He had barely made it through six months during his last stint. Harold told the C Ration Kid he had volunteered for combat to get out of prison and that he had been a good soldier too, for ten cents a day. He had kept going even though he knew he'd be killed. And for a while it

didn't seem to matter. It was all rain and bodies and smoke and screaming. Then, after the Hitler Line, he'd taken off to Rome with some other
guys from the Hasty Ps, just to have a bit of fun and then come back. The
bit of fun went longer than everyone expected. When they got their
hands on Harold, the military police told him he was going away for
three years' hard labour. It was another death sentence. So first chance he
had, off he went.

The C Ration Kid took the story in. He kept talking in his broad
Midwestern drawl. After Cisterna, the C Ration Kid had just said fuck it.

"You only get so many chances and I've had all mine," he might have
told Harold. "If I kept on with it, it'd be like telling God to jump in a lake.
He spared me, brother. I took the hint."

Now there was next week to think about. The C Ration Kid
reminded Harold of the common belief that Italians couldn't be trusted.
"Once the wrong Itie finds out you are at large, they will turn you in,
unless there was lire in keeping you around. And how long are these
signoras going to go letting the absentees lounge around while they
worked? Face it, Joe. You're an absentee. Forget the war. Forget the army.
The war will be over in six months anyway and by then all the absentees
will just melt away and turn up back home. You did your part, and that
is a hell of a lot more than most of those bastards did back home. You
need protection and it is out there, available. Italians and Allied soldiers
are working together. There is money to be made and fun, of sorts, to be
had." Face it. You're an absentee. You've left society. To live, you must
operate beneath it.

8.

RE DI ROMA

As August 1944 began to wind down, Rome shed the vestiges of the Nazi occupation. Collaborators were rooted out and tried; those deemed guilty enough were executed in Forte Bravetta. The war moved north. While Harold and the C Ration Kid were meeting on the Via Appia, only a two-hour drive away the Allies and Germans were slammed up against each other in a succession of bloody melees on the Gothic Line. Towns such as Rimini and Russi were being blown to pieces, and more refugees were streaming into the city, this time from the north. Rome was full of soldiers either resting from action at the front or on the way back, and mixed in with these men were the deserters. Estimations of their numbers ran wild. English writer Evelyn Waugh speculated that there were 9,000 American soldiers at large.[1] In the British army, convictions for desertion rose from 160 in July to 251 in August to 245 in September. At the same time, convictions for absence without leave climbed to 944 in September and to 905 in October, peaking at 1,200 in November. It was a familiar story. Battle-hardened veterans cracked up or burnt out; fresh reinforcements were of a low calibre and many could not cope with combat. Disposal of deserters became a problem; the British authorities had to construct special prisons, courts and provost units to accommodate them.[2]

For soldiers on the run, Rome continued to provide the ultimate sojourn. Yet, wrote George Powell, although banners reading "Welcome to the Liberators" still hung above the streets, the "local belles no longer throw their arms about each and every Allied soldier to plant a kiss on his liberating lips."[3] Feelings among the troops were also cooling. They liked the Italians, but at the same time they were aware that since 1943 Canadians had been dying, all in the name of liberating these enemies-turned-friends. Meanwhile, the Italians had surrendered by the thousands and were getting away with their lives. "If the Italians could make war as they sing opera, they could have licked the world by now," declared the *Union Jack*. The newspaper described the typical Italian male as possessing an "over-ready smile, the eagerness to agree with everything you say, the unnatural readiness to fall in line with anything that may be suggested…and the cold greasy fear which peeps out of a man's eyes when an argument arises."[4] Italy was "nothing but mountains and fountains," wrote one Canadian private.[5]

The ill will was reciprocated. Rome could be a rough town, with a population that increasingly displayed a deep-seated animosity toward the Allies. Yes, the *Americani* and the *Inglesi* had rid the city of the Fascists, but they were an occupying force nonetheless. Italian men resented seeing Allied soldiers cavorting with Italian women, and Allied officers on leave carried pistols at all times to ward off attacks. One Canadian captain recalled returning from the opera with his Italian girlfriend, only to be surrounded by a throng of young, angry Romans. Nonplussed, he did what any self-respecting Canadian officer would—he gunned his way out. A few warning shots cleared the crowd swiftly.[6] This was the intangible that made military men with front-line experience both intimidating and unpredictable. To the seasoned soldier, violence was no longer a reluctant reflex, it was a tool ready for use.

Of course, after years of war, it would have been illogical to expect the two sides to lock arms and embrace. The tone had been set before the invasion of Sicily when General Bernard Montgomery gave a speech telling his troops, "Someone said to me a few days ago that the Italians are really decent people and that if we treat them properly they will come over to us. I disagree with him. Our job is to kill them. That is what we have to do. Once we have killed them we can see if they are good fellows or not. But they must be killed first."[7]

In *The Long Road Home*, a memoir of his life serving in the Cape Breton Highlanders, veteran Fred Cederberg describes a similar speech given to Canadian troops. A general told the Canucks, "The Eyeties are officially considered our Allies. That's the word. They've surrendered and they're on our side. Bully! Well, I'm telling you this: As far as I'm concerned, they're just defeated enemies and you can treat them as such. So help yourself to anything you want, providing it isn't nailed down or guarded. And if that's the case you'll know how to handle it."[8]

The most extreme form of "handling it"—killing Italian civilians—was a frowned-upon but accepted fallout of hostilities, and the closer the incident was to the front line the more legal it became. Civilians killed during combat were unavoidable casualties of war, the price of doing business. There were, however, more than a few incidents behind the lines, and by 1944 this sort of damage became an issue for the British Foreign Office. In a memo examining violence by Allied soldiers against Italian civilians, a British diplomat stationed in Rome reported that it was seriously harming relations with the Italian interim government and undermining the confidence of the general population.[9] To illustrate the sort of violence he was worried about, he outlined three randomly chosen incidents. In October 1943, two British soldiers woke up Giuseppe Garufi and his wife and then robbed the house. It was the second tragedy to befall the Garufi family: three weeks earlier a British truck had run over and killed the couple's youngest son. In December 1943, three off-duty gunners became drunk in a restaurant. They demanded more wine and the proprietor, Rudolph Mastrominico, refused. The gunners shot him dead, fleeing the restaurant. They returned shortly afterward, however, and ordered Mastrominico's widow to hand over all the restaurant's cash. On February 13, 1944, four Canadian soldiers set out from their billets to find some cheap wine. One of the party said he knew of a villa that sold it. Armed with an empty jug and a rifle, they drove a truck to the house. One of the soldiers knocked on the door and asked the owner, Nicolas Testi, to sell them some wine. Testi replied that they had no wine for sale, but offered the man a free glass. The soldier drank it and left. He soon returned with another soldier. Testi agreed to fill their jug with wine in exchange for cigarettes and matches. The soldiers left but returned a third time and tried to force their way in. This time they shot Testi. The Canadians left with more wine. One of the soldiers was eventually identified and charged with manslaughter. Since he was fighting at the front, he was tried in absentia. He was found not guilty.

Still, many Italians adored the Allies, or at least appreciated what a North American or British accent could do. These were the profiteers who ran black market gangs. To an Italian living outside the law, Allied friends were essential assets. With the proper paperwork, a soldier could pass through road checks and in and out of Allied camps. After Rome was captured, Allied drivers were highly coveted. Ivan Gunter remembers how Italian black marketeers scoured the city looking for them:

> They had Italians who were on the lookout for drivers, as long as they were in the army. They would find these fellows on leave and then a girl or two would approach them. The soldiers would be brought back to a house and then they would be kept drunk for a week or two, all the while being seen to by these girls. Just a grand old time. By then, the soldiers had overstayed their leave and were AWOL and going back to their units meant a heavy penalty. The Italians would make them an offer. Stay and drive trucks for the black market. With a Canadian accent or whatever, they were perfect for moving contraband.[10]

The system worked well. Back in December 1943, three months after the capture of Naples, a *Union Jack* editorial had declared, "Everywhere I have been in Italy, I've seen the Black Market flourishing. The authorities are trying to stamp it out but it is a crime which only the people as a whole can destroy. And that's the point. The people are accepting it."[11] By 1944, the black market had grown exponentially. A random check on the route from Avellino to Bari caught fourteen military trucks transporting black market goods. Seven Americans, four Frenchmen, two Englishmen and one Canadian were arrested. "These," the officer in charge reported, "were the unlucky ones who had not been tipped off about the posting."

In total, sixty-six charges were laid against British and American drivers.[12] "The scale on which this illicit trade is being carried in Allied
Military vehicles is disgraceful and the result of slackness and ineffi-
ciency. It is very possible that the bulk of black market grain is being
carried by Allied military vehicles." In one month in 1944, 212 British
and Commonwealth soldiers were fined a total of $97,000 (US), and
another 419 were charged with sequestering contraband.[13]

Both deserters and military personnel were active in the enterprise.
In 1944, the Criminal Investigations Division of the Provost Marshall
General's Office conducted a survey of two thousand cases of various
activities connected with the black market. They found that fifty per cent
of black marketeers were civilians and fifty per cent servicemen:

> The extent to which AWOLs are involved in black marketing is
> not accurately known but is believed negligible. The rigid controls
> at various supply installations preclude the illegal removal of sup-
> plies in substantial quantities. AWOLs attempting to sustain
> themselves and remain at large generally engage in petty crimes
> and occasionally serious crimes of violence such as robbery etc. It
> is felt that, due in part to publicity of a few cases, wherein AWOLs
> engaged in large scale black market activities, an erroneous and
> overrated conception of this phase of the problem exists.[14]

IN AUGUST, A TWENTY-YEAR-OLD petty officer from the British navy
appeared in Harold's neighbourhood on the Via Appia. His name was
William Robert Croft, and he was from Grimsby, a town in northern
England. Bill was a handsome fellow, with straw blond hair, a fair complexion and smiling blue eyes that lightened when he laughed. He had
left school at age fourteen, working in a steel foundry and then a biscuit
factory. He then went to sea as a galley boy, working the route between
Immingham and the Norwegian city of Narvik. He was fifteen when the
war broke out and he immediately volunteered for the Royal Navy. Croft
was clever; he managed himself well in the navy, learning how to play the
system to his advantage. He was always looking to make a little extra

cash, always ready for a scheme. As a hobby, Croft loved to read pulp thrillers and he spent many hours dreaming of a glamorous life lived on the edge.[15] He was particularly mesmerized by the exploits of American gangsters such as John Dillinger. Bill Croft came to Italy in 1943 to join the ship the *Empire Ace*. In March 1944, his ship was sunk and Croft volunteered to join the *Patroclus*, which was heading to Anzio. Croft spent four weeks there under fire and returned to Naples, where he joined the *Empire Griffin*.

Also in March 1944, Bill Croft met a young Italian woman named Maria Fedele. She was a Neapolitan beauty with night-black hair, full lips, chocolate eyes and a lithe figure. Friends remember that Maria had a soft, melodious voice. Bill and Maria had been introduced at a party in Naples, where, she would later recall, "a love sympathy arose between us."[16] For the next few months they carried on an affair. In June, Maria discovered that she was pregnant and was terrified of the shame she would endure in the eyes of her friends and family. Bill decided to spare her. He would drop the war in favour of love. Living like the characters in the thrillers he read, he would take his girl and go on the run. Bill Croft deserted on July 28, and he and Maria moved up to Rome.

In August, Bill Croft entered a restaurant on the Via Appia and ordered himself a glass of wine. He was dressed in his petty officer's uniform and a white peaked cap. Seated not far away were two American soldiers. One was a tall fellow, with blond hair and a scar that ran down his face to his mouth. The other was shorter and better looking. He had a perennial smile plastered across his face, as if it had been planted there since birth.

9.

SUMMER ON THE VIA APPIA

The three deserters talked at length, each spinning out how he had left the military and why. Croft had an easy assurance about him. He seemed worldly and clear-headed, and his take on life in Rome jibed with that of Williams, the C Ration Kid. Any long-term stay would only be possible if a steady—and sizeable—income could be ensured. Some deserters were "going Itie" and partnering up with Italians. Bill Croft told Pringle and C Ration that he had had a close look at the black market while stationed in Naples. There, contraband goods such as US-issue army blankets were sold openly on the streets. The Camorra was well entrenched, thanks to the group's anti-Fascist efforts during the occupation. Organized crime had gathered intelligence for the Allied landings in Sicily and later in southern Italy, and had played a key role in sabotaging the Fascists and in organizing an armed rebellion in Naples during the autumn of 1943. Now that the Nazis were gone, the Camorra ruled with cruel efficiency and unofficial Allied approval—so long as its exploits did not harm the war effort. And the Camorra was popular. It showed more interest in working-class Italians than so-called legitimate politicians did, distributing food to the starving and protecting church property. When Moroccan troops raped Italian women in Campania, it was the Camorra, not the Allied military police, who rounded the soldiers up and executed them.[1]

But Rome, Croft noted, was not yet under Camorra control and was unlikely to be so. The Romans would never allow a southern Italian crime family to run their city. This created an environment that was ripe for freelancing. Already there was a deserter gang in operation. Known as the "Lane Gang," this group was said to contain upwards of forty deserters from every army in the field: American, British, Canadian, Polish, South African, even German. The Lane Gang earned its profit by hijacking vehicles in Rome's tiny streets and by waylaying both civilian and army trucks on the highways around the city. Rumour had it that they had even held up a train. The Lane Gang trafficked in drugs and ran prostitutes, and their exploits made them rich men. They lived luxuriously in spacious apartments and fuelled themselves on a steady diet of girls, *vino* and spaghetti. Croft's logic was confirmed by official military reports. "Get a truck one day," the Canadian officer in charge of black market investigation told *The Maple Leaf*, "and you're rich the next, in this town."[2]

Croft believed there was room for another gang, though on a much smaller scale. A few men doing the occasional job would not raise too much interest from the military police since the MPs were busy tracking down deserters and AWOL soldiers. Together, five or six men could live longer on less because the proverbial pie would be cut into fewer pieces. A small group of friends could sit out the war nicely, spending a little of their time relieving the city's citizens of their possessions and most of it enjoying Rome's charms. To ensure their survival, Croft concocted a twist: this gang would target black market vehicles. They would steal jeeps that had already been stolen. In this way, they would remain unknown to military authorities.

Croft's plan won over Harold and the C Ration Kid. For starters, it was a plan, and that was more than they had going. Nothing concrete was yet established. "It was just sort of a talk," Harold would later say. "And we all joined up."[3] The C Ration Kid brought in another American deserter, a soldier from New York named Walter Glaser, who, thanks to his rake-thin frame and his height—over six feet—went by the nickname "Slim." He was regular army and, like C Ration, had fought at Anzio. After Rome opened up, Glaser became a habitual

AWOL; he had been arrested so many times that he had lost count. Like Pringle, he had an Italian girlfriend on the Via Appia. Her name was Anna, and she lived on the Piazza Tuscola in a flat with her mother. Slim was in love with her; each time he escaped from detention, he went straight to her door.

Over the month of September, Croft, the C Ration Kid and Harold Pringle travelled around Rome, investigating its neighbourhoods and the surrounding cities. The trio spent a night on a Liberty ship in the harbour at Civitavecchia, the port north of Rome, and there they encountered a face from Pringle's days in England. Harold noticed John Norman McGillivary, otherwise known as "Lucky," sleeping on a nearby cot. The two Canadians had been in prison together and had developed a casual friendship.[4]

Lucky and Harold had a lot in common. Both their fathers were veterans of the First World War. Both their mothers were named Mary. Both soldiers came from large families. Lucky had been born on March 22, 1922, in Cape Breton, the second eldest in a family of eight brothers and four sisters. He had an unremarkable scholastic career. His army report sarcastically stated that his one intellectual achievement was "truancy," but Lucky had managed to reach the sixth grade. He was an avid athlete; he swam, boxed and played hockey (defenceman), basketball (guard) and soccer (fullback). Prior to the war, he worked at odd jobs, such as store clerk and farm labourer. Lucky had enlisted at Inverness, Nova Scotia, in March 1940 and joined the Cape Breton Highlanders. At enlistment he was 5 foot 7 inches tall, with black hair and what the army doctor described as "black eyes." His vision was perfect and he had a dark complexion. In 1942, an army psychiatrist evaluated Lucky and described him as "neat and cheerful." Lucky told the doctor that he had joined the army in search of "adventure and experience."[5] He found both, but not in the form he had expected.

Military discipline was not to Lucky's liking. Almost from his first day in the army Lucky was running afoul of his sergeants and officers. His military record is stuffed with page after page of charges. He was punished for everything from failing to sweep under his bunk to possessing a rusty bayonet to breaking windows to going AWOL. In

September 1941, he was charged with using "insubordinate language to an NCO when he was awakened after the reveille started." In 1942, he was charged with "conduct to the prejudice of good order and discipline"; when told to sit down at the breakfast table, he had said to his sergeant, "Make up your fucking mind." Lucky's psychiatrist reported that "this man is impulsive and at times is not very keen on discipline. Started as a rifleman and is beginning to realize that he isn't getting anywhere by losing his temper. Fundamentally sound but young and impulsive. Should make a good soldier with careful handling."[6]

By 1943, however, the army had tired of Lucky's rebellious temper and he was sentenced to one year's detention in the Glass House. In January 1943, Lucky escaped but was picked up again. This time he was sentenced to twenty-two months and scheduled for a May 1944 release. The commandant of the Glass House reported that Lucky was "sorely in need of a stiff lesson" and that his time in prison would provide that education. Lucky's conduct while in prison was poor; he was on report twelve times. Each month, a prison officer interviewed Lucky. Each month, Lucky had one constant refrain: "Says that he is very anxious to get into action with his unit."[7] He wanted to be on the front fighting. Pringle met Lucky in the fall of 1943 when McGillivary had already spent one year in the Glass House.

In December 1943, Lucky made good on his ambition. He broke out of prison, smashing in the prison staff sergeant's teeth before making his escape. Lucky went to London on foot and then stowed away on the SS 'H. T. Tegelberg', a ship bound for Italy. Lucky was discovered on board, but he informed the crew that he was making his way to Italy to rejoin his unit. He arrived in Italy on March 3, 1944, and thanks to the shortage of reinforcements, he was not sent to prison, after all. There was no sense wasting a healthy boy who was so eager to fight that he busted out of jail and jumped a ship. Within days, Lucky was en route to the Canadian reinforcement depot in Avellino. A few weeks later he was with the Cape Breton Highlanders and in action. There was, however, a catch: thanks to pay stoppages, Lucky would not be eligible to draw his soldier's salary until 1946. That did not bother Lucky, not to begin with—at least he was out of prison.

March 1944 found him battling his way up the Cassino Front in, no doubt, a state of ecstasy. The Cape Breton Highlanders were holding a line across from German positions. It was tense work. Barrages would drop down without notice. Once a group of Italian refugees ran through the Canadian lines; half an hour later the Germans threw up a bombardment, killing many of the Highlanders. Canadian intelligence determined that the civilians had returned to German lines and revealed the Canadian position. A week later, eight more refugees approached the Canadian line. The Highlanders yelled at them to stop and turn back, but the Italians kept coming, leaving the Canadians no choice—they opened up with their Bren Machine guns, killing all eight. After the killings, the Highlanders paused for a snack of bully beef. To no one in particular, Sergeant Fred Cederberg remarked, "We'll have to get a burial party out here tonight to pick up those dead civvies. A couple of days under this sun and they'll start to stink and it won't smell nice around here."

A private said, "I don't think I like this war any more."

"Nobody likes it," replied another, while opening a tin of beef. "It's just a temporary way of life."[8]

After the breakthrough at the Hitler Line, the Highlanders went on to attack the Germans along the Melfa River. As always, the fighting was prolonged, bitter and worse than expected. Lucky's comrades, those who knew him from Cape Breton, noticed a change in the boy. John Norman McGillivary had always been hot-tempered, but prison had turned him into a brooding fellow who clung to past wrongs the way a child clings to a blanket. In the Glass House, he had begun keeping a little black book. In it, he would record every slight or offence committed against him. Next to these transgressions he would inscribe a suitable retribution, to be administered physically by Lucky McGillivary. Lucky called it his "ledger." He claimed it had great value as it gave him a glimpse into the future. In June 1944, Lucky decided he was finished with the army and took off, looking for a different shape of adventure.

At Civitavecchia in August, before drifting off to sleep, Lucky showed Harold his ledger, pointing out that Harold's name was not in there. The following morning, Harold and Croft returned to Rome. Lucky went on his way.

During September, Bill Croft spent much of his time out on the Via Appia looking for soldiers who might fit in with his family of deserters. The deserters stopped on the Via Appia because it was the last neighbourhood before Rome's ancient city walls, and it was outside the military checkpoints situated on the roads leading into the city. The Via Appia was checkered with bits of suburban countryside. There were beautiful pine and walnut trees in the round park at Re di Roma. Soldiers on the loose could spend warm, cloudless afternoons occupying a bench and drinking in the local sights, far from the gaze of the military police. As the absentee population grew, the Via Appia became known for its strange colony of burnt-out Allied soldiers.

Bill would sit for hours sipping coffee or wine, perusing the stragglers as they strolled up and down the street. Croft had a good eye, and there were plenty of possible candidates. To him, deserters were not too hard to spot. They were generally thin and nervous, with a dullness to their eyes. Soldiers just off the front displayed a scattered confusion when confronted by civilian life. Watching women buy vegetables or children running amok in the streets disturbed them. They grimaced, as if they were trying to figure out which world they were in. And, of course, there was the noise factor. The deserters, most of them from combat units, came from a world of incessant shelling, a world where men hid in holes while rabbits roamed freely. Slam a door around one of those fellows and he was likely to crawl under a bed.

Sometime in mid-September, Croft was set up in his favourite restaurant, Bar Trieste on the Via Appia, when he spied a soldier drinking crème de menthe, alone, at a table near the back. The soldier was filthy, as if he'd just come off the line, and the sunken rings around his eyes showed that he had not slept for days. He had a round face and brown hair. He spoke Italian but with a British accent. Croft approached him carefully. When he engaged a prospective candidate in casual conversation, Croft listened for slight discrepancies in the stranger's story. The soldier looked up, not knowing whether he was about to be arrested. Croft, in a circumspect manner, introduced himself. Perhaps the dirty soldier sipping crème de menthe had been a bit overenthusiastic about his leave. Perhaps he was not too keen to see its conclusion. Perhaps he needed a friend.

What he needed most urgently, it turned out, was a meal—he had not eaten for two days. Croft said to come along. He had a place not far away where he could wash up and have something to eat. The soldier introduced himself: "Charlie Honess."

Croft thought for a moment. "That may be a bit hard for the *signorinas*," he said. "I think we'll call you...."

"I'll be Carlo," Charlie said, smiling for the first time.

Charlie was, in fact, Cecil Henry Frederick Honess, a twenty-two-year-old from the east end of London who, though having only reached the sixth grade, spoke both French and Italian. He was a sapper in the Royal Engineers and been in Italy since 1943. Honess had spent time clearing minefields in North Africa, had invaded Sicily and had spent four months at Cassino, with all that that entailed—smoke, rotting shit-smeared corpses, screams, rain, men weeping, shelling, German soldiers stacked by the side of the road, a tiny hand peeking out beneath a pile of bricks that had once been a house, a cat as calm as anything staring at them while they ran for cover, lying on your back in a slit trench staring up at the sky and wishing you were a bird, building bridges under machine-gun fire, hammering nails while bullets buzzed by like so many bees. The action at the Gothic Line finished Charlie Honess off. In August, he went absent.

In a staccato voice, he spun out his story for Croft:

> I was loose about nine days then I walked down to Vine Street
> and gave myself up. I was sent to the Court Martial Holding
> Centre at Perugia and then it was moved to Mascerata and I went
> with them. Then I escaped out of Mascerata with some other fel-
> lows. Then I was picked up down at Anzio about two days later. I
> was brought back up to the Rome Guardroom again and at twelve
> o'clock that night I was moved out with some other fellows. I was
> sent away on a truck and on the way I escaped with another
> fellow. Then I came down to Rome with him and left him
> outside Rome.[9]

Bill Croft brought Honess back to the apartment he shared with Maria at 28 Via Pistoia. It was a small, two-storey building that reminded Croft of an English country house. It had a tall pine tree in its front garden, which had been hit by an Allied shell prior to Rome's being made an Open City. The shell had blown a wall down and left a pile of rubble in front of the house. Croft introduced Honess to Maria, who by this time was six months pregnant, and to the landlady and her daughter, who cooked and cleaned for Croft. Honess ate a simple meal of pasta and spinach, and Croft gave him an American GI uniform and ten dollars. Honess thanked him, promising to repay him at the soonest opportunity. Croft assured him that that was unnecessary. Honess said his good-byes. Croft said he would see Honess around the Via Appia. Maria and the other women said, "*Buona sera*, Carlo."

Three weeks later, Honess met Croft again. By this time, a new addition had been made to what was now known as "The Sailor Gang." Lucky McGillivary had turned up in Rome, little black book and all, and it had not been too hard to convince him to join. He took up residence in the first-floor bedroom at Via Pistoia. In early October, Honess met Bill Croft on the Via Appia. The Sailor was in a jeep with two soldiers in American uniforms whom he introduced as Joe and the C Ration Kid. Bill suggested that Honess come for a ride. After a night spent on the roads outside Rome, the men returned and found Lucky "in one of his moods." A fight broke out, and Croft and Lucky stripped off their shirts and raised their fists. Honess would later learn this was a regular occurrence and an accepted means of resolving a dispute. After the fight, Lucky and Croft shook hands and the men settled down to drinking—everyone, that is, except Joe, who was not fond of alcohol. The following morning, Lucky took Honess for a ride in one of the gang's two jeeps and suggested that Honess move into the basement room at Via Pistoia. Honess, who was living with a woman on the Via Appia, agreed. As the first week in October passed, the gang firmed up: two Americans, the C Ration Kid and Slim; two Canadians, Lucky and Joe; and two Brits, Charlie and Bill the Sailor.

The Sailor Gang became a bridge between the army and the black market. Thanks to a series of shady deals, Bill Croft and his men consorted freely with the regular army. Croft befriended an American supply sergeant from Indiana who was stationed at the Airborne Training Center just outside Rome. Bill allowed the sergeant to bring his girlfriend to the house on Via Pistoia and use one of the rooms. In exchange, the sergeant gave Croft bunches of blank US army three-day passes, about forty-eight at a time. These passes, which were superior to the counterfeit ones printed on the black market, were critical to the gang's survival: if a deserter was stopped by an MP and had no pass, he would be picked up. Croft distributed these passes among the Sailor Gang. He would fill in the particulars with false names, ranks, units and serial numbers, leaving the date blank. That way if one of the gang needed a pass quickly, all he had to do was scribble in the details.

The fake passes also allowed the Sailor Gang to move easily in and out of military compounds. In mid-October, for example, Lucky came down with venereal disease. Bill Croft filled out a pass listing Lucky as a Sergeant Frazer of the American 5th Army, and the Sailor Gang dropped him off at the 73rd General American Hospital. Lucky told the doctors that he had come up from Naples on a three-day pass when the disease had broken out on him. The American treatment for VD was eight shots of penicillin given over a thirty-six-hour period, which was just enough time to be treated before the three-day pass expired. Lucky was back in no time, little black book and all.

The sergeant from Indiana was not the only regular army soldier to fraternize with the gang. Lucky had many friends in the American army with whom he would socialize when they went on leave in Rome. None of the soldiers worried too much about the Sailor Gang's illegal activities. Everybody was trying to have a little fun and survive the war, and no one liked the military police; in fact, as far as the average soldier was concerned, an MP was a maggot. They were vultures who got to trot around behind the lines beating up on the guys who were doing the actual fighting, and they were corrupt buggers. In *Execution*, Colin McDougall noted that if a prison guard were returned to his combat unit, his former prisoners "would undoubtedly try to murder him." Everyone knew an MP who was on the take and who was trading a little on the black market. Thus there was an unwritten code that any soldier would shield almost any other soldier against an MP, provided the offence wasn't too great. And so the Sailor Gang spent many evenings drinking at official military messes, even in clubs reserved for senior ranks. Lucky and Honess, who were becoming good friends, were regulars at the South African and New Zealand officers clubs.

In October 1944, Rome was opening up for Joe Pringle, who kept track of the war news by reading the *Maple Leaf*. On October 2, the paper announced that the United States was dropping three tons of bombs on Japan and Germany every minute. A survey conducted by a scientist in Stockholm found that in the previous two months, fifty thousand Germans had committed suicide. Meanwhile, in Portsmouth, Esmee continued her letter-writing campaign. She sent one letter to Canadian Military Headquarters in London every two weeks demanding the return of her twenty-one pounds. As far as the army was concerned, Harold Pringle was still fighting with his unit. They informed Esmee that locating him and retrieving her money was not possible.[10]

On most nights Harold went out in American army uniform, but during the day he preferred to venture forth in civilian clothes. Pringle made frequent visits to the Coliseum and the Forum. Rome was glowing in sunshine, and the female company he enjoyed so much was his. Even the way Romans dressed meshed with Harold's personality. This was a culture in which presentation mattered, and despite their poverty, Romans made great efforts to dress elegantly. Harold Pringle, the dapper envy of his regiment, was now just one in a well-dressed crowd. His Italian improved thanks to his girlfriend's tutelage, and his feelings for her seem to have grown serious. Betti Michael recalled that he wrote home saying that he "had met a person and that he hoped his mother would forgive him if he'd chosen someone and wanted to get married."[11] The women at Via Pistoia laughed when they heard him speak and told him that "*Le lezioni notturne sono le migliori*"—"Night lessons are the best lessons."

The black market Italians were friendly, and like Harold, they were constantly smiling. Italians in general were like that. You didn't work your way up to a smile the way you did in Canada—you came right out with it. When you ordered a cappuccino you grinned from ear to ear.

Frowning you could do later. The Italian black marketeers spoke some English and kept their conversation focused on life in Rome: "The Italian woman, *la donna italiana*, is good, yes. *Molto* friendly." Or, "You like the Italian way of coffee?" They explained their underworld activities with a shrug and a self-pitying admonishment that "everybody must live. *E vero?*" The Italians said they preferred dealing with the Allies to the Germans. The Germans were too rigid. They did not understand that life in Rome was meant to be fluid and adaptable. That is why they were gone and the Allies were here now. The Allies understood life. They understood business.

When a deal was made, contact was brief. Bill Croft would let it be known on the Via Appia that the gang had something to sell, and that message would work its way through the underground economy. Then, at night, a man, generally wearing a black trench coat and hat, would turn up with cash. There would be smiles and handshakes in Rome's darkened back alleys, which twisted and spiraled like a drug fiend's nightmare. The goods would be transferred and the loot divided up. "*Vivono tutti.*" Profit margins were big. Four tires pulled off an Allied jeep would fetch seven hundred dollars. Across town, the Lane Gang continued its operations. Jeeps and trucks were held up and stolen. An officer at Allied Headquarters in Rome estimated that almost all black market olive oil and grain was now being carried on Allied vehicles.[12] The Canadian Intelligence Corps conducted field research and determined that there were one thousand Canadian army vehicles missing and presumed in Italian hands—this when the Canadian army in Italy was trying to requisition seven hundred vehicles.[13] In September, outside Avellino, Canadian soldiers stopped a US army truck laden with olive oil. In it were four Italians and three men dressed in American army uniforms. One of the men claimed to be sick and was slow getting out of the truck. His friends seized the opportunity and opened fire on the Canadians, wounding one in the shoulder. The men ran off into a wheat field, escaping.

In mid-October, the Sailor Gang made a night trip at around nine in the evening. Lucky was driving the gang's jeep, with Bill Croft riding beside him, while Charlie Honess and Harold were in the back. Lucky and Harold were carrying guns, Lucky a .38 revolver and Harold a

Beretta. The gang drove out toward the Tiber River, and as they approached, the jeep drove up a narrow bridge and Lucky spied a civilian car coming toward them. It was a large black four-door saloon car with the letters "ACC" on its front.

Lucky said, "Let's stop that car, it's coming the wrong way." He told Honess to get out and tell the driver to follow them. Honess did so. He returned to the jeep and the civilian car drove behind them, back to the roundabout where Route 2 entered Rome. Honess supposed that they were going to "fine" the driver a few dollars. A few weeks before on the same bridge, Lucky had robbed an Italian of thirty dollars. But this time Lucky had other ideas.

"Let's take the car," he said.

At the roundabout, all four men left the car and approached the driver. He was an Italian, and he claimed to be the chauffeur of an Allied officer, but the driver was dressed as a civilian and no one believed his story. None of the gang, it appears, knew that "ACC" stood for "Allied Central Command." Honess told the Italian they were going to take him to a prison camp. Harold and Bill got into the civilian car and they followed Lucky and Honess in the jeep. They drove for five kilometres and turned off to the right down a small side road. Lucky stopped the jeep and told Honess to get into the civilian car with Joe. Bill brought the Italian to the jeep. Honess and Joe drove the civilian car back to Via Pistoia and then hid it in the garage on Via Rimini where the gang kept its jeeps. Later, Honess asked Croft and Lucky what had happened to the Italian.

"We took him off the road a ways, kicked him out of the jeep and fired a couple of shots at him to scare him," Bill told him. Honess checked the gun. There were two bullets missing. Four days later an Italian came around to Via Pistoia and bought the civilian car from Croft for seven hundred dollars American.

NOT ALL OF THE SAILOR GANG's activities were so lucrative, or so harsh. A week before hijacking the saloon car, Lucky and Honess made a trip up to Tivoli, a small city outside Rome. They met a couple of girls, took them driving and stopped in a small village for some wine and food.

On the way back to Tivoli, Lucky decided that he wanted some chickens and, leaving the girls to wait by the side of the road, Lucky and Honess approached a farmhouse. Lucky asked for two chickens and wrote the Italians a bogus military receipt. They drove the girls home and returned to Rome.

After they stole the saloon car, Lucky, Honess, Bill and Harold drove out to Tivoli again. They returned to the farm and as Honess grabbed a turkey, some Italian women came running out from the fields, yelling at the soldiers to leave the birds alone. "Never mind her," Lucky said. "Get on and get those chickens." Lucky, who was wearing Bill Croft's sailor hat, pulled his revolver out and fired a shot in the air. Bill and Harold went to the front of the farmhouse, while Honess entered the cold shed and gathered up an armful of onions. When Honess came out of the shed, he saw Lucky standing behind the jeep and an Italian man walking down the farmhouse steps, frantically trying to load a rifle. Lucky rushed the man, but the Italian managed to get off one shot. Honess grabbed the rifle, but as he did another Italian rushed him with an iron bar, striking him across the arm. Honess looked around and saw the other three pulling out in the jeep. He ran after it and jumped in. The Sailor Gang sped off, leaving Bill's sailor hat lying in the dust.

On October 22, Bill Croft was in Bar Trieste, passing time, when he saw a British soldier who was looking the worse for wear. His uniform was dirty and he had obviously not eaten for some time. After the usual introductions, Croft invited the soldier back to Via Pistoia.

His name was Bill Holton, and he was with the Hampshire Regiment. Holton had enlisted in 1940, and was heading for Italy in 1943 when he contracted pneumonia. After a few months in hospital, Holton finally arrived in Italy in March 1944 and spent time fighting at the Gothic Line. At twenty-one, he was one year older than Bill Croft. Holton was a handsome kid, like Harold. He had blond hair and blue eyes and fine English features. Holton had gone on leave on October 1, but once his time ran out, he had decided that he was not interested in going back. He had worked as a batman (a valet for officers) and had saved twelve thousand lire. He went to Rome, just looking to have a good time. He tried not to attract attention and to live quietly off his savings. The money lasted two weeks.

Croft gave Holton a pair of trousers, a pair of socks and a tie. Holton had his own shirt and shoes. This time, Croft was less circumspect in his offer. Holton had two choices: throw in with the Sailor Gang or get picked up. Holton followed Croft's logic. Bill Holton became the final member of the Sailor Gang.

Harold liked Holton and offered him a place in his apartment at 40 Via Cesena. Holton took up with Harold's girlfriend's friend and the two deserters lived together, away from the crowd at Via Pistoia. Harold was less and less enamoured with the Sailor Gang. The boys at Via Pistoia were always drinking, and he did not approve of such carelessness. Still, they were the only friends Harold had.

Meanwhile, on October 14, Harold's old friends, the Hasty Ps, had been thrown into a fray at the village of Bulgaria near the Fiumicino River in Ravenna. The regiment had lost thirty men but had gained the town and fifty-five prisoners with it. The Allies pressed on, but by late October they were stuck. The Canadians would spend another winter in Italy, with no reinforcements, no equipment and very little of anything else.

As October progressed, Croft began to realize that the Sailor Gang was gathering a momentum he could no longer control. In the thrillers he read, the criminals operated with cool efficiency, but his gang was becoming bolder. Lucky's little black book was filling with more and more names, and he was growing dangerously reckless. One night Lucky had returned to Via Pistoia with a gold watch and a load of maize. He told Bill that he had been speeding down a road when he saw an Italian driving a horse and cart. Lucky got out, shot the horse and took the man's watch. Thanks to their nocturnal revels, all the members of the Sailor Gang were becoming well known on the Via Appia. Like the gangsters in Bill Croft's thrillers, they were magnanimous when drunk, and they befriended soldiers who were on leave. They continued to socialize with officers and other soldiers.

Life at Via Pistoia became more and more unruly and it was worrying Maria, who was now seven months pregnant. Lucky and Honess were almost constantly drinking, and with drinking came fighting.

Harold, who disliked the boozing, came over to the house only when business required it. The C Ration Kid was growing more and more aggressive. When he was over at Via Pistoia, he would offer Maria one hundred dollars if she would sleep with him. Maria turned down the offers. Croft just laughed it off, but beneath his calm, resentment was beginning to simmer. The fellows he had helped out of the war were now thinking that they had gotten themselves out of it under their own steam. Sooner or later something was going to give. The Sailor began to think of a way to relocate.

Then, in late October, Slim was picked up again by the military police. Bill Croft went to his girlfriend Anna, who was short of money, and offered to move into her house and pay rent. She agreed. Croft made plans to move on November 2 but did not tell the rest of the gang.

10.

28 VIA PISTOIA

Throughout the last week of October 1944, Rome was drenched by rain and the streets off the Via Appia became muddied between their cobblestones. On November 1, the rain stopped, the sun broke and a warm, clear day began. Up north, Tony Basciano and the rest of the Hasty Ps were heading to the town of Miramare. Eight had been killed and seven wounded the previous day. Forty-one reinforcements arrived while soldiers from "A" Company went to the movies in the town of Riccione.[1] In Avellino, the scent of pine needles filled the head of Captain Hugh Ramsay Park as he sipped coffee and smoked a cigarette at a café in the town square. At 28 Via Pistoia, Maria paused as she prepared breakfast for Bill and thought of her family. Today was Tutti Santi, All Saint's Day, and all the families in Naples would be going to church together. On Via Cesena, Joe Pringle and Bill Holton slept with their women beside them, secure in bedrooms ringed by shuttered windows that cut the Italian sun. Tom Jamieson, now a captain, reported in at Allied 1st Echelon Headquarters in Rome. After spending the fall attached to the 8th Army up near Ravenna, running supplies up to the front, he was in Rome helping to organize the next big push. He was soon to be sent to Greece to meet with partisan guerrillas. Private L. G. Doiron, from Nova Scotia, who had spent time in the Glass House and who owed the government fifteen months' back pay, was listed as a deserter.[2] After being sent to Italy and serving at the Hitler Line and the Gothic Line, he had gone AWOL from the West Nova Scotia Regiment on October 1. A Private Fried, who had escaped from the 2nd Canadian Field Punishment Camp in Avellino, was reported killed in action. The commandant at the Field Punishment Camp learned that, after escaping from military prison, Fried had caught up with his regiment, the Seaforths, and returned to the front. He crossed him off his list.

Charlie Honess woke up in his damp, dirty basement bedroom and stared at the ceiling. His pillow was soaked with sweat, and up his spine he felt an uncomfortable tickling, as if a snake were coiling and uncoiling itself in the small of his back. Honess dressed quickly, at least as quickly as he could, but his head spun and his balance was off and he had trouble putting on his shoes. Once his shoes were on, Honess stuck his gun in his coat pocket and walked up the stairs to the ground floor. He was dressed as an on-duty GI, a typical disguise for him. Charlie saw Maria in the kitchen with the landlady and her daughter. The women were cutting open pomegranates, which had come into season in October and had become a staple of the Sailor Gang's diet. Lucky in particular craved the orange-shaped fruit with its tough rind and acidic reddish pulp. Honess stepped to the counter, grabbing a few seeds and popping them in his mouth.

"*Buon giorno*, Carlo," Maria said. "*ti piacciono i melograni?*"

"*Buon giorno, si, si,*" Honess told the women. "*Come va?*"

"*Bene,*" the landlady replied. "*E te?*"

"*Non c'e male,*" Honess said. "*Non c'e. Vado al bar.* Okay?"

"Okay, Carlo," Maria told him.

Honess walked out the front door, glancing up at the pine tree that stretched over the front garden of the house on Via Pistoia. He strolled down the short street, turned up Via Taranto and gazed at the apartment buildings lining it, five and six storeys high. At the corner of Via Orvieto he saw the post office, built by Mussolini before the war but now in the hands of the Allies. From Via Taranto he crossed along Via Pinerolo and stopped, sitting down for a cigarette in the round park at Re di Roma. The pinching in his back began to knot up again. The snake tightened its coils and Honess worked his shoulders, trying to shake it. He was up again quickly, heading for Bar Cecchelia on Via Appia, which he could see a little in the distance. There were soldiers sitting at tables out in the sunshine with coffee and liqueurs. It was only eleven o'clock, but who was counting?

At eleven thirty, Bill Croft and Maria met Charlie, and the three decided to go to a restaurant on the Via Appia for a lunch of pasta and spinach. Afterwards, Bill suggested that they walk to a bar near the Entertainment National Service Association (ENSA) Cinema on Via Rimini. They arrived at the bar at about one in the afternoon and spent the rest of the day drinking rum and coffee. Lucky appeared that afternoon at four o'clock. He had a few drinks and then he and Honess went off to another bar to buy a couple of bottles of liquor. At four thirty, they came back to the bar near the cinema. Honess would later describe the rest of the afternoon:[3]

> Lucky said that he had got a party on that night and would I like to come with him. He also asked Bill. I said, "Yes, all right." Well, we all came out of the bar, walked across the road to the ENSA cinema and a garry [a military jeep] came along and there was an American and two girls. One of the bottles was open and Lucky asked the American would he like a drink. The garry stopped and we gave the American a drink and then the American asked where we were going, so Lucky said we were going to a party. The American asked us if we would like to go down with him for a drink, so we got into the garry, drove round somewhere and we finished up, I am not certain of the name of the club, but it was either the New Zealand Officers Club or the South African Officers Club, and right opposite the officers club there was a café, but when we got there the café was not open.

By this time Lucky was pretty drunk. Honess, by his own confession, was half drunk.

> We had been there some time waiting for this café to open and then Lucky got fed up with waiting and he threw a bottle up

against the wall, one of the empty bottles, and said, "Come on lads, let's go to this party."

I said, "All right, we will go to the party," and Lucky tried to get a garry. He could not get a garry, and a jeep came along with an American in, and the American gave us a lift back to where we had started from, just near the ENSA Cinema.

Lucky went to the bar and bought a bottle of anisette, a colourless sweet liquor flavoured with aniseed. It was half past five. Honess and Lucky went along Via Rimini and found a bar. Lucky told Honess to open the bottle and "give the boys a drink": "There was lots of GIs in there and sailors and Italian women and he told me to give anybody a drink who wanted one."

Lucky and Honess spent two hours there.

"When we got in there," Honess said, "there was a table reserved and we sat down and then there was about six or seven GIs came in, an Englishman and an Italian girl. They all came over to the table and they all knew Lucky, and Lucky introduced me to them, and they all sat down and then some food Lucky ordered came over and there was also a lot of drink on the table." They spent the evening drinking, singing and eating. Lucky ordered twenty bottles of wine, just for himself and Honess.

The bar filled up and the party continued into the night. Lucky and Honess joked and traded songs. Lucky sang Cape Breton ballads and Honess sang east London music hall songs. Somewhere around eight o'clock an accordion player came into the restaurant. Lucky was over-joyed; he gave the man five dollars and told him to play. The crowd at the restaurant clapped and laughed, and soon people on the street were clamouring to get in. Lucky delighted in the scene.

Then the proprietor of the place wanted this music fellow to go away after playing a couple of tunes because the music was attracting a lot of people and the place was very crowded. Lucky did not speak Italian at all. I speak a bit, and if Lucky wanted to say anything he would tell me what he wanted to say. This propri-etor was telling me, and I was telling Lucky, about the music fellow. The music fellow was not gone, but Lucky went to pay his bill and he had not got enough to pay it and he asked me to give him some money.

I gave him fifteen dollars and he said that would be enough. Then when I was looking at the bill that the Italian proprietor had given me, Lucky had moved over to the end of the table, and the next thing I knew Lucky had shot the table up in the air, and all the bottles were flying around, and then Lucky started tipping the other tables over. I do not know exactly why he tipped it up. He was in a temper, that was all. I imagine it was to do with the amount of the bill, because he was saying how much he had spent there and how much he had drunk and what he had given the music fellow to play music.

Some more fellows, some GIs over in the corner, picked up some bottles and came at Lucky. I was trying to smooth Lucky down, to pacify him a bit, and they came at me with a bottle. I took a pistol out of my back pocket and I told the fellows who had the bottles to back up in the back of the bar, and I said to the American fellows and Lucky: "Come on, we will get out of here." But the American fellows moved against the stairs but Lucky said no, he had hurt his wrist or something, and he said, "I am going to find the fellow that cut my wrist."

Honess backed up the stairs with the Americans he had been drinking with, all the while trying to talk Lucky out of the bar. Lucky was having none of it. He handed Honess his wristwatch and told him to take care of it. Honess told Lucky, "If you don't come, Lucky, I am going to get away and leave you."

This did not sit well with McGillivary. "If you take off on me, Charlie," he swore, "I will kill you next time I see you."

As he was going up the stairs for the last time, Honess saw a Canadian soldier, pistol in hand, going down into the bar. Earlier in the night, Lucky had given the Canuck a drink from his bottle. The Canadian told Charlie, "All right, I will look after him."

That was all the encouragement Charlie needed. He backed out of the bar and then ran down the street, sprinting for about twenty minutes. The flickering lights from the cafés and bars blurred as he passed. Charlie made for Joe and Bill's apartment, on Via Cesena and walked through the large porch archway at the apartment's front door, climbing the stairs. He banged on the door. In a few moments, Holton opened it. He and Pringle were both sober; they had decided to turn in for the evening with their girlfriends. Holton saw Charlie standing there, his hair rumpled. He had blood on the left side of his shirt and he was out of breath.

"Where's Joe?" Honess asked, and he pushed past Holton in a stagger.

Charlie walked down the hallway and saw the Canadian, whom he knew as Joe Pringle, half-dressed, standing beside his bed. Harold's girlfriend was lying under the covers. Pringle came out and asked Honess what the trouble was. Charlie rushed through the events of the evening; he'd been in a fight with Lucky on the other side of town and he'd left Lucky there. The three men talked briefly. Just what sort of trouble had it been? Finally, Joe said that they might as well go round to Via Pistoia and see what had happened to Lucky. They fetched the jeep from the garage on Via Rimini and drove over. It was around nine-thirty.

They parked the jeep in front of the house, and Joe removed the rotor and coil wire to prevent the jeep from being stolen. Inside, the landlady and her daughter were cleaning up the kitchen; they greeted the women in Italian. The three men then went upstairs to Bill Croft's room and found him and Maria asleep. Joe sat down in a chair by the room's window, waking Maria. Bill, who had gone to bed drunk at seven o'clock, kept on snoring. Even in his own inebriated state, Honess thought Croft looked "pretty drunk." Charlie crawled onto the bed and gently picked up Croft's pistol, which was tucked behind the mattress. He handed it to Harold, who set it on a small table near where he was sitting. Bill was fully dressed, lying on top of the sheets, with his shoes off. Honess told Holton to get a glass of water.

As Honess and Holton tickled his feet and sprinkled water in his face, Croft gradually awoke. He would later recall seeing "Pringle grinning at me."[4] Charlie asked, "Where is your gun, Bill?"

"Down there by the bed," Croft said.

"Are you sure?" asked Honess, smiling.

Croft looked in its usual hiding place, the dresser drawer beside the bed. "Maria must have shifted it," Croft said. Then Honess laughed, grabbing the gun from the table and tossing it to him. Harold sat silently and watched as Honess showed Croft Lucky's wristwatch and recounted the story about the fight in the bar. "Lucky told me, 'Get to hell out of here, I can take care of myself,'" Honess said. A soldier had rushed him with a bottle, but another Canadian had been there and had helped Honess escape. "I pulled out my pistol, but I don't remember firing a shot," he said. Honess realized that he had lost his jacket.

Harold Pringle was not impressed by the theatrics. He told Honess, "I think you had better go down to bed."

"I will see Lucky later," Charlie said and went down to the basement, where he dug up a bottle of crème de menthe that he had been saving. Honess poured himself a few drinks.

The landlady brought coffee up to the bedroom, then she and her daughter left for home, which was a few doors down at 11 Via Pistoia. The men each smoked a cigarette. Holton brought out a deck of cards and began playing solitaire at the foot of the bed. A half-hour passed, and then they heard Honess holler up.

"Joe, there is someone fucking around the house."

Croft told Holton to "nip down there and see who it is."

Holton went downstairs and opened the front door, and Lucky sort of "fell into" the hallway. He had blood on his hands and face and he was not wearing shoes. "Shut the door and lock it," he said. As Holton locked the door, Charlie came up from the basement. "Get upstairs out of the way," he said to Holton. "This is nothing to do with you." Holton went back upstairs to Bill Croft's bedroom.

"What's all the noise at this time of night?" Bill wanted to know.

"Oh, Lucky has come in and looks the worse for wear," Holton answered.

Croft was not worried. He closed his eyes and declared, "Let them fight it out between themselves."

The men could hear an argument beginning downstairs. Lucky was yelling. Maria started to cry, and though she could speak very little English, she thought Lucky's voice sounded "annoyed." He and Honess were quarrelling about the incident at the bar. Lucky told his friend he was a "yellow bastard. I told you what I would do to you." Then Lucky moved into his room and toward his chest of drawers. Honess remembered that that was where he kept his revolver.

Meanwhile, Croft was fed up. "Go down and tell them Maria is crying," he said. Holton rushed down but as he reached the foot of the stairs, he saw Honess and Lucky struggling. He saw Honess grab hold of Lucky, pulling him back, at the same time pulling his pistol from his pocket. Honess stuck the pistol in Lucky's ribs and said, "Shut up and don't move or I'll shoot."

Lucky replied, "You haven't got the nerve, you chickenshit bastard."

At midnight on November 1, 1944, Gabriele Di Biagio was preparing for bed. Di Biagio was a farmer who lived in the village of Torre Gaia, a small hamlet outside Rome. That night he had attended celebrations at a friend's house. As every Italian knew, today had been Tutti Santi, All Saints' Day. It was a holiday reserved for worship and for feasting. Every Italian also knew that after Tutti Santi, right at the crack of *mezzanotte*, at midnight, came Tutti Morti, the Day of the Dead.

That was why Di Biagio had returned home well before midnight.

At midnight on Tutti Morti, Italians believed, all the dead from all the thousands of years past rose up from their graves and walked the roads. They could move freely but could not pass through a crossroads. That was one reason why all Italian graveyards were located outside city walls.

The dead had no specific malice against the living on Tutti Morti. They were not seeking revenge. But they might cause trouble for those among the living who dared to venture out on their night. Bad things happened to those who were on the roads after midnight on Tutti Morti.

At midnight, Di Biagio heard a truck drive down the main street of his village and past his house. His dog barked at the noise. About ten or fifteen minutes later he heard a truck drive back in the opposite direction. Di Biagio assumed it was a truckload of bandits out to steal. He rose from bed and went to his window. From there he saw the shadow of what seemed like a small military vehicle with its lights off. It passed down the main street and out of view. Di Biagio returned to bed.

The next day, one of Di Biagio's grandsons went out after breakfast to play in the fields near Di Biagio's house at Torre Gaia. The ground was muddy from the rain and a slight drizzle was coming down. The boy followed the water as it ran through ditches and irrigation wells and then he saw something that stopped him cold. He fetched his grandfather.

Gabriele Di Biagio, his brother and his brother-in-law went back with the boy to the field. There they saw the branch of a pine tree and a little grass resting on a dead body in an old irrigation ditch. It was a man's body, dressed in an olive green uniform with American sergeant's stripes. The corpse's head leaned on its chest. The body was seated with its arms folded and its legs running down the ditch. It wore socks but no shoes. Its toes were sticking up into the air.

11.

AUTUMN ON THE VIA APPIA

Late October 1944 was a busy month for the Special Investigations Branch (SIB) of the British Military Police in Rome. The unit, which was responsible for solving serious crimes such as rape and murder, had cases pouring in. On October 16, the SIB arrested a British major who worked at Allied Headquarters. The officer had been embezzling welfare funds; he was charged with forgery and writing fraudulent cheques. On October 22, there was a report of the murder of an Italian civilian near Tivoli by four Allied soldiers. On October 23, a café proprietor in Rome was reported killed by two Allied soldiers. The motive was robbery, the method shooting. Long-term deserters were suspected. On October 27, the SIB received a report that a Polish corporal had murdered a woman by strangulation. They apprehended him and turned him over to the Polish authorities. On October 28, the SIB picked up thirteen members of a band of armed robbers operating between Naples and Rome. The group was made up of civilians and Allied deserters. On October 31, six members of a second band of armed robbers were arrested; all the men were deserters from the US and British armies. The SIB believed the six were connected with the murders of the café proprietor and the Tivoli civilian. Like those picked up a few days earlier, these deserters operated on the roads between Rome and Naples. Then, on November 2, the SIB received a telephone call regarding the discovery of the body of a soldier, believed to be American, at Torre Gaia. The body was as yet unidentified but the soldier appeared to have been be murdered.[1]

Sergeant Joseph Ryan of the SIB drove out to investigate. He arrived at Torre Gaia on the afternoon of November 2 and met a British officer from the local base who had appeared at the crime scene. Ryan inspected the body, which lay on a blanket by an irrigation ditch. It was a thin young man with dark, curly hair, and Ryan noted that he was wearing a US-issue uniform with sergeant's stripes on the left sleeve, but he found no identification. A piece of cloth covered a wound just above the left lung, in its centre a ringed powder burn. Ryan cut the cloth from the shirt, then telephoned for an ambulance to transport the body to the 104 British General Hospital. On November 4, an autopsy was performed; the doctor concluded that death had been caused by multiple gunshots. He also noted that the man had been in the early stages of tuberculosis.

At ten o'clock in the morning on November 2, Bill Croft went to the bar at the corner of Via Pistoia and telephoned for a taxi. He returned to his house, packed up some food and his and Maria's belongings, and, when the taxi arrived, loaded them in. The landlady noticed that the normally affable Bill was very "hurried" and did not take the time to chat. That afternoon, Bill and Maria arrived at their new apartment at 4 Piazza Armenia. The life of a gangster was no longer romantic, and Bill Croft was becoming rattled. By leaving Via Pistoia, he wanted to give the impression that the Sailor Gang had disbanded. Croft decided to cut himself adrift from the rest of the boys, at least as far as robbery was concerned.

On November 2, Charlie Honess awoke at Pringle and Holton's apartment on Via Cesena. The three men stayed out of sight for a couple of nights, but on the third day, Honess, Harold Pringle and Bill Holton armed themselves and went to the garage on Via Rimini to check on the gang's jeep. When the men entered the repair shop they found two American MPs waiting in the jeep. The police immediately drew their pistols, yelling, "Let's go!" The Sailor Gang scattered as the MPs fired their pistols at them. Holton and Pringle turned right, while Honess turned left. He kept running until he was on the Via Appia and then ducked into Bar Cecchelia, running through the lounge and into the toilet. Honess saw a ledge and placed a watch—the one Lucky had given him on November 1—and a pistol there. He hid. After ten minutes, the bar's owner came into the toilet, wanting to know what was going on. Honess was "in shock and out of breath" and told the man *"Sono un disertore"*—"I am a deserter"—and that the military police were after him. An American soldier who was in the toilet at the time looked around and told Honess that there were no police out there. Shaken, Honess walked out into the bar, sat at a corner table and ordered a bottle of anisette. He began drinking, noticing that a young Italian was sitting nearby with a girl. Honess thought he could sense the police coming in at any moment, and the anisette had little effect on his racing heart. He was desperate to get rid of the gun and watch. He told the young Italian he did not want the police to find them on him if he were caught, and asked him, "Do you want these things?" The Italian gave him twenty-five dollars for them. The Sapper then waited out the afternoon in Bar Cecchelia, and when dusk came he slipped back out onto the Via Appia.

For the next few days Honess stayed with an Italian girl he knew. Then he rented a room near Bar Cecchelia. Bill Croft, who had been keeping an eye out for the gang's other members, learned of his whereabouts and left a note asking him to telephone him at his new apartment. Not long afterwards, Honess, Croft, Holton and Pringle agreed to meet together at Bar Cecchelia. The C Ration Kid and Slim also turned up. The men discussed the arrests, the police, Lucky and their respective futures. Someone said that the military police were cracking down on the Lane Gang. It was the Italians, another said, they didn't need deserters anymore and so they were letting the MPs do their dirty work for them. It looked like the good times were going to dry up. Pringle, never one to panic, was happy at his apartment. Not everyone was so calm. Honess told Holton that he was finished with Rome and that he was "getting out of here." The two Brits decided to escape to Florence; they left that night. The pair arrived with ten dollars between them; they slept in parks, had nothing to eat and lasted only two days before catching a ride back to Rome. They split up just outside the city walls. Holton melted away into a crowd by the Castelli Romani, and Honess found himself on his own. That week, he saw Croft near San Giovanni di Laterano, but the Sailor gave him a cool reception. Croft did not mind saying hello, but he would

not tell Honess where he and Maria were staying; in fact, all he would say
was that they were finally getting married. Meanwhile, there was trouble
at Pringle's apartment. The police had turned up, and now Pringle was
out on the street. He holed up with Honess in his room on the Via Appia.
All the while rain came pouring down.

Meanwhile, the SIB continued to investigate the mysterious death
of their Torre Gaia corpse. A check determined that it was not an
American, and the multiple shooting suggested a killing connected with
the black market. In Italy, multiple gunshots were the murder method
of choice for organized crime: they signified that responsibility for the
murder was shared. With no regiment stepping forward to claim the
body, the detectives at the SIB also began to suspect that they had the
body of a deserter on their hands, but although they suspected that it
was a Canadian, they had no leads. As far as crime went, November continued at the same pace as October. On November 7, the SIB received a
report of the killing of an Italian civilian by a member of the Allied
forces. A British private had stabbed the man to death with a penknife.
They picked the soldier up. On November 8, a British soldier was
arrested for posing as a Roman Catholic chaplain. The soldier had been
taking donations from civilians and using his ecclesiastical dress to gain
access to their daughters. On November 17, detectives arrested an
American soldier for holding up a café in Rome. On November 18, the
SIB captured five hundred kilograms of silk that had originally been
destined to make parachutes in England. A black market gang had
stolen it and planned to sell it in shops throughout Rome. That same
day, the SIB found an Allied soldier walking the roads outside Rome. He
was suffering from complete amnesia.[2]

On December 8, the Canadian Military Headquarters offered two
hundred US dollars to any civilian who could provide information
regarding the deaths of two Canadian soldiers that would lead to the
apprehension of their murderers. On November 19, the SIB got their first
break in the Torre Gaia case. Detectives arrested one British and two
American soldiers outside a barber shop on the Via Appia. At first, the
soldiers pretended to be Italian. "*Non capito*" was the reply to the question, "Are you boys absentees?" The trick did not fool the MPs, who were

accustomed to such antics. The three deserters were brought in and interrogated—vigorously. Detectives at the SIB were convinced the three were involved in several cases of armed robbery on the roads running from Rome. Word got out on the Via Appia: Bill Holton, Slim and the C Ration Kid had been arrested and were sitting in cells at the American Army Central Intelligence Division prison.

Not long afterward, the SIB descended on the house at Via Pistoia. Photographers were brought in, and the landlady and her daughter were interviewed. Frightened, the women eagerly co-operated. The SIB went directly to Bill Croft's new place on Piazza Armenia but did not find him. On November 21, captain John G. Rutterford of the British Provost Corps picked up two men in the town of Monte Romano, north of Rome. Rutterford had spotted the pair riding in a South African Air Force vehicle. He questioned the men, who told him that they were Americans returning to their units after being on leave. Each man was carrying a duffle bag. Inside one bag Rutterford found a service revolver that was very dirty, with fouling in the barrel and chambers. It contained one live round. The American said that he must have picked up the wrong bag while travelling in another truck. Rutterford was not buying the story; he arrested both men. One of them turned out to be Bill Croft. A few weeks later, on December 4, Maria Fedele gave a statement to the SIB outlining the events of November 1.

By the beginning of December, only Harold and Honess were still free, although they were not in contact with each other. The winter was a savage turn from the ease of the summer, yet throughout it all, Harold seems to have maintained his relationship with his mysterious Italian girlfriend. He may have met her secretly at the park in Re di Roma or at the apartment of a friend. Harold must have known that his time was trickling away. Had he been clear-headed, he might have fled Rome. He did make an aborted attempt to make it to Livorno, the port from which Allied troops ships were setting sail, but the roads were clogged and they were rife with military police.

Then again, things could have been much worse.

Harold could have been up at the front with Tony Basciano and the rest of the Hastings and Prince Edward Regiment. Throughout

November, the Hasty Ps were, as they almost always seemed to be, right in the thick of it. By December 4, 1944, the regiment was inching its way up the spine of the Adriatic coast, pressing on to the northern town of Ravenna. On December 5, at one in the morning, the Hasty Ps commenced their crossing of the Lamone River. From the beginning, the attack (dubbed Operation Chuckle) was a costly fiasco. Farley Mowat would later write his father saying "the regiment has been to hell...Most of the few old friends I still had there are gone."[3] Like all military failures, the plan had seemed logical on paper. The Lamone sector was a series of canals cut by expanses of open ground, small woods and buildings. The Hasty Ps were to advance under a creeping barrage with the rifle companies leading the way. This sort of artillery fire required precision since the shells were timed, according to a schedule, to land a few hundred yards in front of the advancing troops. On December 5, the lead-off units, "B" and "C" companies, formed up by a dyke. When the barrage commenced they were to follow it in. Unfortunately, however, they had formed up on a dyke too far forward.[4]

Consequently, at zero hour, the Canadians came under direct fire from their own artillery. Forty-eight men were killed or wounded in a matter of minutes, a thirty-three per cent casualty rate. Crippled, the companies fell back, unable to advance because of what the regimental war diary describes as "low morale." In truth, the men, who knew they had been shelled by their own troops, were in a state of outrage and shock. The regiment's commanding officer ordered the attack to continue. Harold's old outfit, "D" Company, was given the assignment of breaking through the same ground. Out they went with tracer bullets, one veteran would later remember, flying at them like a snow flurry.[5] And so the day progressed. The Canadians made a series of mad attacks in driving rain along canal banks and dykes against shelling, mortars, sniper fire and German efficiency. Troops streamed back and forth from the front lines; by the end of the battle sporadic machine gun fire was used to slow the enemy advance, and keep the Germans from mounting a successful counterattack.

Shortly afterward, Canadian Press reporter Bill Boss published a narrative of the attack, which fifty-five years later he still remembered as "an utterly crazy waste of life." Boss was respected by the troops for his fearlessness while covering combat, and he had gotten close to the battle lines. His report depicted the Lamone attack as a poorly conceived squandering of men. In retaliation, the Canadian High Command tried to have him banned from reporting on the Italian campaign. However, the British high commander, General Harold Alexander, saved Boss. He ordered the Canadians to keep the plucky journalist at the front and is said to have told the Canadian commanders that if they did not like his coverage, then "they should stop fucking up."[6]

Had he known about the Lamone, Harold might have felt a little better about his own predicament. Truth be told, the certain death that he had envisioned at the villa in the Arielli Valley would likely have happened on the Lamone, if not earlier at the Gothic Line. No matter what hand fate played him, Harold Pringle could congratulate himself for buying at least one more day.

AT SEVEN THIRTY IN THE evening on a cloudy December 12, Sergeant Major Arthur John Brown of the SIB was staking out an apartment on the Via Appia. As Brown waited outside the building, he saw what, thanks to an artist's depiction, had become a familiar face. The man was dressed as a civilian. Brown approached him and told him that he had reason to believe he was an absentee from the British army. The man replied, "*Non compesco,*" in convincing Italian. But after a little prodding, he confessed, shrugging, "I am." There was an air almost of relief in his voice. Brown instructed another detective to take Charlie Honess into custody, and the Sapper was brought to the US Army Central Intelligence Division office.

Brown remained on the Via Appia. Thanks to his sources, he knew there was one more suspect to pick up. He waited outside an apartment on Via Cesena. At ten in the evening he saw his target enter the main entrance accompanied by a young woman. After a few moments, Brown followed the couple in, climbing the stairs. He found their apartment and knocked. The young woman answered. Brown walked past her and began asking questions about a "*disertore.*" In the bedroom, dressed in civilian clothes, he found Harold Pringle. At first, Harold tried to hold Brown off with "*No capito,*" but it was no use; he eventually gave himself up, admitting to the detective, "I am absent." Brown escorted him to the American prison where Honess was being held. At that exact moment, up near Ravenna, "D" Company was exchanging small fire with the Germans. The Canadians would take six prisoners.

On December 15, Brigadier General Alban Low, deputy commanding, RAAC, called a meeting to discuss, with the Canadian officer in charge and with Lieutenant Colonel Carrick, the disposition of four Canadian soldiers who were involved in international gangs in Italy. Thanks to the SIB and to assistance from Italian black marketeers, they had captured members of both the Lane and the Sailor gangs. "A considerable number of very serious charges are being brought against Private McFarlane, Private Vizina and Gunner Ceccacci," the war diarist for Canadian 1st Echelon Headquarters wrote. "Private Vizina was injured almost immediately after he joined the gang and is presently in hospital and it is unlikely that any serious charge will be laid against him."[7]

The arrest of members from the infamous Lane Gang was a major coup for the SIB. Along with the Canadians, the detectives had arrested American and British deserters and Italian civilians. The gang, they learned, had been run by an Italian known to the deserters only as Scarface. During the Nazi occupation, he had been incarcerated in Via Tasso, and it was in the infamous apartment there that he received the scar that earned him his nickname. Scarface loathed Fascists; he insisted that the Lane Gang rob only Fascists and Fascist sympathizers. This, he joked, still left plenty of people to rob.[8]

Jose Ceccacci had joined the gang in September 1944. Ceccacci had grown up in Toronto and spoke fluent Italian. He had had an unfortunate childhood. When he was five, a car struck him and broke almost every bone in his body. When he was seven, his mother died. When he was sixteen, in 1940, Ceccacci had enlisted, using his crippled brother Clement's enlistment notice. He was made a gunner, and after Italy was invaded became a translator for the Canadian headquarters at Naples. He had a poor record, piling up twenty-nine charges for AWOL and other offences.

In April 1944, Ceccacci went AWOL again from the Canadian army and after some time on the loose, joined up with an American unit, the

3rd Division Quartermasters Corps. He and his unit came to Rome two days after the liberation. Ceccacci kept meaning to return to the Canadians. "But you know how it is," he told the SIB when they questioned him. "I figured I was doing just as well with them."[9] When his unit pulled out of Rome he stayed, with just ten dollars. The money disappeared quickly and Ceccacci wandered around Rome for a few days. He was in and out of detention. Then in August he met an American GI named Cramer at a bar. Cramer told him that knew how to make easy money; he gave Ceccacci a place to stay and some money, and told him he had a date with an Itie and wanted Ceccacci to interpret. This was the first time Ceccacci met Scarface, who when he saw him asked, "Who's the kid?" Ceccacci adopted an alias, calling himself Jose "Spick" Lopez.

At nine the next evening, August 27, Ceccacci participated in his first robbery. Scarface, along with five Italians and five deserters dressed up as American military police, burst into the home of a suspected Fascist. As they barged in, Scarface accused the man of being a Fascist, yelling, "Stop in the name of the Allies!" While the deserters held the man and his wife at gunpoint, Scarface and his henchmen searched the house. They stole 319,000 lire, two rings, a silver watch, a firearms certificate and an Italian pistol. Each of the deserters received $350 for their work. "I felt rotten," Ceccacci said of the robbery. "But when the Itie accused them of being Fascists they didn't deny it."[10]

Following this robbery, Scarface began to trail a teller named Armando from the Bank of Napoli. He learned that the teller walked back streets when carrying an attaché case of money to the Bank of Italy. Scarface claimed that the man was a Fascist and had earned his money by turning in patriots; he organized a plan in which Ceccacci, riding a stolen bicycle, would pass by Armando and grab his attaché case. Ceccacci was then to ride to Scarface, who would be sitting on a running motorcycle. At 10:40 on the morning of September 12, right by the Trevi Fountain, the plan was put into action. It was a farce. Ceccacci fell off his bicycle but tried nonetheless to wrestle the case from Armando. The bank teller called for help; in an instant the Italian Carabinieri were there. Ceccacci was handed over to American military police.

While at large, Ceccacci had been posing as an infantryman from the 349th Infantry. The MPs sent him to the American Stragglers' Post, from where he was sent to the 349th, which was fighting up at Bologna. Ceccacci spent three days fighting with the American outfit, and when the 349th came back to rest, he once again deserted.

He returned to Rome and lived by selling rations that he procured from the American dump. He slept in parks and on the street. Ceccacci again met Cramer, who had escaped from the stockade, and the American enlisted him in a counterfeiting scheme. The deserters bought fake 1,000-lire notes from Scarface for 500 lire and exchanged them for real money. In November, Ceccacci passed a bad note to an American bomber pilot who was on leave. The next day the pilot saw Ceccacci on the street and had him arrested. Ceccacci was charged with two counts of AWOL and sentenced to eighteen months in prison. No charges were laid relating to the robberies. Ceccacci's antics were a small part of the Lane Gang's activities, which included robbing garages that Scarface suspected of Fascist leanings.

Along with the Lane Gang, there was the case of a Canadian soldier who was in serious trouble. "C5292, Private Pringle, was a member of a gang of five known as the Sailor Gang," it was reported, "and four of this gang will probably be charged with the murder of the fifth member of the gang."[11]

What exactly Low and his fellow officers discussed at their December 15 meeting is uncertain. They probably debated whether the Allies should make a public display of having finally picked up members of these deserter gangs. The Lane Gang, for example, was famous through-out the entire military theatre; there was not a soldier in the country who had not heard the stories of their high living and disregard for authority. In fact, the very name "Lane Gang" became a catch-all symbol of illegal activity, and its exploits were reported across the Mediterranean theatre of operations. An American, Chaplain E. V. Johnson, had even reported that the Lane Gang was active on the island of Corsica.

The autumn of 1944 had been one of continuing unrest among the Romans, and there was a visceral anger against the black market and the foreigners involved in it. Despite the arrests that had been made, the Allied authorities could not expect crime by AWOL soldiers to decrease.

There were no reinforcements, and the fighting up north was turning out to be as bad and demoralizing as that of the previous winter. Military psychiatric wards were filled. Soldiers on the line were cracking up and bugging out, and when these men went on the loose they inevitably turned to crime as a means of funding their excursions. In late November, the provost marshall, RAAC, informed Allied Headquarters that "lorries have been held up and drivers relieved of their cash, spare tires, and products stolen." These hold-ups were so common that "the Servize Italiani Autotasporti have now refused to operate at night without armed escort." Two days after Pringle's arrest, the SIB had captured an Italian counterfeiting ring that had 725,000 lire worth of fake 500- and 1,000-lire notes in their possession. Caravaggio's painting *Susannah and the Elders* was discovered in an artist's studio in Trastevere; the priceless painting had been looted from Monte Cassino before the bombing in 1944 by a German officer who had then given it to an Italian musician as the price of a concert. On December 21, four civilians were murdered when a truck pulled up and machine-gunned them from the rear of the vehicle. There was more outrage.[12]

The Romans placed the blame for such crimes on the black market, and some of them were organizing the "Lega della Fame," the Hunger League. This group had thousands of members already and was growing each day. The Hunger League wanted bread rations raised to 300 grams a week, macaroni rations to 100 grams and oil rations to 1,000 grams. Members of the Hunger League were turning over stalls that sold black market butter, bread and eggs. The League's organizers were furious that the black market had continued to thrive under the Allies, and they planned a protest march through Rome. Such a march would be an embarrassment. Diplomatically speaking, the Allied officers agreed that something had to be done to show the Italians that something was being done. They decided that the deserters would be put on trial, quickly and publicly, and in Rome. The story of the arrest of the infamous Lane Gang would be passed on to the press.[13]

On December 29, high-ranking officers from the Canadian, British and American central commands met to discuss the fate of the Sailor Gang. An official report from the meeting states that the men under

investigation—Croft, Honess, Pringle and Holton—were "alleged to
have committed a number of crimes in this area, including three murders."[14] The officers were given the results of investigations conducted by
both the SIB and the American Military Police, and a copy was sent to
Canadian 1st Echelon Headquarters, Allied Field Headquarters. The officers agreed that now that the investigation was over, a separate summary
of evidence should be taken in each individual case. All summaries
would be taken simultaneously. The Canadian Judge Advocate General
(JAG) at first suggested that Colonel William Gunn prosecute the case
with Captain John Bourne, a lawyer from British Columbia, acting as his
assistant. Instead, the JAG made Gunn the court martial's judge advocate
and left Bourne to prosecute the case himself. The SIB gave Bourne three
statements, those made by Pringle, Holton and Honess. He was also
given testimony from Maria and from the landlady at Via Pistoia. One
month later, on February 5, Bourne had his case set. A trial date was set
for February 14.[15]

The JAG selected Michael Cloney, a thirty-year-old lawyer from
Toronto, to represent Harold. Cloney, who had been defending in courts
martial in Avellino, had never lost a case and was known as one of the
brightest minds in Canadian military law. Some of his defence strategies
had become legendary at the JAG. In one case, Cloney defended a soldier
who had been charged after an altercation at an officers' mess. The soldier had been ordered to leave the mess but had returned later and begun
drinking; for this he was charged with disobeying an order. In his
defence, Cloney asked the officer who issued the order, "Did you order
this soldier to leave?" Yes, was the reply. "And did he leave?" Cloney asked.
Yes, was the reply. "And did you," Cloney asked, "order him not to
return?" No, was the answer. The case was dismissed. The judge advocate
in charge of the trial told the court, "If I ever find myself in trouble I
hope young Lieutenant Cloney will be free to defend me." After the war,
Cloney would go on to a distinguished career in military law and eventually become an Ontario Appeals Court judge.[16] He was the best, most
logical choice to defend Harold.

But on February 6, the JAG removed Cloney and assigned the case
to a lawyer and son of a Manitoba judge, captain Norman S. Bergman.

No explanation was given. With only seven days to prepare a defence, Bergman scrambled.

Meanwhile, a panel (the military equivalent of a jury) was selected: five officers pulled from the Rome area. The president of the panel was Colonel R. W. Richardson, a doctor from No. 5 General Hospital in Rome. Bergman objected strenuously to the selection of a non-combatant doctor as president of a murder trial because he believed that Richardson's expert knowledge would prejudice the rest of the panel. Bergman had legal weight behind him. The King's Regulations, the law that governed the Canadian military, stated that "an officer, other than a combatant officer, will by virtue of his rank, or his position, be entitled to precedence and other advantages attached to the corresponding rank among combatant officers. Such rank or position will not, however, entitle the holder of it to the presidency or courts-martial or to military command of any kind."[17] Bergman's objection, however, was overruled without explanation.

On February 14, 1945, at ten on a sunny, mild morning, Harold Pringle's General Field Court Martial began. The charge was murder.

12.

A CRAZY THING TO DO

Harold Pringle's court martial was Captain Norman Bergman's first murder trial.[1] In fact, it was his first trial of any kind. Still, Bergman was confident; he came from a lawyer's family and saw this trial as a golden opportunity to distinguish himself. With only seven days to prepare, he worked feverishly to build a case. By the time the court martial began, he was convinced he could win.

Yet it quickly became clear that he was waging an uphill battle. The first day of the trial was spent establishing basic legal facts. A witness, for example, was called to identify Lucky's picture as that of John Norman McGillivary. Sergeant Joseph Ryan was called in to testify about the discovery of the body. On February 16, 1945, the prosecution called Harold's former flatmate Bill Holton to testify. The British deserter's testimony seemed so perjured that it enraged Bergman. On February 17, in the midst of his cross-examination, the lawyer from Manitoba was so furious that his disdain for Holton poured off him. It was not just Holton Bergman was angry with; he was incensed by what he saw as a panel and president slanted against his client. He took this anger out on Bill Holton.

"Do you realize today what you are saying?" Bergman asked Holton, who sat on the witness chair looking well scrubbed and fresh.

"Yes."

"Do you realize someone's life hangs on what you are saying?"

"Yes."

"You are off scot-free so it does not matter what you say," Bergman continued. He paused. The disgust registered on his face. He spoke to Holton as a nasty schoolteacher might address a child. "Does it?"

Here, the court martial's judge advocate interrupted, saying, "That is a matter for the Court."

If so, it was a mere technicality. Bergman was right: Holton was not going to spend one minute in prison. The British Judge Advocate General had given him complete immunity in exchange for his testimony, and they were getting their money's worth. Holton was proving a measured witness, at ease and yet not overconfident. While he testified, Holton avoided Harold's stare as best he could. Harold, who was under close police guard, sat and listened to the man he had invited into his flat off the Via Appia do his best to incriminate him. Like Holton, Harold was clean-shaven and decked out smartly in his uniform. Yet the boy from Flinton was not smiling anymore. That grin had disappeared at ten in the morning on February 14, when the panel had been brought into the courtroom for the first time. The charge had been read: "That the accused, C5292, Private Pringle, H. J., did commit a civil offence, that is to say, murder, in that he, in the Field, in Italy, on or about November 1, 1944, murdered F55044 Pte McGillivray [sic],[2] J. N., a soldier of the Canadian Army Overseas." Harold had entered his plea: not guilty.

By the trial's third day, both former members of the Sailor Gang sat before the seven-man panel. Along with the president, Dr. Richardson, there were three lieutenant colonels, J. H. Zeigler from the Canadian Supply Company, D. C. Warnica from 1st Armoured Brigade and R. L. Tindall from the 5th Canadian Armoured Division. The panel was completed by two majors, W. A. Boothe from the 3rd Canadian Armoured Reconnaissance Battalion and W. McLaws from 1st Echelon Headquarters. At the panel's centre sat Bill Gunn, the judge advocate for the trial. It was his job to explain points of law to the panel and to decide on legal matters such as admissibility of evidence. Gunn was an intelligent and qualified lawyer who after the war would become one of the most respected judges in his home province of New Brunswick.

The court martial was being held at the Canadian 1st Echelon Headquarters, which was located off Rome's posh Via Veneto. Many in the army were curious to get a glimpse of one of the men who had been terrorizing the roads around Rome; those who had official reason to watch the trial crammed into the courtroom. Among them was a Canadian liaison officer attached to the British army, Lieutenant Tom Jamieson.

As the trial continued, the military public propaganda machine geared up. Prior to the court martial, the British Eighth Army public relations unit had decided to lump all deserters into "the Lane Gang," and it publicized the group's capture with glee. Its army newspaper, *The Crusader*, ran a two-page spread on the apprehension of the Lane Gang. The black market in Italy had been smashed and Italian roads and highways, the paper declared, were safe once more. Meanwhile, the murders continued. On January 14, members of an outlaw gang killed a British corporal. Three Italians were arrested. On January 15, the homicide of an Italian civilian was reported. Two British soldiers were arrested. That same day, a fifteen-year-old Italian boy was reported dead. A New Zealand soldier was picked up and charged with his murder.[3] But those were cases for other panels and other lawyers.

At Harold Pringle's trial, the story Bill Holton told of the Sailor Gang was so strange and so sinister that it managed to grip the attention of a panel of war-weary officers. Holton's words ushered those in the courtroom into a dark world whose moral compass spun frenetically. It was the world every soldier knew existed. In fact, it was the one they walked through every day. Yet in the telling of the events of November 1, 1944, this secret war-made civilization obliterated the image of the clean, wholesome world the Allies were supposed to be bringing to Europe.

The prosecutor began by trying to establish a context for the crime; he explained how Bill Croft had recruited the Sailor Gang. Holton described meeting the Sailor on the Via Appia and how Croft gave him clothes and money. Holton said he eagerly joined the gang and then met man he knew as Joe Pringle, who invited him to live in his flat on Via Cesena. Holton said he met Lucky four times in total: the first time in a bar, the second in a different bar, the third out in the jeep and the last on November 1. He told the panel that on the evening of Lucky's death, he and Joe Pringle had not been drinking and were "feeling about ordinary." Honess came to the apartment and stumbled in, asking, "Where's Joe?" Honess then told Holton and Pringle about Lucky and the music fellow and the fight and the Canadian with the pistol. Holton noticed that Honess had been drinking, was not wearing a jacket and had blood on the left sleeve pocket of his shirt. His hair was rumpled and he was out of breath—from running, Holton presumed. All three men drove in the jeep to Via Pistoia; they went upstairs and woke up Bill Croft by sprinkling water in his face. Pringle told Honess to "sleep it off," and then Holton heard a noise downstairs. He went down and pulled the door open, and Lucky fell in against the wall, saying, "Lock the door." He was wearing US-issue trousers and shirt. No hat. No shoes.

Lucky started to walk to his room along a dark patch of hallway. He opened the door to his room and went in. Honess walked past Holton, following Lucky, and as he entered Lucky's room, the Cape Bretoner began berating him. As Lucky reached for the cupboard, Honess drew his pistol and grabbed him. He stuck the gun in Lucky's ribs, telling him not to move, but Lucky did not back down. He dared Honess to shoot and called him a chickenshit bastard. "When I heard the shot and I saw the flash in the muzzle of the pistol," Holton told the court martial, "I saw Lucky fall from the doorway of his room into the passageway where I was standing. As he fell it appeared that he had his hand across his body. A position like this"—Holton demonstrated the collapse, cocking his elbow and holding it at a right angle to his body. Holton said Lucky looked mournfully at Honess and said, "What did you want to do that for, Charlie?" Then Lucky said, "It's okay, it's only my arm."

Pringle and Croft came running down the stairs. Maria was up in the bedroom crying.

Joe Pringle said, "We've got to get him to a hospital."

Croft said, "Yes, we will have to get him out of here."

Holton said, "That was a crazy thing to do."

Honess said, "Somebody get the jeep."

Everything sped up. Bill Croft dashed up the stairs and Joe ran out the front door and began fixing the jeep. Holton and Honess carried Lucky outside. Holton had his upper body, Honess his feet, and as they lifted Lucky into the back seat of the jeep, he sagged in the middle. They laid Lucky out across the back seats. Joe started the jeep, Charlie Honess riding beside him and Holton sitting in the back with Lucky's legs across his lap. Just as they were pulling out, Bill Croft appeared in his stocking feet; he climbed into the back seat and rested Lucky's head on his knees. Lucky's feet stuck out the jeep's side.

The Sailor Gang drove out into the night. It was Tutti Morti, and the Romans had all gone in for the evening. The streets off the Via Appia were deserted. The night was dark and a slight drizzle drifted down. At the Re di Roma roundabout, Joe saw an MP's jeep. Somebody said, "Pull Lucky's feet in; they're sticking out." Holton turned to grab them, but Lucky drew them back in himself. Holton told the gang, "Lucky has pulled them in himself." Holton said that the four men remained silent for most of the trip. The road was very bumpy, and a couple of times Lucky said, "Take it easy." The jeep drove out of Rome along Via Casilina, the main road connecting Naples with Rome, which the men knew as Route 6. They drove for around twenty minutes, and then someone said, "Pull off here." Joe Pringle extinguished the lights and drove about five hundred metres along a muddy dirt road until they reached a field surrounded by a barbed-wire fence.

Joe stopped the jeep. Holton told the jury that he, Croft and Honess lifted Lucky out of the vehicle. Croft had Lucky's upper torso, Honess his middle and Pringle his feet. As they moved Lucky, Holton heard a grunt but was not sure who made it. The men laid Lucky on the ground two yards from the jeep. His feet were pointing toward it and his head rested on the ground. Holton stood near the rear left wheel of the jeep, about two yards from Lucky. It was almost midnight; he described the night to the panel as "half dark and half light." Ten yards away stood an olive tree, and beyond that he could make out buildings. Holton was about to get back in the jeep when he saw Joe Pringle walk up to Lucky's right-hand side. Joe took out a pistol, bent over and pointed it at Lucky. He was one foot away from him. "I heard a shot and I saw the flash of the gun coming out of the muzzle of the gun and I believe I saw the gun sort of jerk in his hand," Holton said. Lucky made no movement.

Joe stepped back from where he had been standing, gun in hand.

Croft jumped around Lucky's body. "I then saw Croft take out a pistol and pointing it at Lucky's forehead squeeze the trigger twice but there were no reports of a shot, only a clicking sound similar to a gun being fired on an empty chamber. He then said to the accused, 'Lend me yours.' I then saw the accused pass over a pistol to Croft."

Bill Croft pointed the pistol at Lucky's forehead and fired. The bullet pierced Lucky's skull but he showed no movement. The men were about to get into the jeep when Pringle said, "No, wait a minute. Put him over there." He pointed to a brick trench, located just past Lucky near the barbed-wire fence. Holton would not say who moved Lucky to the trench. He saw Pringle walk to the pine tree, break off a branch and then place it on top of Lucky. Holton, Croft, Honess and Pringle climbed back into the jeep and drove off. Joe and Honess were in the front, Croft and Holton in the back. They drove back to Route 6 and Joe turned the headlights back on. After a while, Joe Pringle asked if anybody had taken Lucky's dog tags.

"I never knew he had any," said Bill Croft.

"You should have taken them."

Honess turned around. "If anybody asks where he is, say that he has gone to Naples," he told them. Then Honess looked at Holton, speaking with a measured grin. "Don't get telling anybody or you might join him in Naples."

Croft laughed, "No, I think he's all right."

The Sailor Gang drove back to Via Pistoia. Upon arriving, they assembled in Lucky's room and divided his belongings. As they began, an Italian woman who had been Lucky's girlfriend came in. She spoke to Croft in Italian, and Holton made out part of the conversation.

"Lucky *ospedale niente ritorno qui,*" Croft told her: Lucky's gone to the hospital and won't be coming back. Then he gave her Lucky's boots and some cash. She left, silently. Holton, Pringle and Honess returned to the flat on Via Cesena. The next day, Croft moved out of the house on Via Pistoia and the Sailor Gang broke up.

It took Holton one and a half days to tell this story to the panel. The look on Harold's face as Holton spun his tale alternated between shock and horror. Bergman, in contrast, remained calm. Though he was seething inside, he waited eagerly for his opportunity in cross-examination. It became instantly clear as he commenced that Norman Bergman was determined to shred William Holton's story into thin strips.

Bergman believed that Harold Pringle was innocent, but despite this he decided to keep Harold off the witness stand, saving him from cross-examination by the prosecution. There were similarities between Harold's and Holton's accounts, but there were also enormous differences. Bergman believed he could tell Pringle's version by using it to cross-examine the chief witness against him.

Up to the shooting, the two stories were more or less identical. Honess shot Lucky, who asked him, "What'd you want to do that for, Charlie?" Pringle said, "We have to get him to a hospital." In Pringle's version, however, Croft ran upstairs to his room to make out a fake pass for Lucky. Then he ran out to the jeep in his stocking feet and jumped in. As the jeep sped through the Via Appia, Croft told his friends that they could not take him to the nearest hospital, the American 73rd, because Lucky had been treated there two weeks earlier for venereal disease. If they returned it would be suspicious. Pringle and Honess knew of a hospital down Route 6 near Lebano. So the Sailor Gang drove that way.

As the jeep sped through the empty streets and out onto the ancient highway, Lucky began to fade. He told Harold, "Take it easy" a couple of times. Croft took Lucky's pulse. "He's going," he told the men in the jeep, and a few minutes later he felt Lucky's pulse again. This time he felt nothing. "He's gone," Croft pronounced. "He's gone."

Honess let the news sink in. He saw a turning and told Harold to take it. "Turn here," he said. Harold drove off the road and shut off the jeep's lights. The gang rode for a few hundred yards and then stopped. Holton, Croft and Pringle removed Lucky's body from the jeep and laid it out on the ground. The field was quiet and the night was dark, but one could make out shapes in the distance. It was midnight. They decided to disfigure Lucky to prevent whoever found the body from identifying him. Harold stepped forward, and to no one in particular he said, "If you fire at a dead body it won't haunt you." Then Harold aimed his Beretta at Lucky and turned his head to the left as he fired, flinching. The bullet sailed into Lucky's left lung. Harold stepped back, his head to the ground.

Honess leaned against the jeep, shaking, and Holton stood by Pringle looking on. Now Croft stepped forward. He stood beside Lucky's body and drew his silver-plated revolver, aiming straight for the head. He squeezed the trigger and the gun clicked six times, empty. "Lend me yours," Croft said to Harold, who handed him his Beretta. Croft aimed once again. He drilled a bullet into Lucky's skull. Throughout this gruesome process, in both Holton's and Pringle's stories, there was no movement, not a single twitch, from Lucky.

Then the gang carried Lucky's corpse over to the ditch and lowered him in. Harold pulled down a tree branch and set it on top of Lucky's body. He scattered some grass. The men returned to the jeep. As they did, Croft said, "A waste of bullets but I owed him that one." The attempt at disfigurement was a failure. The Beretta left small holes, one the size of a quarter in Lucky's forehead and one the size of a quarter in his chest. That didn't matter. The real purpose behind the shooting was to make the killing seem like a black market hit. The Sailor Gang knew that death by multiple gunshots was the signature of the Mafia. If the police ever found Lucky, they would pick up on that immediately. "Don't worry," Croft told Honess. "They'll think the Italians did it."

Bergman introduced this story by carving away at Holton. Before deserting, Holton had been employed as an army batman (a sort of valet attached to officers), working for up to four officers at a time. Each one paid Holton extra money for his services, which gave him "an income over and above what the army paid." Bergman maintained that the offer to join a black market gang had been tempting. He painted Holton as a greedy schemer who had grown accustomed to having money while in the army: "When you joined this group of fellows they did not have to talk you into it, did they?" Holton answered, "No."

Next, Bergman established that Holton had a fluid memory. The British man had given a first statement on November 22, a few days after his arrest. At that time, he was still being considered for prosecution. In fact, Holton was on the suspects list until late December. Once he was made a witness, it seems that his story grew like a garden, tended by the detectives who interviewed him. After his first statement, in which he made no mention of the shooting, the police had gone back to him on

December 4 for more elaboration. "Why did they come back to you and get another statement?" Bergman asked. The court president objected, saying, "I do not think that is a fair question." Bergman was not backing down. "The court knows that this witness is an important witness. In the question of fairness of the Defence I do not intend to be fair in the questioning. I can ask why he gave a certain answer."

Holton replied that the police wanted to know if he was "actually present when the second part of the shooting took place." Under Bergman's cross-examination it became clear that Holton had, in fact, given four separate statements about what occurred that night. Each time the detectives returned to Holton, he groomed his story to fit their needs. They needed to know more about the actual shooting; he provided details. Holton, however, was far from rock-solid. Bergman explained to the panel that "there are inconsistencies in the four statements." Holton admitted as much.

If true, Holton's story was rife with what can best be described as incredible events. During a thirty-minute ride with a dying friend, Holton recalled only two sentences being spoken—"Pull his feet in" and "Take it easy." Bergman was not buying it. "I am going to suggest that there was a lot more conversation in that thirty minutes," he told Holton. "When did you hear Croft say 'He is going'?"

"I never."

"When did you first hear Croft say 'He is gone'?"

"I never."

"After you had left Lucky that evening at Torre Gaia did anyone say 'It is a waste of lead'?"

"I do not remember."

"Is it a question of whether you remember or [that you] do not wish to remember?"

"I do not remember."

"How is it you remember some things so well and cannot remember that?"

"Other things sort of stuck in my mind."

"Do you think that four people with a body for one-half an hour can not say a word? Does that seem reasonable to you?"

"It does not sound reasonable."

As Bergman continued his cross-examination, Holton's credibility gradually crumbled. Holton grew evasive and petulant. He seemed willing to embellish any detail, no matter how inconsequential or slight. He even lied about his girlfriend. To the reply "I had just an occasional girl," Bergman asked, "Did you see a girl on the night of November 1, 1944?"

"No," said Holton.

Bergman paused for effect and then asked, "Do you want to think that one over again?"

Holton shrugged, "I was in the presence of a girl."

As Bergman brought his cross-examination toward its close, Holton teetered on the edge of complete collapse.

"Did you or did you not, in the first statement you ever made to the police, make any reference to the shooting of Lucky?"

"No."

"Are you certain of that?"

"Yes."

"How much more of your memory must be refreshed before you tell the complete story?"

"I have told it."

"You changed your mind on this point right now?"

"No."

"You said a few moments ago you referred to the shooting of Lucky in your first statement. You have changed your mind. How far can we trust your memory?"

"I do not know."

"When you heard Croft fire his pistol in the first instance, did you hear clicks or did you count the clicks?"

"I heard clicks."

"It was a clicking noise that you heard?"

"Yes."

"When Croft handed the accused back his pistol there were certain comments, were there not?"

"Yes."

"Will you, as far as you possibly can remember, repeat the exact words used by Croft when he handed the pistol back to the accused?"

"They were words to the effect 'That was one I owed him.'"

"Anything else during that transaction?"

"Not that I remember."

"Could there have been other conversation you do not recall at that moment?"

"Yes."

"Throughout the evening there could have been lots of little bits of conversation that you do not recall at the moment?"

"Yes."

"The conversation I have suggested to you throughout this cross-examination could have taken place and you do not recall the correct words?"

"Yes."

"Could Croft have said, 'He is going'?"

"Could have done."

"Could not Croft have said, 'He is gone'?"

"Could have."

"Could he have said, 'It's a waste of lead'?"

"Could have done."

"You were worried about yourself?"

"Yes."

"About what was going to happen to you?"

"Yes."

"You were trying to find a reasonable answer as to what had happened so you would not get into trouble?"

"No."

"When did you first start to get a story?"

"When the police questioned me."

"Did you try and reconstruct it in Florence?"

"No."

"It was not until November 17, 1944, that you started to get a story together?"

"After."

"How long after?"

"About the twenty-ninth of November."

"That is the date you gave your first statement?"

"No."

"When did you give your first statement?"

"Soon after I was arrested."

"Did you give any statements other than [those] you gave to the police on 28 November and 4 December?"

"I cannot quite remember."

"Did you give more than two statements to the police?"

"I am afraid I cannot remember."

"You cannot or you do not want to?"

"Cannot."

"Who did you give them to?"

"The SIB."

"You just wanted to talk and tell them all?"

"I was asked about it."

"You did not have any thought about anybody else you might implicate in your statement?"

"I just told them what happened."

"You had no thought that you might implicate your friends?"

"When it comes to a man dying . . ."

"Try to remember and answer my last question."

"No, I was thinking completely of myself."

"And these people had treated you pretty nicely up until November 1, 1944, and had given you lots of money?"

"Yes."

"And it was just little Private Holton you were thinking of?"

"Yes."

Bergman finished with Holton on February 19. The prosecution next called Gabriele Di Biagio, who described seeing a jeep drive by his house in Torre Gaia on the night of November 1. Then came Maria. Since Bill Croft had been arrested, Maria had been living on Piazza Armenia in Naples with Walter Glaser's girlfriend, Anna. Maria was due to deliver her baby at any moment, and the British and Canadian authorities had brought her up from Naples, giving her three hundred lire a day in expenses. Over the course of February, she would earn fifteen thousand lire testifying. Through an interpreter, Maria told the court how Joe Pringle, Honess and Holton had come to Via Pistoia on the night of November 1. She described hearing the fight between Lucky and Honess. She said that she thought the men were away for about half an hour after they left with Lucky. Bergman continued tough cross-examinations.

On February 20, Bourne called his final witness, Major A. C. Jones from the British General Hospital. Jones had performed the autopsy on Lucky on November 4, three days after his body was discovered. Jones had only been practising medicine for seven years. He had worked two years as a pathologist with the Royal Army Medical Corps and had performed between eighty and one hundred autopsies in that time. Bourne began by offering a photograph of Lucky's body taken on the autopsy table. Jones identified him as the man he had examined. Judging from the trial transcripts, Jones was a fastidious man, proud of his station as a doctor and confident in his judgment. Bourne asked him to read from his autopsy notes: "Describe the body as you first saw it."

"The body was that of a well-built young man of sallow complexion, with black hair and at the time we were looking for identification marks as he was unidentified and we failed to find any. There were no special scars which would serve as a help in identification. I measured the body. It was 5' 8" tall and the penis was uncircumcised, which I noted as it might help in identification."

Jones said that there was an entry wound half an inch above the left eyebrow and a hole in the skull at that point exactly one centimetre in diameter. At the rear of the skull was an exit wound, located at the bump one can feel at the back of the head. There was a gunshot wound through the third rib on the left side of Lucky's body. Finally, there was an abdominal wound right below the lowest right rib. The gunshot wound through the lung had gone straight through Lucky's body. The abdominal wound had gone through the liver.

Jones said that the abdominal wound had not damaged any major vessels in the liver but had caused considerable hemorrhage into the abdominal cavity. The bullet to the lung had passed through without damaging the heart. The bullet through Lucky's skull had passed along the base of the brain and had not damaged any major vessels. Bourne asked Jones if he had examined the stomach. Jones said he had but all he had found were "undigested potatoes." Jones also said that he didn't notice the smell of alcohol. Bourne asked if, in such a case, he would expect to. No, Jones replied, "I would not expect the smell of any Italian white wines, for example."

Then Bourne asked the big question: "What was the cause of death?"

"Death due to hemorrhage and shock from gunshot wounds."

Bourne pressed him for details. Jones said that a man might live up to ten hours without treatment for the abdominal wound and up to a week in the hospital. He said that the lung wound was also not necessarily fatal, and that even without medical attention for it, a man might live twenty-four hours. Finally, Jones said that a man might live up to twelve hours with the head wound. If all three wounds had been inflicted at the same time, Jones gave a man two minutes. The prosecution rested.

Bergman began his cross-examination by establishing that Jones's recorded time of death was "purely speculative." He then concentrated on Jones's technique as a pathologist, questioning his examination of the abdominal wound and asking the pathologist to give the court both medical and lay explanations. Jones admitted that he did not measure the length of the bullet track in the liver. He guessed at four inches, with a one-inch diameter. Bergman asked him about hemorrhaging. Jones said that there was "very little" in the lung and not much "gross hemorrhage" in the head wound. Bergman established that a bumpy ride in a jeep would accelerate hemorrhaging in the liver.

With the prosecution's last witness done, it was Bergman's chance to present his case. Harold, as Bergman had instructed him, turned down his opportunity to testify. It was a decision Harold was uncomfortable with. He had begged Bergman to let him tell his side of the story, but Bergman was confident that it would be unnecessary for Harold to take the stand. In order for the panel to find him guilty, they would have to believe he was guilty without any reasonable doubt. Bergman believed that Holton was an opportunistic liar and he believed Holton's testimony would carry little weight. The entire case rested on whether or not Lucky was alive at the time of the second and third shots, and Bergman was sure he had a witness who would establish the events of November 1 unequivocally in Harold's favour. In fact, this witness would be the only one called by the defence. Norman Bergman called Major Edgar C. Fielden of the Royal Canadian Army Medical Corps, Fifth Canadian General Hospital in Rome.[4]

Edgar Fielden had been born in England and had come to Canada with his family at age six. He grew up in Brantford, Ontario, attended the University of Toronto, and did post-graduate work in Pennsylvania and New York. Fielden began working as a pathologist in 1926. In total, he had eighteen years' experience, working at both St. Michael's Hospital in Toronto and with the City of Toronto, and he conducted approximately 250 autopsies a year. Fielden had been in charge of all post-mortems at both St. Michael's and the City of Toronto. In 1941, he enlisted and was eventually promoted to the rank of lieutenant colonel. After the war, Fielden would go on to have an exemplary career. In 1970, he became president of the College of Physicians and Surgeons of Ontario. The day he appeared at Harold Pringle's trial, Fielden was armed, for the first time during his stint in the army, with his service revolver. He had been advised by the military police to bring it as there could be those who might go to extreme measures to ensure that he did not testify.

Fielden was called as an expert witness. He had carefully scrutinized the original autopsy report and he had watched Jones testify. Bergman did not waste time. After establishing Fielden's credentials, he began questioning the pathologist about the abdominal wound. Fielden explained that the wound in the liver had caused a "very severe hemorrhage." He would have expected at least a quart of blood to be lost. The one-half pint of blood that Jones had discovered would be the remnants of whatever blood had not seeped out the entry and exit wounds.

"What conclusions did you draw with reference to Major Jones's statement relating to the lung wound?" Bergman asked.

"The wound in the left side of the chest had passed through the lung. At the level which this wound entered the chest it would pass through the thick portion of the lung and there should have been a large amount of hemorrhage from this wound in the lung into the plural cavity. Major Jones said there was a very, very small amount of hemorrhage present in the left plural cavity, therefore, I believe that this wound was inflicted after death."

"Major Jones traced the bullet track into the brain tissue at the base of the skull," Bergman said. "What conclusions did you draw?"

"Major Jones stated that the bullet track in the head extended along the floor of the brain and out at the back through the right occipital lobe," said Fielden. "He also stated that there was no hemorrhage in the brain tissue along this bullet track and no hemorrhage on the surface of the brain where the bullet track had passed along the floor of the brain. It is my opinion that this wound also was inflicted after death."

With those answers, Bergman believed he had established reasonable doubt.

Fielden went on to explain that Lucky's inebriation would have accelerated his hemorrhaging from the abdominal wound. He said that he would expect a man to live maybe fifteen minutes: "I have seen people die within fifteen minutes of having a ruptured liver in which the rupture was no bigger than this wound described."

The prosecution tried to shake the pathologist's testimony.

"Would that not hold true with the head wound if the person had lived a few seconds after the head wound had been inflicted and the heart only beat a few seconds?" asked Bourne. "Would not the signs you would expect to find be substantially the same as if the body had been dead?"

Fielden answered, "In the case of the heart wound there is one point of great significance—there was no hemorrhage in the brain tissue along the track to the brain. If the heart had been beating at the time of this bullet wound in the head there would have been evidence of concussion and bruising and hemorrhage into the brain tissue itself. Major Jones stated there was no such hemorrhage."

"When you say that you believe that these wounds were inflicted after death, do you mean that either of them [could] have been inflicted at the point of death?"

"I say this—both of these wounds were inflicted after the heart stopped beating—in my opinion that is dead."

Bourne was unable to rattle Fielden, and the pathologist rebuffed all his attacks. If Harold Pringle's and Bill Croft's shots had been delivered while Lucky was still alive, there would have been bruising and blood in both wounds. Jones had found neither. Therefore, Lucky must have been dead when the shots were fired.

This thinking formed the foundation of Bergman's closing remarks to the panel. He told them, "It is impossible to kill a dead man," and he maintained that the prosecution had failed to provide sufficient evidence on which to convict. Bergman directed most of his ire toward two prosecution witnesses: Maria Fedele and Bill Holton. Of Maria he said, "She has made mistakes and in some information she has given she has lied, definitely lied in others." He described Holton as

> one of the most bare-faced liars ever to give evidence before a tribunal. In his own words, he thought only of himself. He admitted giving four statements. He admitted they were inconsistent and his conduct as he described it was inconsistent in the acts of any person taking a part as he alleged. He said he was merely a spectator and in one statement he made he admitted that he had carried the body from the ground to the sump, or assisted taking it there. When questioned on that point he did not bother to answer. I do not blame him. I think he would have been better off if he had not answered in cross-examination. As a spectator he would have been better off if he had gone to the opera and spent his time there, if you would have believed his story.

He noted that if Holton's version of events, in which only two sentences were spoken during the entire thirty-minute ride, were to be believed, then the Sailor Gang comprised "the least talkative group of people who ever enlisted in the army." He made sure to mention Holton's deal: "He has been promised immunity as far as the serious charge of murder is concerned. By what right the British JAG, of the British Army, promises immunity I do not know." Bergman said the reason Lucky was dumped in the field in Torre Gaia was simple: "Having a dead body on their hands, they felt it might be difficult to explain and being caught in a bad spot decided they had better get rid of the body."

The crux of his argument rested with Major Fielden's evidence. Alcohol's acceleration of the heart rate and the resulting increase in bleeding from the first abdominal wound would have resulted in death in under fifteen minutes. The lack of hemorrhage in the lung and head proved that those shots were fired after Lucky was dead. "As the Court will realize it is impossible to kill a dead man, the Court must acquit the accused on this charge."

"It is a very heavy responsibility that has been thrown to the Court," Bergman said, finishing his arguments, "to decide whether or not a man lives. That, however, is the problem of the five of you—your problem alone."

Captain Bourne approached his closing address in a drier and more methodical fashion. He first spent great energy on the legal definition of murder; next he ran through Holton's story, using it to recreate the events of that evening. Bourne used Maria's testimony to back up Holton's and rested most of his case on the statements Honess and Harold had made to the SIB. He connected Honess's contention that Lucky "was still alive" when they laid him on the ground to Harold's statement, "It's just the same from there on. I want to say the truth. I took out my gun and aimed at his body and I just fired only one shot." Bourne tried to dismiss Fielden's testimony as biased. Fielden was "subconsciously an advocate for the accused and his opinions may have been coloured by this." Bourne's address was a long one, running at least an hour and a half.

When both the prosecution and the defence had finished presenting their cases, Bill Gunn, the judge advocate, instructed the panel on points of law. He was hard on Holton's testimony, saying that while even if the jury considered Holton an accomplice they could still admit his evidence, "according to the law it is dangerous to convict the accused on the uncorroborated evidence of an accomplice, although it is within your legal province to convict upon it if you choose." Finally, Gunn suggested that it would be possible for the panel to convict Pringle of manslaughter. This was a very uncommon action for a judge advocate to take as it demonstrated that he obviously did not think the prosecution had proven its case beyond a reasonable doubt for a murder charge.

The panel recessed. The trial had lasted seven days. The panel deliberated for one hour.

The court was called into order and Harold was brought before the judge advocate and the panel. The verdict was then announced: guilty of murder.

Next, Bergman delivered a sentencing address:

> Mr. President, gentlemen, it is my duty now to address the Court in mitigation of punishment. I wish it clearly understood that in spite of the findings of the Court, any comment that I make is not to be an admission of guilt upon the part of the accused. With reference to the history of the accused, I will tender the report of the advisor of neuropsychiatry, which gives you certain information.
>
> The accused enlisted at the age of eighteen. He enlisted in the same unit in which his father was serving and during that time while he was with his father, he was not in any trouble in either military or civilian life. He first got into trouble after his father was returned to Canada in 1941. He had seen active service, and has seen action and served in the line up to the Hitler show. The obvious conclusion for the Court, and for the confirming and reviewing authorities, to consider is the fact that he lost his father's influence on him during his very, very formative years. That should be taken into consideration in deciding whether there should be a commutation of sentence.
>
> With reference to the offence of which the accused stood charged, there is no evidence of any pre-arranged scheme to do wrong on the night of November 1, 1944. The accused took a fairly inactive part right to the moment when he was accused of firing the shot. Whether the verdict of this Court is sound, or not, is a matter not for me but for the reviewing authorities who have access to the legal books and information they have and not to a defending officer, with some two or three books to use as a guide in his defence. I strongly plead, and with proper investigation into all the circumstances into the background of the accused's life, his

regimental history, and any part he took with reference to this charge be scrutinized very carefully and the sentence which the Court passes be commuted.

The court closed briefly while the panel contemplated its decision. It was reopened and Harold was ushered in. The room was still. The judge advocate broke the silence: "Accused, will you come forward and take this? I suggest you see your Defending Officer and he will explain that to you." He gave Harold a sheet of folded paper.

There was not much explanation necessary.

Private Harold Joseph Pringle, CIC, attached F.A.P. to Canadian section 1 Echelon AFHQ.

The Court have found you guilty of the following charge: When on active service, committing a civil offence, that is to say, murder, in that he in the field, in Italy, on, or about, 1 November 1944, murdered Pte. McGillivray (otherwise known as "Lucky")

But not guilty of the following charges: nil

The Court have passed a sentence of death upon you.

The Court have made no recommendation to mercy.

Two days later Harold filed an appeal of the verdict: "I intend to base my appeal on the facts that lying occurred when evidence was given by Private Holton and Maria Fedele, and that contradiction occurred during the evidence of the two medical officers. I also respectfully request permission to call three further witnesses each of whom can give relevant evidence. May Captain Bergman (defending officer) please be detailed to assist me in preparing my appeal."

Bergman made preparations to travel to Naples. He would gather evidence at Bill Croft's trial, which was set to begin on March 12.

13.

THE SAPPER

The day Harold's guilty verdict was passed, the British Judge Advocate General began its trial of Sapper Cecil Henry Frederick Honess at Allied Headquarters in Rome. The British JAG chose an officer from its legal staff, Major S. J. Collins, as its prosecutor. Major J. S. Barnes, from the Royal Ordnance Corps, was selected to represent Charlie Honess. The timing of the trial to begin February 22 was not an accident. The British court intended to call the same witnesses as the Canadian prosecutor had at Pringle's trial. Maria would appear and speak through an interpreter; the detectives from the SIB would give precisely the same testimony as they had at Harold's court martial, right down to the sentences they used. The prosecution would also call its star witness, Private Bill Holton, who would add the usual Holton flourishes. At Charlie's trial Holton would claim he tried to break up the fight between Honess and Lucky, saying that the Sapper had told him to "Get out of the way. This has nothing to do with you." Holton would say that Honess had said, "He asked for it" after shooting Lucky. In hushed tones, Holton would tell the panel that right after the shooting, he was frightened for his life and that Honess had threatened him. Holton was unable to explain why he then accompanied his would-be assailant on a two-day trip to Florence. Before the trial began, Honess was shown a copy of Holton's statement and he was succinct in his assessment. Only two words were necessary: "Lying bastard."[1]

Charlie Honess stared listlessly as his court martial began and the trial's president, Lieutenant Colonel W. J. Bostock, of the Royal Pioneer Corps, told him he was "accused of murdering Private J. McGillivary alias Lucky. To that charge do you plead guilty or not guilty?"

Honess replied, "Not guilty, sir."

Outside, it was a sunny, cool day, and Honess may have looked longingly out the courtroom windows, wondering if he would ever walk under blue skies again. The court was stifling and claustrophobic. The man known to the Sailor Gang as Charlie Honess found himself looking backwards, realizing that somehow over the last five years—five years that comprised one quarter of his life—everything he had ever been had disappeared. Now he was poised to lose everything he had ever once hoped to become.

Despite having grown up in difficult circumstances, at one time his future had seemed promising. Honess had been an above-average student, but he was from a poor family and does not appear to have had a happy home life. He left school at age fourteen. At age fifteen, he ran away from home and joined the army. His father eventually caught up with him and had him discharged. Honess spent the next two years working as a labourer. He had native intelligence and he studied in his spare time, teaching himself to speak both French and Italian. When he reached seventeen, Honess re-enlisted; this time there was nothing his father could do about it. In 1938, he married.

When war broke out in 1939, it was a golden opportunity for Honess. It was a chance to become a hero.

During the Battle of Britain, when the Nazis bombed London, mercilessly killing 40,000 Londoners, Honess volunteered to work in a bomb disposal unit. Bomb disposal meant defusing unexploded bombs and there was no room for error. Miss a switch and the bomb disposal worker became a casualty. Bomb disposal workers were often blown to pieces so small that their bodies could not be found. On one day alone twenty bomb disposal engineers were killed. The job required iron nerves, demanding that a man focus all his concentration on the subtle nuances of the steel eggs dropped from planes by the Nazis, designed to blow him to smithereens. With his creativity and street smarts, Honess had enough confidence to stick it and he became a respected member of this elite unit. Honess's military record states that Honess was "in the thick of it for quite a while in Hackney." The army has a tendency toward understatement; when a military report states that an individual was "in the thick" of it, a civilian can read that he was in the thick of a lot of serious trouble. In 1941, one of the bombs Honess was working on detonated. Honess was seriously wounded and his co-workers appear to have been killed. After this incident, his wife would later report, "his nerves were shaken and he was subject to fits of depression."

Still, shaken or not, to the army Honess was a skilled and seasoned sapper, and as such he was invaluable. In 1942, he was sent to the Eighth Army in North Africa. Normally, a soldier would be given an embarkation leave, two to four weeks to spend with his family before leaving on an assignment that might cost his life. Time before North Africa was tight, however, and Honess did not qualify for leave. This, said his wife, "caused him to write very worried letters." In North Africa, Honess cleared minefields. It was dangerous, dusty work. After Africa came the invasion of Sicily and then the invasion of Italy. Again, the life of a sapper was precarious. Mines were cleared, and Honess also found himself building bridges under enemy fire.

In July 1944, Honess received a letter from his mother saying that a V2 rocket had destroyed his parents' house and that his wife, who had been living with them, had moved out. It is difficult to say what Honess read into this news. The man who wrote worried letters home may have thought there was more to the move than a pragmatic relocation. Whatever his concerns, it is clear that this news was the tipping point. As the Eighth Army prepared to attack the Gothic Line, Cecil Frederick Honess went absent. Beginning at the end of July, all letters from his wife were returned to her unanswered. He drifted, aimless, drinking heavily. A maddening cycle began: when Honess was AWOL, he grew ashamed and despondent, and he turned himself in. When imprisoned, he became indignant and restless, and he escaped. Finally, the wheel stopped spinning: he landed in Rome, adopted the name Charlie, met Bill Croft and joined the Sailor Gang.

During his trial, Honess's lawyer argued that the shot the Sapper

fired into Lucky's liver had not been fatal. He maintained that Pringle
and Croft, whom he described as "assassins," acted without Honess's
knowledge or consent and that it was the Canadian and the Sailor who
decided that Lucky was a liability and needed to be taken on the proverbial one-way ride. "I do not think the accused could by the wildest stretch
of imagination be called a leader of men," Honess's lawyer told the panel.
"And to visualize him taking any part in dissuading this man from doing
something of which he had not had warning I do not think can be imagined at all."

Maria was once again called to testify. Through an interpreter, she
described the Sailor Gang's activities the day of the murder. "What was
the relationship between Charlie and Lucky that afternoon?" she was
asked. "Were they friendly?"

"They did not talk a lot," she answered. "I was with Bill and they
more or less sat. I did not notice if they spoke to each other or not."

Maria said that at about eleven o'clock, Joe Pringle, Bill Holton and
Charlie Honess came to the house on Via Pistoia.

"Did you hear them talking?"

"They woke up Bill; then they started to talk."

"Did you understand what they were talking about?"

"No."

"Did you notice anything about any of the ones that came in?"

"I noticed that Carlo was very angry indeed."

"Was he doing much talking?"

"When Lucky came back he talked to him. I do not know what they
said."

"Did you notice anything about Carlo's dress?"

"It was stained with blood."

Unlike Pringle's lawyer, Honess's defender decided to have his client
testify. Major Barnes asked the Sapper about his relationship with Lucky.
"Well, we were very good friends," Honess answered. "He used to take me
out a lot to learn how to drive." The Sapper described the night of
November 1 in detail. When Lucky came into the house on Via Pistoia,
Honess said he asked him, "Where have you been?" Lucky seemed "in a
hell of a temper" and he began swearing. He said something about

Honess deserting him in the bar. Lucky walked into his room, threw his shoes on the floor and called Honess a "yellow bastard," saying, "I told you what I would do to you." Then he went to a chest of drawers, where Honess knew he kept his gun. Honess drew his own pistol from his back pocket and stuck it in Lucky's ribs. "Shut up and don't move," he said, "or I'll shoot." Lucky grabbed the wrist of the hand the gun was in and threw an arm around Honess's shoulder. "You haven't got the nerve to shoot," he told the Sapper. They struggled for a few seconds and then the pistol went off.

After Honess fired at Lucky, the Canadian stood for a second and then collapsed, as though someone had given him a push. He caught hold of Honess, almost dragging him down. Honess asked him, "Is it bad?" and Lucky answered, "Get a doctor. Get me to a hospital." After a couple of seconds, he said, "What did you shoot for, Charlie?" Then, "It is all right, Charlie, it is only my arm." Pringle appeared, saying, "We must get him to a hospital." He grabbed hold of Lucky, said, "I'll get the jeep," and ran outside. Honess picked up Lucky and dragged him to the front door. There, Holton grabbed Lucky's legs and the two men carried him out of the house toward the waiting jeep. Before leaving Lucky's room, Honess stole a glimpse into the half-open drawer. Lucky had been reaching for his little black book.

Honess described the trip in the jeep as "very bumpy," recalling that Lucky seemed to be in pain and had said "Take it easy" two or three times. Honess said the main reason for the ride was to get Lucky medical attention. "I had not done anything so bad that Lucky could not go to hospital," he maintained. Honess knew the village they were driving toward. "We had all been there two or three times before, Joe Pringle had pointed out this hospital and showed us where he got away from the Military Police."

"What did you think would happen to you if you took him to a military hospital?" The prosecutor asked Honess. He replied, "I did not care what happened to me."

Honess said that the last words Lucky said were "Where are we going and how long will we be?" Then, he remembered, "Lucky never answered me, and he never groaned any more and he was dead quiet."

In the jeep, Bill Croft and Pringle discussed whether Lucky was dying; they decided to pull over and see if the Cape Bretoner was indeed gone. Once they reached the field at Torre Gaia, Croft, Holton and Honess carried Lucky out of the jeep and laid him down. Honess stayed back from the body, leaned against the vehicle and thought he was going to vomit. He said Joe Pringle walked up alongside Lucky and drew his Beretta, bending down double, almost touching Lucky with the muzzle of his pistol. Then Pringle fired into his chest. At the same time, Honess heard clicking. The noise turned out to be Bill Croft's gun. "This won't fire," Croft said. "Joe, lend me yours." Then Croft fired a bullet directly into Lucky's skull, saying, "That was one I owed him." Croft walked to the back of the jeep, where Honess was standing.

"What did you fire those shots for?" Honess asked him.

"It's all right," the Sailor replied. "They'll think the Italians done it."

The memory of that night deeply affected the Sapper; he became weepy under cross-examination.

"You saw Joe take his pistol and go deliberately close to the body and point it at his chest?"

"That is right."

"What did you do when he did that?"

"I just stood there."

"But Lucky was your pal, remember, the one you were going to take to hospital?"

"What could I do; I was flabbergasted."

"You did not do anything at all."

"No."

"You just stood there and let him do it?"

"Yes."

"Were you happy when he did that?"

"I do not know what I thought."

"Or were you happy that you had killed Lucky. Did you do anything when Croft pulled out his silver-plated pistol and clicked it?"

"I could not; I was paralyzed."

"You heard Croft, after his pistol misfired, ask for Joe's?"

"Yes, that is right."

"You knew what he wanted it for?"

"I did not."

"Do yourself justice. You knew what he wanted it for. You knew perfectly well that Lucky's body was going to be dropped off somewhere?" the prosecutor asked him.

"No, I did not know that."

"What did you think was going to happen to Lucky?"

"That they were going to look at him. Myself, at that stage, I did think Lucky had died."

"You thought he had died?"

"Yes, because I spoke to him and he never answered, and he looked queer as he lay in the back of the jeep."

"From that moment onwards did you see anything about Lucky which gave you any reason to believe he was still alive?"

"No."

"He was limp when you took him out?"

"He was limp when we took him out."

"As far as you know from the moment that he never spoke to you he might be dead?"

"Yes."

"Was the idea of going up some turning, or something, to see whether he was dead or not?"

"To examine him, yes."

"To see whether he was dead or not?"

"I do not know that because Joe turned down the side turning."

"You had to keep an eye open for the turning, had you not?"

"Joe told me to look for a turning and then we came to it just as he said it."

"Prior to that you had formed the opinion in your mind that Lucky might be dead?"

"I had thought of it. It was possible."

"And I have no doubt you said something of that sort to Joe?"

"No, I did not."

"Why not, you were all in the party together?"

"No," said Honess. "It was my party."

"It was your party in the sense that you had shot him, and the others were helping you to remove the injured man, or the body, from the house, that is right, is it not?"

"They were helping me to get him to a hospital."

"You thought he was dead?"

"I did not think he was dead. I thought there was a possibility."

"You thought there was a possibility and you thought it would be a good idea to have a look and see. Did you not suggest that to Joe? Joe was your pal, you remember, and he was helping you."

"He was not helping me. He was helping me take him to hospital."

"Joe was helping you. He knew what had happened, had a pretty shrewd idea what had happened?"

"Yes, he knew that I had been the cause of the shot at Lucky."

"Was there no conversation at all in that jeep about what Lucky's present condition was?"

"Not between me and the others. I did not know what was said but Bill said something just as we turned, before we turned off the side turning, about Lucky dying. That was what it sounded like to me."

CHARLIE HONESS'S TRIAL LASTED only two days. In his summation, the prosecutor recounted the events of the night of the murder and maintained that Honess had murderous intent when he shot Lucky. About the friendship between Lucky and Honess, he pointed out that "between men of this character and circumstances the term friendship is probably quite different from the way which we might mean. They hang together not because they liked each other, but they were all in the same boat and had to hang together." In his summing up, Honess's defender said that Lucky's shooting was

a pure accident resulting from the struggle of two half-drunken men. The accused, I suggest to you, is not a criminal. He is a fool, and I say that though he is here in the room, and I think he will be the first to agree with me in the light of what has happened in the past. But a fool is not the same as being a criminal. He got himself into bad company and bad habits, and he is now reaping the fruit of what he has sown. I suggest that, if given a chance and the necessary environment and training, he can become quite easily a very useful member of society and a good husband to the wife waiting for him in England, to say nothing of his parents.

Like Bill Gunn at Harold Pringle's trial, the judge advocate made great pains to caution the panel about Bill Holton's testimony. Knowing "the sort of person he is, it is important that you should consider his evidence very, very carefully indeed before you act upon it and believe it.... If you accept his evidence he is an accomplice and as you well know, gentlemen, it is very dangerous to convict an accused person on the uncorroborated testimony of an accomplice and in a case of this kind that would be a danger which you would not probably be prepared to undertake."

He was wrong. The panel deliberated for a little under half an hour before finding Charlie Honess guilty and sentencing him to death. To the Sapper, the verdict may have seemed like his only real means of escape. Even on the run, Honess had felt trapped and had often found himself wanting to surrender and go to prison. He sometimes thought he could serve his time and have a clean slate. Yet going home must have seemed impossible. His friends and family in England had got on with their lives. They had jobs and children and homes. Meanwhile, if one included the time he had spent defusing bombs, Cecil Henry Frederick Honess had been at war for four and a half years before deserting. Like most soldiers who came under fire, he had collected memories that would dog him for life and he had grown "worldly," as the people at home would say. There must have been visions of battle that he could not leave behind—burning houses in London, fragments of men on the desert in North Africa, mines exploding in olive orchards in Italy. At first, he thought time and alcohol might wash them away, but as the months passed the visions only grew more vivid. It was as if his memories were outraged by his attempts to quiet them and they were rising up, demanding his attention. Booze helped muffle them, but it always wore off.

Honess's final adventure had been a month running wild in an ancient city. Yet that time spent on the Via Appia and the terrible events that followed it were the only tangible life Honess now possessed. The Sailor Gang had become more real than anything he could now imagine waited for him back home. They were family. "I did not know anybody else," Honess said of Bill Croft and the rest. "I had not any money and if I wanted some and they had some they would give it to me. They were the only people I knew. It was the only way I could eat or sleep."

14.

THE SAILOR

On March 15, the British Admiralty began its court martial of Petty Officer William Robert Croft. His trial was enormously significant to the British Royal Navy, since no sailor in living memory had been tried for murder and no sailor had been executed since 1861. Normally, when a sailor got into trouble, he would be handed over to civil authorities and tried in a British court. Croft, however, was accused of committing a crime on foreign soil during wartime, and regulations dictated that the navy had no option but to try him in Italy. The prospect of a capital case sent the Royal Navy "to panic stations," according to a 1994 *Daily Mail* article written by Anthony Gardner and Anthony Babington. The Mediterranean Command was determined to ensure that the trial and the accompanying proceedings were beyond reproach.[1]

The trial was held in Naples in a lavish palazzo hung with chandeliers and mirrors; the officers sitting on the panel wore full dress uniforms, complete with swords. The surroundings were so surreal, Gardner and Babington wrote that "one might have been stepping into another century."[2] The Royal Navy chose a thirty-year-old lieutenant named Jeremy Hutchinson to act as prosecutor. He had never tried a case, let alone a murder trial, but he had plenty of potential. He went on to become a celebrated barrister—so successful, in fact, that he eventually became Lord Hutchinson of Lullington.

It was fitting that Bill Croft, the young man who had organized the Sailor Gang, was being tried in Naples, for it was Naples, as much as anything else, that had given birth to all the hapless violence on which the gang of deserters embarked. Not so much Naples the city nor the people of Naples—rather, it was war-made Naples, what Naples became, first under the Fascists and then under the Allies. During the Second World War hundreds of cities in dozens of countries were devastated, but there was something about the humiliation of Naples that burrowed deep into the minds of the men who passed through it on their way to the front. At least a half dozen books were written about the iniquity that transpired there.

"In the broadest sense we promised the Italians security and democracy if they came over to our side," wrote John Horne Burns, an American officer who recounted his own disillusion in his 1948 book, *The Gallery*, a collection of short stories set in post-liberation Naples. "All we actually did was knock the hell out of their system and give them nothing to put in its place. And one of the most tragic spectacles in all history was the Italians' faith in us—for a little while, until we disabused them of it. It seemed to me like the swindle of all humanity, and I wondered if perhaps we weren't all lost together. Collective and social decency didn't exist in Naples."[3]

That had not always been the case. Naples was a city dedicated entirely to the sweet things in life, with thousands of years of art, cuisine, architecture and music in its history. Originally a Greek colony, Naples predates the city of Rome; its name derives from the Greek for "new city," *neo metropolis*. Before the Allies and the Germans arrived, Naples had been conquered ten times, and every time the Neapolitans had turned conquest into a force that eventually invigorated their city. In essence, Naples ignored and finally overcame all its conquerors. The German occupation of 1943 and the Allied liberation, however, finally kicked the life out of the city. Today, Naples is again a vibrant, chaotic, mesmerizing place, but there is evidence everywhere still of the degradation that thrived there during the war.

Naples suffered most because it was one of the only Italian cities to resist the Fascists from the beginning. It is fair to say that

Neapolitans generally resent being told how to conduct their lives, and Fascism did not exactly click with civic sentiment. Goose-stepping Germans and coiffed Fascists held no attraction. Neapolitans regard most authority as a meaningless manifestation of vanity. This attitude is embodied by the story of an elderly Neapolitan gentleman who, as he watched the Americans unload their tanks on the docks, declared, "What beautiful rust!"[4]

Naples became an important strategic goal for the Allies in the autumn of 1943 after the successful invasion of Sicily. One of the world's great natural harbours, Naples was considered by British and American planning staff to be essential for a successful military operation in Italy. The Allies were confident the city could be taken since there was an active resistance movement in Naples; there were reports that even young Neapolitan boys were arming themselves and fighting the Germans guerrilla-style in the streets. The Germans repaid this aggression in characteristic fashion, imprisoning and murdering hundreds of people. Meanwhile, the Allies conducted extensive bombing missions against Naples in an attempt to dislodge the Germans. These raids caused great damage, claiming many civilian lives, and as the bombing runs continued, the city was cut off from supplies of food and medicine. Starvation set in. Gradually, the entire population of the Naples Zoo disappeared, and diners found themselves feasting on tropical fish and zebra. There were rumours of cannibalism. As starvation spread, typhoid epidemics wiped out entire streets. The poor, who never had much on which to subsist, suffered most.

Norman Lewis, a British intelligence sergeant, tried to exorcise his memory of the city in his book *Naples '44*:

> Here, to all intents and purposes, we were living in the Middle Ages. Only the buildings had changed—and most of those were in ruins. Epidemics, robbers, funerals followed by shrieking women, deformed and mutilated beggars, legless cripples dragging themselves about on wheeled platforms—even raving lunatics they'd no room for in the asylum. People walked the streets with handkerchiefs pressed over their mouths and noses

as they probably did in the days of the plagues of old. This morning I actually found myself in a little square tucked away among the ruins where women were dancing to drive the sickness away.[5]

The Allies won Naples in September 1943, but the city they occupied was hardly a prize. Before retreating, the Germans had wrecked almost all the city's public works. The water system was utterly destroyed. The arrival of the Allies halted German atrocities and the bombings stopped, but the Allies brought a new pestilence. The injection of an enormous well-fed, well-paid army created an economic disparity that triggered a moral mudslide.

In his 1952 memoir, *The Skin*, Curzio Malaparte, who served with the Allies as an Italian liaison officer from 1943 to 1945, wrote that he considered the effect of the liberation to be a plague: "Everything these magnificent soldiers touched was at once corrupted. No sooner did the luckless inhabitants of the liberated countries grasp the hands of their liberators than they began to fester and to stink. It was enough that an Allied soldier should lean out of his jeep to smile at a woman, to give her face a fleeting caress, and the same woman, who until that moment had preserved her dignity and purity, would change into a prostitute."[6]

There was a sex-trade district to suit every lurid impulse. Soldiers lined up outside houses, and once inside they were led into a rooms where they found a dozen or more women willing to perform any sexual act for the smallest of sums. Sometimes money was not even involved. Norman Lewis describes happening upon such a display on the way into Naples. He saw several trucks drawn up by a half-derelict building. Soldiers were grabbing tins of beef from the trucks and carrying them into the building, where "a row of ladies sat at intervals of about a yard with their backs to the wall. These women were dressed in their street clothes, and had the ordinary well-washed respectable shopping and gossiping faces of working-class housewives. By the side of each woman stood a small pile of tins, and it soon became clear that it was possible to make love to any one of them in this very public place by adding another tin to the pile."[7]

Sexual commerce was so common that virginity became an oddity.

For the price of a dollar, soldiers could visit one of the "Virgins of Naples." After paying a fee they would have one minute to stare into a telescope that was stuck in the vagina of a preteen girl. Malaparte described such a show:

> The girl threw her cigarette on the floor, grasped the fringe of her petticoat with the tips of her fingers and slowly raised it. First her knees appeared, gently gripped by the silk sheath of her stockings, then the bare skin. She remained for a moment in this posture, a sad Veronica, her face severe, her mouth half-open in an expression of contempt. Then, slowly turning on her back, she lay at full length on the bed. Like the odious lobster when it mates, gradually opening its pincer-like claws, staring at the male with its small, round, shining black eyes, motionless and threatening, so the girl remained staring at the spectators. A profound silence reigned in the room.[8]

In April 1944, the Bureau of Psychological Warfare sent a bulletin stating that 42,000 women in Naples were engaged in prostitution—this out of a "nubile female population of 150,000." Norman Lewis was ordered to interview Italian women who wished to marry Allied soldiers; he found that "nine out of ten Italian girls have lost their men folk, who have either disappeared in battles, into prisoner-of-war camps, or been cut off in the North. The whole population is out of work. Nobody produces anything. How are they to live?"[9] Malaparte included boys and young men in the prostitutes' ranks. There was also, he recalled, a special "market for children." This, he maintained, was a new breed of vice:

> From time immemorial all kinds of things had been sold in Naples, but never children. Never before had children been sold in the streets of Naples.... One could say anything about the Neapolitans, but not that they sold their children. And now the piazzatta of the Capella Vecchia, situated in the heart of Naples, beneath the noble mansions of the Monte di Dio, the Chiatamone and the Piazza die Martiti, and close to the Synagogue, had

become the resort of Moroccan soldiers, who came to buy
Neapolitan children at the price of a few soldi.[10]

Venereal diseases such as syphilis and gonorrhea spread. Rates of
incidence of VD in the British army rose from twenty per thousand to
sixty per thousand after the liberation of Naples. The army tried to
fight this outbreak by distributing condoms and educating soldiers on
the risks of sexual activity. They also attempted to monitor the women
the soldiers were visiting, using "vice squads" of military police to
round up suspected prostitutes. A post-war report states that the civilian system was "largely ignorant and wholly corrupt." The entire Italian
staff at a Naples civilian hospital dedicated to controlling venereal disease was arrested and charged with bribery and corruption. Spot
inspections by British doctors of women cleared by Italian medical
boards found fifty to eighty per cent infection rates in groups of
women listed by Italian authorities as twenty per cent infected. The
British concluded that little could be done to prevent the spread of
venereal disease. Education and prophylactics were the best defence,
although the author of the report noted that in future attention should
be paid "especially to regimental officers."[11]

Today those Neapolitans old enough to remember the war see a kind
of bittersweet nobility in the city's willingness to preserve itself at any
cost. Oreste Schiano di Zenise, who was a young teenager during the war,
comes from an aristocratic line that has been in Naples for 2,700 years;
he and his family escaped the city before the worst of the bombing,
becoming refugees. "They gave up nothing, those women," he said of
those who turned to prostitution. "And they have nothing to be ashamed
of. They were trying to feed their families." War, Oreste observes, was the
unthinkable becoming the unavoidable. "Think of the most terrible
thing you could do. Think of something so horrible you can't, even in
your wildest nightmares, ever imagine it coming true. In war, it is not
only possible, but you do it," he says. "In war, it is possible."[12]

This sentiment also applied to the Italian wartime black market,
which began in Naples. The city's citizens became so adept at theft and
retail that any product could be obtained. Entire tanks disappeared in a

matter of hours. The black market stole a Liberty ship from the harbour. A train and seven rail cars disappeared. It was possible for a person with the right amount of cash to purchase a complete crated American fighter plane. Allied security officers estimated that the equivalent of one in three cargo ships went missing. Rumours circulated that the black market was planning a large-scale robbery of the harbour using the protective smoke-screen triggered by the air-raid siren as cover. Stolen goods were sold openly on street stalls. Ever mindful of good taste, Neapolitan black market merchants arranged their wares attractively, with ribbons or a vase of flowers to attract customers. They advertised. Lewis describes seeing placards attesting to the value of contraband goods: "YOU CAN MARCH TO KINGDOM COME ON THESE BEAUTIFUL IMPORTED BOOTS…IF YOU DON'T SEE THE OVERSEAS ARTICLE YOU'RE LOOKING FOR, JUST ASK US AND WE'LL GET IT."[13]

Yet, even more than by the depravity itself, the soldiers who experienced Naples seemed most shocked by the inhuman callousness that misery bred. Naples was a place created for celebration, but it was mired in suffering. The city was like the young mother a British soldier described burying her small child. "Her mouth, I thought, was made for laughter," he wrote in the *Union Jack*, "but now her cheeks were drawn in sorrow as she cried."[14] In one passage, Norman Lewis describes a lunch he had in October 1943 in the Neapolitan neighbourhood of Vico Chiatamone:

> Suddenly five or six little girls between the ages of nine and twelve appeared in the doorway. They wore hideous straight black uniforms buttoned under their chins, and black boots and stockings, and their hair had been shorn short, prison-style. They were all weeping, and as they clung to each other and groped their way towards us, bumping into chairs and tables, I realized they were all blind. Tragedy and despair had been thrust upon us, and would not be shut out. I expected the indifferent diners to push back their plates, to get up and hold out their arms, but nobody moved. Forkfuls of food were thrust into open mouths, the rattle of conversation continued, nobody saw the tears.[15]

Lewis learned that the girls were from an orphanage, a place where conditions were very bad. They had been brought to the neighbourhood for a day's outing and their attendant had been unable or unwilling to keep them away from the lure of the smell of food. "The experience changed my outlook," Lewis wrote.

> Until now I had clung to the comforting belief that human beings eventually came to terms with pain and sorrow. Now I understood I was wrong, and like Paul I suffered a conversion—but to pessimism. These little girls, any one of whom could be my daughter, came into the restaurant weeping, and they were weeping when they were led away. I knew that, condemned to everlasting darkness, hunger and loss, they would weep on incessantly. They would never recover from their pain, and I would never recover from the memory of it.[16]

It was against this backdrop that Bill Croft met Maria Fedele in March 1944. Presented against such misery she must have been a startling sight. Maria was a young, well-bred woman who met Bill by accident, she later told military police, at "the house of a friend whose name and address I do not remember."[17] To Bill, Maria was a ravishing Italian beauty with warm brown eyes. To Maria, Bill was exotic, with worldliness beyond his years. He was handsome and well put-together. The first time Maria saw Bill he was dressed smartly in a khaki British uniform and a white peaked cap. Maria said that a "love sympathy" developed between them that night.[18] Like most young people who fall in love, Bill and Maria must have felt like the only two lovers in the world. In fact, in Italy during the war, these kinds of couplings were not uncommon. The war's instability could have an aphrodisiac quality that transcended both reason and language. For instance, in January 1945, a Canadian chaplain reported that he had been asked to marry a Canadian private to an Italian woman. On arriving at the scene, "it was discovered that the girl is only sixteen years of age; she could not speak English nor he Italian."[19]

Bill and Maria fell passionately in love. They began to meet once a week, either at her friend's house or out in the street. Soon they were meeting three or four times a week. Maria began teaching Bill Italian, and he learned quickly. Bill brought Maria aboard his ship, the *Empire Griffin*, and she was impressed. Shortly after this date, Bill was sent up to Anzio for four weeks. The experience was disturbing, and the shelling and bloodshed got under his skin. His decision to desert, however, was not motivated by fear or shell-shock. In June 1944, Maria discovered she was pregnant and was terrified of the derision she would receive from her family and friends. Bill decided to protect her: they should leave Naples. They could be married in Rome, he told her; the war would end soon, and when it did—and after the child was born—they could return to Naples. In this way, they could save Maria's reputation. On July 28, Bill left his ship, and together he and Maria hitchhiked along the Via Casilina to Rome. When they arrived, Bill began introducing Maria as his wife and they moved into the house on Via Pistoia.

In the annals of the Royal Navy, Maria is perhaps the most unusual witness ever to testify at a court martial. On March 16, 1945, at nine thirty in the morning, she took the stand for Bill's trial. Maria brought her baby, and as she began her testimony, she began breast-feeding. "In typical naval fashion," wrote Gardner and Babington of the incident, "nobody batted an eyelid."[20]

As in the trials of Honess and Pringle, the prosecution wanted to use Maria's evidence to corroborate Bill Holton's story and to establish a credible sequence of events. The fact that she was giving evidence against her lover, however, gave her testimony at Bill Croft's trial an extra melancholy. Croft's defender tried to use her pained replies to soften the character of his client.

"Miss Fedele," he asked her, "why did Bill take you to Rome?"

"I do not know why."

"Did you pass as his wife?"

"Yes."

"Whose baby is that?"

"His, Bill's."

"Was it your intention to be married to Bill?"

"Yes."

Croft's defender had Maria describe life at Via Pistoia; her evidence painted a picture more applicable to a cozy homestead than to a den of thieves. The defence even suggested that Lucky, the perennial trouble-maker, offered to purchase clothes for her baby. "What was Lucky's attitude towards you and towards the coming birth of Bill's child?" Maria was asked. "He was very kind to me," she replied.

Croft's defender had the advantage of having attended Harold Pringle's trial, and he built his case on the gaps he saw left open. For instance, when the prosecution once again called Holton, the defence was ready to chip away at his character. Croft's defender described him as "the gentleman who turned King's evidence" and under cross-examination forced Holton to admit he made "lying statements." The defence made Holton concede that, though he was a late arrival to the Sailor Gang, in the seven days he spent with them he committed three robberies. He also established that Holton had what could most charitably be described as a very hazy recollection of the events of the night of November 1. In his opening exchange, the defence rendered Holton's testimony almost worthless.

"You have made various statements to people about the affairs which you had witnessed of this particular gang?"

"Yes, sir."

"In other words, you have not proved at all consistent in any of your statements?"

"I do not quite understand."

"Your statements are not consistent, are they?"

"No."

"In other words, you are not a person to be believed, are you?"

"That is a matter of opinion."

"Yes, it is quite right. You, I believe, are now serving a sentence as a deserter, are you not?"

"As an absentee."

"As an absentee, yes. Were you asked to come here to give evidence against Croft?"

"Yes, sir."

"Do you know that Croft said that you had nothing to do with this particular crime?"

"No, sir."

"You are quite prepared, in order to save your own neck, to come and testify against your erstwhile friend, are you not?"

"Yes, sir."

"That is the sort of man you are?"

"Yes, sir."

"That is the sort of man the Court is expected to believe here today?"

"Yes, sir."

"Despite all the contrary and inconsistent statements?"

"Yes, sir."

In its summation, the defence catalogued Holton's inconsistencies. The effect was almost comical. In his first statement to the police Holton had maintained that "Honess appeared when we were at 28 Via Pistoia." Under cross-examination he admitted, "He first came to the house Pringle and I lived at." In his first statement Holton had claimed that Croft said, "Let them fight it out between themselves." In court Holton conceded, "I cannot definitely swear that he said that." In his first statement Holton had maintained that Croft had taken Lucky's revolver. In court he conceded that he had taken it. Holton had originally told SIB detective Brown that after Honess shot Lucky, Joe Pringle said, "That was a crazy thing to do," and that Croft said, "Stop arguing, we have to get him to hospital." Croft's defender had Holton acknowledge that he had changed his story to "Someone behind me said, 'Let's get him to a hospital,' Pringle I think," and claimed that it was he, Bill Holton, who had said, "That was a crazy thing to do." Croft's defending officer revealed to a stunned panel that in his first statement to police, Holton had sworn that he exited the jeep before it drove to Torre Gaia. Holton had maintained that he "stayed there for about twenty minutes, when I heard the jeep coming back." Under cross-examination, Holton admitted that his first statement was a "fairy-story."

Croft's defender called another medical expert, Major John Cunningham from the 92nd British General Hospital. Cunningham had fourteen years' experience as a pathologist, twelve of which he had spent doing autopsies; he had performed between 1,500 and 2,000 autopsies in his career. Like Fielden, Cunningham concluded that Lucky had suffered a wound to the liver, which he considered "particularly dangerous… early death is always likely in any wound of the liver." He said that both Harold Pringle's and Bill Croft's shots were likely administered after death. Cunningham explained that it would not be possible to guarantee Lucky's state at the end of the ride from Via Pistoia; the most a doctor could do was to "surmise." Cunningham said that the treatment Lucky received—a ride over rough roads at high speeds—was the worst possible given his wound. He estimated "death within an hour."

At Croft's trial a complete account of what happened the night of November 1, 1944, was finally given. Croft gave evidence—and for the first time, so did a jittery Harold Pringle. The stress of living under a death sentence was taking its toll. Croft's and Pringle's versions of events had similarities to those that had preceded them, but their versions, unlike the others, had a convincing mixture of panic, self-interest and fate.

Up to Honess's shooting of Lucky, the stories matched. Harold came down the stairs from Bill Croft's room to find Lucky on the floor bleeding. Honess was kneeling down beside him. Holton was there; he said, "That was a crazy thing to do." Then Harold Pringle declared that they had better get a doctor, and he went to get the jeep. By this time, Croft was downstairs. The gang always had a supply of half-complete passes ready in case of emergency, and Croft raced back up to his room to get a pile of trip tickets and a pass for Lucky. Croft tried to slip on his paratrooper's boots, but it took too much time so he ran out the front door of Via Pistoia in his socks just as the jeep was driving off. Before he left, Maria tried to convince him to stay home. "Don't go," she said in Italian, "I am afraid." Pringle saw Croft as he was pulling out of the driveway and he stopped the jeep, noticing that Croft had no shoes on and was carrying a white slip of paper. Croft said that his "intention was to give them the pass and let them go to the hospital with it, but then I jumped in the jeep." He got in and rested Lucky's head on his lap.

Bill Croft had decided that he was not going to let Joe Pringle and the rest be responsible for Lucky. When they arrived at the military hospital, somebody with a little tact would be needed to smooth Lucky's admittance; otherwise they might tip the military police to the fact that they were deserters. They had trip tickets and passes, which should have sufficed, but other strange questions might need to be answered with a bribe. Throughout the trials of the Sailor Gang, various prosecutors tried to undermine the gang's stories by suggesting that a gang of deserters would never willingly venture into an army base hospital—they would be too afraid of arrest. Viewed in the context of the gang's habits, this point was unfounded. Yes, the Sailor Gang feared the military police, but they socialized regularly with other ranks. Lucky, in particular, made a habit of drinking with GIs and Canadians; the soldiers would carouse with Lucky, then he would chauffeur them back to base. Once, after driving a group of drunken soldiers back to their barracks, Lucky had his gun confiscated by an officer who disapproved of his having left it sitting on the passenger's seat. The officer had simply examined his fake pass and then taken his gun.

At Re di Roma, Harold saw a jeep that he thought was a military police vehicle because it slowed down as they passed it. He turned and told someone to get Lucky's feet back in. Croft grabbed Lucky by the shoulders and pulled him in. Then the men in the jeep became quite quiet. Nothing was said as the jeep raced through the empty, ancient city. They drove out along the Via Appia, noticing that even the prostitutes, who usually worked this strip hoping to greet soldiers on their way into the city, were gone. Along the road there were ruins, Roman columns and medieval arches. Umbrella pine trees, the flat variety found all around Rome, lined the road. The night was black, but not completely: one could make out shapes.

"Take it easy, Joe," Lucky said when the jeep crossed some tramlines. He repeated this request twice more, each time sounding more faint. Then Lucky was very still. Croft reached down and felt his pulse. "He's going, Joe," he said to Pringle.

"What was that?" asked Honess.

"I said he's going," Croft answered back.

Croft continued reading Lucky's pulse. "He's going."

Harold drove faster while Honess looked over his shoulder back toward Lucky. Holton sat quietly, with Lucky's feet across his lap, as night closed in around the Sailor Gang. Croft pressed down harder, trying to raise a pulse. Nothing. "He's had it, Joe," he said. "He's gone." Somebody said to look for a turning. Honess saw one and told Joe to turn off to the left. The jeep's lights were turned off, and they drove down a very bumpy patch of muddy road, so muddy that Harold had to put the jeep into four-wheel drive. When the road ended, Harold stopped the jeep. Holton, Honess and Croft jumped out, while Harold stayed a moment and reached back to feel Lucky's pulse. He had learned how to take a pulse while he was in hospital in England; Harold would help the orderlies out. He too felt no pulse. Harold sat there a second, frozen: Lucky was dead.

Harold was pulled back to the moment by the feel of Lucky's body being removed from the jeep. The men lifted Lucky out and carried him a few yards, laying him face up in front of the jeep. In the distance, you could see a few farmhouses. There was a pine tree not far away.

Harold stepped forward and drew his Beretta. He pointed it at Lucky's face. Harold stared at the face of his friend. Croft told him, "If you fire at a dead body it won't haunt you." Harold kept looking at Lucky lying on the ground. Then he repeated the words: "If you fire at a dead body it won't haunt you." Harold pointed his Beretta at Lucky's head and squeezed the trigger, but he flinched as he did so, turning his head away, and instead of firing into Lucky's skull, the bullet passed into his chest. There was no movement. At the same time, Croft was standing on the other side. "I leveled the pistol at the face of the corpse, tightened on the trigger and I balked," he testified.

"How do you mean, balked," the prosecutor asked him.

"Looking into the face of a man who had been my companion for two and a half months, sir."

"Yes?"

"I did not relish the job I was doing."

Croft's gun misfired six times. It was empty; Pringle, Honess and Holton heard clicks.

"Lend me yours, Joe," Croft said.

Harold gave him the Beretta. Croft knelt and fired, point-blank, into Lucky's head. Again there was no movement.

For a moment, the four men stood motionless as they tried to comprehend what they had just done. Honess and Holton walked up from the jeep, where they had been standing. The men lifted Lucky and carried him over to an old irrigation ditch. Honess and Holton lowered Lucky in until he was completely submerged, in a sitting position. Pringle appeared with a tree branch in his hand. He laid it on top of Lucky. The others pulled up some grass and threw it on him. Then they returned to the jeep. As they got in, Holton said, "A waste of a bullet, but I owed him one."

The Sailor Gang then drove back out of Torre Gaia and onto Route 6. There was little conversation. Croft lit a cigarette to quiet his nerves. Honess said, "If anybody asks, tell them Lucky's gone to Naples." Then Honess caught Holton's eyes: "And don't get any ideas about telling anybody, or you're going to join him in Naples."

"Oh, don't worry," Croft said. "The kid's all right."

When the men returned to Via Pistoia, they immediately went to Lucky's room and searched it, looking for any of his possessions. Honess claimed Lucky's winter jacket. Holton grabbed his revolver. Pringle got his shoes. They gave Lucky's Italian girlfriend a little money and his boots. Then Croft made a small fire and they burned the rest of Lucky's belongings. Holton, Honess and Pringle went back to their flat on Via Cesena. The following morning, Croft and Maria moved out and the Sailor Gang dispersed.

To counter this story, the prosecution called a new witness, former Sailor Gang cohort Walter Glaser, otherwise known as "Slim."

Glaser appears to have been picked up on November 19, along with Holton and Bobbie Williams, the C Ration Kid. The men were suspected of armed robbery, but the SIB had been unable to find enough witnesses to make it stick. Nevertheless, there were plenty of other charges to lay. The SIB wanted to wrap up investigations in a number of murders, and they let the soldiers know that anyone who could be of assistance would be given a walk. Holton stepped up with his story of Lucky's murder. The C Ration Kid kept silent. Slim was evasive; he told what he knew, which wasn't much. The police recorded his statement and placed it on the pile. When Croft's prosecutor discovered it, he thought he had found the testimony that would seal his case for reasonable doubt.

Glaser was called, and the defence had him relate a number of meetings that had been held by the Sailor Gang shortly after November 1, 1944. Glaser described Lucky as "hot-headed and bad-tempered. He would fight anyone all the time.... He thought he could rule everybody. We were all pretty good friends with one another except for this Lucky." Glaser spoke about the C Ration Kid's crush on Maria, and his cruel teasing. Glaser said that C Ration had offered her one hundred dollars to sleep with him. He told the court that C Ration had gone to 28 Via Pistoia when Croft was not around and told Maria, "Croft ain't coming back. Bill ain't coming back no more. He's leaving, you know. I want you to live with me. I'll give you money and buy you clothes. Croft is no good." Glaser recalled meeting Croft at his girlfriend's house in early November. "I asked him why everybody was up there," he said.

"What did he say when you asked him why he was up there?"

"'Better place,' sir."

"And what else did he say?"

"That's about all I remember."

"What other conversations did you have with him?"

"I don't remember. I was just talking."

"Yes, but what did you talk to him about?"

"Well, everything in general, I guess. Talking about me mostly."

"Did Bill talk to you about his friends?"

"No, he didn't do that, sir."

Glaser said that he and Croft discussed going up to Leghorn, the Allied name for the seaport of Livorno. The soldiers were interested in getting on a ship leaving Italy. That night, Glaser said, the men met at a bar on the Via Appia.

"Now can you tell us what the conversation after that was about?"

"About this fellow, Lucky."

"What was the conversation about Lucky?"

"Well, they said he was dead."

"Who said he was dead?"

"I do not recall who said it, because it was said in a bar, and while we were drinking."

"Who was present then?"

"Myself, Bill Croft, Joe, Charlie, and Bill Holton."

"And you were in a café?"

"Yes."

"And somebody said Lucky was dead."

"That is right."

"Was anything said about how that came about?"

"He had an argument with this guy Charlie."

"And then what was said?"

"That Charlie shot him, it was not only that, it was all drawn out over a space of a few hours."

"Do you mean the conversation in the bar, or do you mean the…?"

"I am speaking of the shooting."

"It was drawn out over a few hours?"

"The way it was explained to me, that is."

"Yes, the way it was explained to you. Was anything said as to how he was shot?"

"There was."

"What was said about that?"

"They said that he had gotten into an argument in this restaurant. That was Charlie and Lucky. Croft was not present."

"Not present in the argument?"

"Not present in the restaurant."

"And then what was said?"

"They said this fellow Lucky left this fellow Charlie in the restaurant and took off, went out, and then Charlie left later on and went back to the house and waited for him in Lucky's room."

"Yes, and then what happened?"

"Well, they was explaining that he come back to the room and got into another argument there and this guy Lucky started calling Charlie names and then Charlie started calling him names back and then I do not know, they were both half drunk in the hall, and something about pulling out guns, and how that one guy Charlie told him to pull out his gun, he pulled out his gun, then he pulled out his gun and bang and shot him."

"And then what was said as to what happened?"

"Well, they said he was a trouble maker, that's all."

"Who said that?"

"We all agreed on that, we all said so, no one specifically."

"Was anything more said about what happened after that shot was fired?"

"After the shot was fired it woke Croft up, the shot and he come running down the stairs to see what was the matter and Lucky was there bleeding, says he wanted to be taken to a hospital, this guy Lucky said that; then Croft left and went up to get his shoes to take him to hospital and from there on I am rather hazy about what happened, and I do not quite recall, except something about putting him in a jeep and I know they finally got him into a jeep and took him outside Rome and I think he was shot again."

"Try and remember, if you can. You say you think he was shot again?"

"I know he was shot again."

Glaser told the court that at the bar on the Via Appia, Charlie Honess had said that Lucky was threatening to turn the Sailor Gang in to the cops. It was tough for him to remember, "we was all drinking very heavily." Glaser said that Pringle had shot Lucky but he (Honess) could not be sure of the timing of the shot.

"Well," Glaser said, "he was put in the jeep, and he was taken out about 20 kilometres or 25 kilometres—I don't remember the exact distance— and he was put on the ground. He was dead when they laid him out on the ground. Then they told me that they made Croft shoot him after he was dead, but this fellow Charlie made it clear to me that he was already dead. He say'd that they did that more or less to have everybody in it."

"Yes. Now was there anything else you want to say? You were telling your own story."

"Well, yes, they made it clear that they always wanted to hold Croft under the impression that he had shot him—that Croft had killed him. But they stated that Croft did not kill him."

"Was anything else said? About the events that took place?"

"No, I guess that covers it."

It was damaging testimony from a witness who was supposed to help the case for the prosecution. Glaser tried to correct his mistake, after recounting an entire story that maintained Lucky had been dead, by professing that "I did not believe that this fellow was dead." It was too little too late. "Private Glaser," observed Croft's defender, "was an important witness for the prosecution and yet he said Honess told him in a bar that Lucky was dead."

In his closing address, Croft's defender touched on many of the points Bergman had accentuated in his defence of Pringle. He noted that Holton was an accomplice and that it was dangerous to convict on the evidence of an accomplice. He stated that two medical experts with vastly greater experience than the prosecutor's pathologist had determined that Lucky was dead when he was laid on the field. He tried to explain Harold Pringle's jittery testimony. "In view of the circumstances and mental strain under which Pringle has been living since his arrest shortly after the crime was committed," he said of the Canadian, "one may think that he gave his evidence as well as could be expected from a man who is naturally in a state of nervous tension." Croft's defender explained why Pringle had not read Honess's statement fully: "In effect, he said, 'Yes, I agree with that, it has really got nothing to do with me, he was already dead, yes, it's just the same from there on.'" Croft's defender brought to the panel's attention inconsistencies in the interrogation made by the SIB: Croft refused to give a statement until February; his defender said that Croft had asked to see a naval legal officer but had been denied the opportunity. Sergeant Brown testified that "he did not ask me if he could see a Naval Officer." But his partner, Sergeant Swetnam, testifying about the same meeting, said that Croft "said something about seeing a Naval legal officer."

"I suggest," said Croft's defender, "that Brown and Swetnam, and especially Swetnam, were not carrying out their duties as they should."

"One last word," Croft's lawyer argued in his closing address.

> Members of the Court, I would like to say this, that if Croft were being tried in England for the charge of murder, he would have at his disposal the finest legal brains in the country, he would be defended by King's Counsel, with a junior barrister to assist him; further his Solicitors would have at their disposal all the textbooks and learned tomes on the subject, and a Case Law from

which to choose; it is Croft's misfortune that he should of neces-
sity be defended by me, who, I am in the unfortunate position of
having little experience and no access to the works I have referred
to. I therefore, members of the Court, entreat you not to let him
suffer on account of any lack of knowledge, or lack of compe-
tence on my part, and that any shortcomings which can be
imputed to me, that they go in his favour and that those few
grains of mercy which we so often hear about, if there is in your
minds any reasonable doubt in this case, that may be thrown on
the side of the accused, William Robert Croft. I do finally say to
you that here we have a man who in the next few hours will at
your hands either be returned to the world, or will be sent to his
death. It is probably, Members of the Court, the first time in
which you have held a man's life upon your shoulders—well, I am
quite sure that you will give this matter all the consideration that
it deserves, and the burden I have carried for the last four days—
and it has been very heavy—I now assign to your shoulders.

The panel retired for two hours. They returned, and the verdict was
read: Guilty. Croft's defender made a plea for mercy:

I informed the court this morning that Petty Officer Croft was
born 21 years ago and that at the age of 15 he was thrown into a
position where he had to fend for himself. The court has heard
his history, how he left school at the age of fourteen and at fifteen
he went to sea. Croft, gentlemen, has been thrown into this unfortunate net. He is the child of an unhappy age when, almost from
the time that he could begin to understand things, men have been
killing each other. I do suggest to the members of the Court that
his extreme youthfulness be taken into consideration in considering and deciding the sentence and the lack of opportunity that
he had.

The panel assembled twenty minutes later and sentenced Croft to
death.

15.

AN INVIDIOUS POSITION

Norman Bergman filed a petition against Harold Pringle's guilty verdict on March 26, 1945, ten days after Croft's trial ended. The young legal officer put great effort into preparing a three-page summary, written in the first person as if spoken by Harold and accompanied by trial transcripts from the Sailor's court martial. In the petition, Bergman maintained that the evidence brought forth at subsequent trials proved that Lucky was dead at the time that Pringle and Croft fired at his body. He wrote that Glaser's testimony and Fielden's medical evidence established substantial reasonable doubt as to Harold Pringle's guilt. The evidence shows, the petition stated, "that there was no preconceived idea to take Lucky for a ride....Our sole concern was to get Lucky proper medical attention." It argued that Holton should have been tried as an accomplice for the murder, since he aided and abetted the transport of Lucky's body. "To uphold my conviction for murder," it concluded, "would amount to a substantial injustice."[1]

Harold was held at Number 1 British Military Prison and Detention Barracks while he waited for the Judge Advocate General to consider his petition. The compound was located north of Rome, along the Tiber River. In *Execution*, Colin McDougall described its grounds: "Everywhere was the constant, pervading scent of pine trees. Between the buildings one walked on a carpet of sweet-smelling needles and cones. To the

Canadian soldiers this forest might have seemed reminiscent of home, except that the stand of pines was too deliberate, too consciously cultivated."[2] Since Harold was facing a death sentence, he was considered an escape risk and was kept under close guard and received no visitors. During the day, soldiers in the general population sometimes saw him looking out his cell window into the exercise yard below. A Canadian soldier under sentence recalled running laps in the prison yard and calling up to a man who spent every afternoon at his window. "The next time I come around, tell me your name," the soldier yelled up. On his next trip by, the figure called down, "Harold Pringle." The British sentries, with the exception of a Staff Sergeant Murphy, were not fond of their Canadian charge. Another former Canadian soldier remembered how Harold sometimes extended his hand through the bars as the other prisoners walked past. The men would slap his hand as a form of solidarity. Once, after this particular soldier had greeted Harold, a British sentry struck the soldier's hand with a billy club and then smashed the club against Harold. After the war, whenever he was out in public, this soldier made a habit of looking for the sentry, hoping that he might have a chance at revenge.[3]

Since January, Number 1 Military Prison's chaplain, a Canadian named Father B. S. Farrell, had ministered to Harold. Under Father Farrell's guidance, Harold began dedicating himself to Catholicism, praying daily and accepting mass each morning. The priest was the only company Harold was allowed while in detention, and the pair became friends, playing cards together and chatting about life back in Canada. In March, Father Farrell sent a letter to Major A. L. Louden, an officer at headquarters in Rome. Norman Bergman included it in Harold's petition:

My dear Major Louden,
I sincerely hope you will accept this letter in the spirit in which it is written. If in writing it, I offend against any canons of Military Law or legal procedure, I confess my mistake and plead ignorance of these matters. If, on the other hand, this letter can be of any use in any way, I ask you to use it as you will and if there is any other further course of action that you think I can take to supple-

ment and substantiate what I have written, I most earnestly ask
you to advise me whenever you can.

My purpose in addressing this letter to you is to plead for the
life of the Canadian soldier Harold Pringle who has been convicted of a capital charge. God forbid that for a moment you
might think that I am unaware of the gravity of the offence with
which Pringle has been charged and found guilty, nor is it my
slightest intention to question in any way the procedure whereby
this verdict has been reached. My plea is a plea for mercy based
on what I venture to claim as an intimate knowledge of the general character of the man himself. For some considerable time
now I have made a practice of spending about half an hour a day
alone with Pringle. I may have started these visits out of a sense of
Christian charity and of my duties as a Chaplain to the prison
where he is detained, but as my acquaintance grew I began to be
attracted to the man himself and now I can say with the greatest
sincerity that I look forward to the periods I spend with him.
Nothing will ever convince me that he is in any sense of the word
a criminal by nature. It would certainly appear from the account
of the trial that he got himself mixed up in some very wicked
company but the lad, I am convinced, is good at heart. During the
whole time I have known him, I have been struck by his obvious
desire to give not one whit of trouble to those in charge of him
and I have no complaint from him despite his long hours alone
both before and after his trial. The only thing he asked for with
any persistency has been the permission to smoke.

His whole concern seems to centre on his father and mother
and on the terrible blow that will befall them when they hear
what a plight he has got into. He often tells me of his father who
was a Sniper Sergeant throughout the last war and who volunteered to come to England with the Canadians in this in order,
amongst other things, to be near his son and so to look after him.
I believe they were in the same unit in England though his father
returned to Canada some time ago. As a priest I have been gen-
uinely edified at the generous and appreciative way he has

responded to real genuine prayer and devotion which simply cannot be anything but absolutely and completely sincere. I have been a Chaplain now since the outbreak of the War and I have met all types and conditions of men and I have never felt more convinced of a man's fundamental goodness than I have of Pringle's. For myself, if Pringle were a free man tomorrow, I should jump at the chance of employing him in any capacity.

Before God then and as a Minister of God whose sole charge is the betterment of man, I assert without hesitation that this man Pringle can and will make good if those whose difficult and responsible duty it is to judge finally on his case can see their way to extending to him something of the Mercy of Christ and so commute the death sentence to one less severe both for Pringle and those dear to him. Maybe the thought of the victory which now is ours will help soften the hearts towards one who as a lad of eighteen started bravely to serve the cause even though he had since fallen by the way.

I may add in conclusion that Pringle himself is entirely unaware of the fact of my having written this letter.

I remain, my Dear Major,

Yours sincerely,

B. S. Farrell, C. F. Roman Catholic Chaplain.[4]

Father Farrell was not the only one writing letters. By early April, Harold had written his parish priest in Flinton and asked him to explain his situation to his parents. On April 6, Harold sent a letter home. The grammar and spelling are Harold's own.

My Darling Mother + Dad,

Just a few lines again to say I am well and in the very best of health. And I sure hope and pray this few lines fine you all in the best of health. Well Mother Darling it is about three months since I first written but received no answer yet. So I sure hope you are getting my letters ok now. And if you are please write real soon. How is everyone around Flinton I sure hope they are all in good

health also give them my best regards. The war news is looking
much better now. There was a Canadian officer down to see me
to day and is trying to trace my mail for me. And will I ever be
glad when I hear from you it seems like years since I last had a
letter so please write real soon. By the way has Father Kinlin been
up to see you yet. Well Mother Dear I havent heard anything
more about my trial yet. But I will let you no just as soon as the
papers come back which I dont think it will be much longer. And
again Mother please dont worry about to much. How are all the
folks down at Grandmas I sure hope they are all well. Give them
my best regards. Well Mother the Catholic Priest of the camp is
very good to us all. And his name is Rev Father Farrell. I have
been going to Holy Communion every morning so please
dont worry.[5]

Harold's friend Charlie Honess was not so optimistic. On April 4,
the British army informed his wife and parents of his impending execution. The Honess family was shocked. They responded by writing the
British military authorities in London and informing them of their son's
distinguished military record. Prior to deserting in Italy, Charlie had
never had any disciplinary action taken against him. A British officer
relayed their plea to Rome:

Husband wounded in back in 1940/41 London Blitz while in
bomb disposal unit. Thereafter nerves shaken and subject to fits
of depression. Later sent overseas without embarkation leave
causing him to write very worried letters.

Last July home of Honess's parents with whom wife lived was
destroyed by enemy action and wife had to leave it. Honess's
mother informed him of this and all letters from wife to Honess
since that date have been returned to her.

Wife represents that these troubles must have unbalanced his
mind as he was placid type and never showed any signs of running riot.[6]

The officer asked British Headquarters if the sentence had already been carried out. If not, he wanted to learn if the panel at Honess's court martial had been aware of his record before it sentenced him to death. The officer directed the British in Rome to have a military psychiatrist examine Honess, and the Royal Navy's legal department, which was handling the case against Bill Croft, was also notified of the Honess assessment. The navy was told that if Honess were to be found mentally unstable, he might not be executed. A naval legal officer, however, reported that "it was not anticipated that this [assessment] was likely to materially affect the case and subject to this it was intended to carry out the sentence."[7]

The following day, his prediction proved true. A British military psychiatrist, Major H. A. C. Mason, interviewed Honess. He reported that the Sapper had left school at age fourteen and at age fifteen had enlisted in the army but had been discharged after his father objected. The doctor found "no signs of thought disorder or an abnormal emotional state, though I judged him to be a somewhat restless individual liable to moods."[8] In short, Honess may have been messed up, but he was certainly sane enough to be executed.

On April 11, 1945, Lieutenant Colonel A. Winter, the commandant of Number 1 Military Prison, met with Charlie Honess and told the Sapper that the army had confirmed his sentence and that he was to be executed on April 13. Honess met briefly with his lawyer, Lieutenant Barnes, and discussed possible courses of action. Barnes may have told Honess that to press on against the verdict would be futile and would cause undue embarrassment and suffering. Then again, he may have tried to convince Honess to fight the conviction. Perhaps the Sapper had no confidence in his own innocence—after all he had been drunk that night, and his had been the first shot to hit Lucky. It was, as he said at his trial, his party. Perhaps Honess was unwilling to spend a long stretch in prison. And when he got out, what then? Back to England? To do what? Perhaps Cecil Henry Frederick Honess began to see his time in Rome as a sort of limbo, and if it had been nothing more than a stopover there was no reason to delay the inevitable. He dictated a short note and signed it:

The sentence of death awarded by the Court and confirmed by the Supreme Allied Commander has been promulgated to me. I have discussed with Lieutenant Barnes, my Defending Officer, the desirability of submitting a petition against the sentence and I have decided that I do not wish to do so.

C. H. F. Honess.[9]

Two days later, at Forte Bravetta, where the Nazis had held their firing squads, a party of thirty soldiers from the Cheshire Regiment assembled in the courtyard. Present were Lieutenant Colonel Winter, along with a chaplain, a medical officer and two majors from the Provost Corps. Before Honess was brought out, the doctor offered him an injection of morphine, which he accepted. In death, Charlie Honess meant to be no trouble to anyone, not even himself.

Honess's arms were tied behind his back and he was blindfolded by a sergeant, who noticed that the Sapper's hair was neatly combed. Brown earth clung to Honess's boots as he was marched out a short distance to a stake that had been anchored in the ground in front of a wall pocked with bullet holes from previous executions. The doctor had given him a strong dose, and as the morphine began to kick in, Honess became woozy and had to be propped up by two soldiers. The firing squad stood silently, waiting for their target. If the men had a chance to look upwards, they would have seen pine trees and palms poking their bows above the walls of Forte Bravetta beneath a grey sky. Lieutenant Colonel Winter, a decorated veteran of the First World War, stood at attention. At precisely eight in the morning, a British major gave the order to fire. The shots rang out and Honess slumped over dead, like Lucky, of multiple gunshot wounds.

Honess's body was quickly removed; the Cheshires were dispersed and marched off to the mess for an issue of rum. The Sapper's body was prepared for burial and driven to the military cemetery in the southwest end of Rome. The graveyard was opposite the famous Protestant cemetery where Percy Bysshe Shelley and John Keats were buried. "It might make one in love with death," Shelley once wrote of the surroundings, "to think that one should be buried in so sweet a place."[10] Honess was given a small service, attended by the chaplain, the men who dug his grave and, strangely, the commandant of the prison. Lieutenant Colonel Winter had no official reason to attend the funeral, but perhaps there was something about the plight of the troubled Sapper that led him to pay his respects. Eventually, the cemetery would hold 429 servicemen. At the time of Honess's burial, no one realized that he was being interred a few feet from the man who had once given him driving lessons and whom he was convicted of killing. Lucky McGillivary's grave lay only three rows away.

AT THE SAME TIME THAT the army was executing Honess, the Royal Navy's legal branch was examining Bill Croft's trial, trying to determine if the proceedings had been fair and if the sentence of death should be confirmed.

The head of the legal branch, N. J. Skelhorn, believed that there was no doubt as to the propriety of the conviction, although he allowed that if the trial rested entirely on medical evidence then there might be reasonable doubt. The testimony of Major Fielden and Major Cunningham had more than established that Lucky might have died in the jeep on the way out of Rome, Skelhorn noted. He reported that the Canadian authorities were trying to determine if there was a military hospital in the vicinity of Torre Gaia, as this might support Croft's and Pringle's alibis. He observed, however, inconsistencies in Croft's and Pringle's testimonies, specifically the statements that were made to the SIB in December. He said that Croft's explanation—that the shots were an attempt to disfigure Lucky—was a "very unlikely one." The summary was circulated at British Legal Headquarters.[11]

This was not, however, a clear case of confirming a sentence. Honess had been found guilty of Lucky's murder, but it was possible that the other suspects were innocent. Skelhorn and the Royal Navy's legal department were very mindful of the fact that there were two soldiers accused of participating in the same crime after Honess's shot, and that it would be diplomatically uncomfortable if one side were to execute their man and the other did not. "An invidious position might arise if the sentence of death on Croft were to be carried out and the Canadian Authorities were subsequently to commute the sentence on Pringle,"

Skelhorn explained in a three-page summary of the case. "The part taken by the Canadian soldier in this crime was in all material respects the same as that which the accused took, and I have been keeping in touch with the Canadian Military Authorities here with a view to, if possible, co-ordinating the decision as to whether this conviction should be confirmed with their decision."[12] In short, it would be ideal if the Canadians and British would both execute their men at about the same time.

When this report was sent to the Royal Navy's upper ranks, the contradictory medical evidence set off alarm bells. One reader noted, "It would appear to be quite without the scope of the ordinary doctor to express an opinion that would be of value or carry sufficient weight. The Police Research Laboratory, Sir Bernard Spilsbury or someone similar would be more appropriate to advise."[13]

Sir Bernard Spilsbury was a British pathologist who had pioneered the use of forensics to solve criminal cases and whom many considered to be the father of modern pathology.[14] Spilsbury became famous at the beginning of the century through his work on the 1910 Crippen case. Subsequently, many of the most infamous and complicated British homicide cases of the 1930s and 1940s were solved by Spilsbury's analysis. In honour of these achievements, he had been knighted in 1925. On May 11, 1945, the sixty-nine-year-old pathologist examined the original autopsy report made by Major Jones and read through the transcript of Bill Croft's trial.

In a three-page handwritten report, Spilsbury concluded that the first wound to Lucky's liver was inflicted in the upper part of the organ. He said that this wound would not produce extensive bleeding. He observed that Lucky's comment, "It does not matter, it's only my hand or my arm," demonstrated that he was not severely shocked. Spilsbury did not consider Lucky's other reported comments, including "Take me to a hospital," to signify that the liver wound was life-threatening. The second wound, to the lung, should have caused ready bleeding, but Spilsbury determined that the shock from the wound had delayed the flow of blood. He concluded that the lethal wound had been the last gunshot, the one fired by Bill Croft into Lucky's head: "My opinion therefore is that McGillivary was neither killed nor rendered unconscious by the bullet wound in the abdomen but that he was killed instantly by the bullet through the brain." Spilsbury ended his report by expressing his "appreciation of the care and thoroughness with which Major A. C. Jones R.A.M.C. carried out his examination of the dead body."[15]

Spilsbury's report was circulated to the British Navy's top legal minds, who, with the reputation of Britain's greatest forensic scientist behind their verdict, felt certain of Croft's guilt. Nonetheless, the report was kept secret. Croft's lawyer was never informed of its existence, and it was never tested by any sort of cross-examination. Any doubt that the Royal Navy might have had about Croft's guilt was also assuaged by their belief that this was not just a case of a single murder. In a handful of documents on Croft's case, there are frequent references to other alleged wrongdoings. "It may not be improper to take note of the Commander in Chief's statement that there are many other charges," wrote a Royal Navy officer, "including two of murder and several of armed robbery, outstanding against the man."[16] These murders were, in fact, unsolved cases that had occurred in and around Rome in 1944 and in which deserters were suspected. It appears, however, that no official charges were ever laid against Croft or any of the other men in the Sailor Gang. It may be that the SIB's detectives, who knew they had little chance of solving these cases, seized the chance to pin them on deserters who were already in custody and heading for a firing squad.

Armed with a report from Sir Bernard Spilsbury and a suspicion that if not entirely guilty of one crime Croft was probably guilty of others, the navy was ready to confirm its verdict and sentence. The British Admiralty determined that "no ground is seen for differing from the conclusion reached by the court and if the conviction was proper, there appear to be no mitigating circumstances which would justify a recommendation to His Majesty that the sentence should be commuted."[17]

What the British Admiralty did not know, however, was that it had based its judgment on the observations of a mentally spent pathologist. By 1945, the war had taken its toll on Sir Bernard Spilsbury and he was a man in trouble. Spilsbury had suffered a stroke and was living in comparative poverty; his testimony was no longer considered unimpeachable by the scientific community. In 1940, his son Peter Spilsbury, a doctor working in London, had been killed during a bombing raid. "From that day," wrote Douglas G. Browne and E. V. Tullett in *Bernard Spilsbury: His Life and Cases*, "as more than one [friend] has put it, 'he began to fail.'"[18] That year, his eldest sister also died. In 1945, Spilsbury's friends noticed a growing decline in his health and in his mental alertness. They still considered his medical conclusions to be sound, but the process was taking longer. He suffered from insomnia, and a few months after reviewing Croft's case he suffered another stroke. By 1947, it was too much. Spilsbury locked himself in his small laboratory office, turned on the gas and committed suicide.

BOTH HAROLD PRINGLE and Bill Croft lived to see the end of the war in Europe. On May 7, 1945, the day Germany surrendered, Harold wrote a letter home:

> My Darling Mother,
> Just a few lines again to say I am well and in the very best of
> health And I sure hope and pray that this few lines fine you all in
> the very best of health. Say Darling Mother I sure was glad to hear
> from Dad. But he sure didnt give much news. The war is sure
> looking much better now. And I think it will be over by the time
> you get this At least I sure hope so. How are all the Folks down at
> Grandmas I sure hope they are all well and in good health. Also
> give them all my best regards. Dad was telling me in his letter that
> he thought Neil Freeburn was dead. But I sure that it is not so. As
> Neil sure was a good friend of mine. I guess Demore Bosley had
> some bad luck with his wife. But I guess he will get over it If you
> see him tell him to drop me a few lines also give him my best
> regards. And is he still in Flinton yet or where. Say sure hope that
> Charlie doesn't have to go in the army But if he does it wont be
> for long anyway.
>   Well mother have you seen Father Kinlin lately. And if he has
> told you please dont worry. Father Farrell wrote to him some
> time ago so I sure hope that he got the letter Say Mother Darling
> I sure am glad you are getting my letters ok again And please

forgive me for not writing before. By the time you get this letter I
think I will have some news about my trial And I will let you no
just as soon as I find out. But in the mean time please dont worry
How are all the folks around Flinton I hope they are all in the
best of health. Also give them my best regards. Say Mother
Darling where is Father Kinlin now Is he still in the same place I
sure hope so as that is the address I gave to Father Farrell. Say
how are all my sweet brothers + sisters I hope all in good health. I
guess they have all forgotten me haven't they. Mother Dear if they
have any photos around the house please send me some of you
all. As I lost all which I had in the front. Try and get one taken
all together.

Say Mother did you every get those last pictures I sent you. If
so what did you think of them. There sure isnt much new to
night. But I will write again real soon. I sure hope Marion is in
the best of health also. Barbie and husband. And what is Howard
doing. Also how does he like married life. I hope ok.

Well Mother Darling I guess I will ring off for to night. But I
will write again real soon. And hope to hear from you again in the
mean time. So ontil then I will say cheerio for now. With the very
best of luck. And God bless you all and everyone. With lots of
love to all from your lonesome son Harold Pringle.

Answer real soon soon soon.

They have just told me the war is over.[19]

THE NEXT DAY HAROLD wrote home again:

I am more than glad to be getting your longed for letters which
help me a great deal and how. But Im awful sorry to hear your
sick. I sure hope and pray that this few lines find you in the very
best of health. For myself Im in the very best of health. But getting awful lonesome for you all. Well Mother Darling I have just
been told the war is all over at last. I have just mailed another letter to you and I think I said something in it about it being over.
But I think you will likely to no before now. But thank God it is

over at last sure has lasted much longer than any of us thought hasnt it. But I think we can safely say it is over now. I sure hope that Grandma is feeling better and I also hope that Leo Lessard's wife is well again. Also hope that it isnt any thing serious. Say I sure was surprised to hear they have three children. I sure would like to see them. And do they still live in the same place. I guess things have certainly changed alot in old Flinton. I guess I wouldnt recognize anyone. But hope it hasnt changed that much.

I think you said one of your letters it has been very cold in Canada. Well the weather in Italy is just wonderful now. But as a rule it is very nice one day and the next its raining like every thing. But just the same give me old Canada any day. Say I sure hope that Charlie doesn't have to go in the army. But if he does: probably it will only be for a short time. Say where is Miss Bennette teaching now. Also do you no were she is living. She sure was wonderful to us. She certainly sent us all lots of cigs. So I sure hope that she got some of my letters ok. Also where are the Andrews now do they still live in Flinton I suppose Geraldine is married by now. I suppose most of the girls are married around there now. For myself I've come close to it about three times now.

Again mother darling please dont worry about me I no it is very hard not to. But certain thats whats making you sick all the time and it also makes it much more harder for me. To think that you are worrying all the time So please don't worry any more for I will be ok. And I go to mass every Sunday also to Holy Communion every Sunday and also Father Farrell has lots of prayers said for me. He sure is wonderful to me. I will also get him to write to you right away.

Well Mother Darling the Boys are really singing to'night. I guess they are all quite happy *and how*. So I guess I will ring off to night.[20]

When news of Germany's surrender reached the Canadians in Avellino, "the reaction of our troops," wrote the camp's war diarist Captain Hugh Ramsay Park, "was a matter-of-fact reception and a composed, quiet celebration."[21] The festivities in London, England, were euphoric and prolonged. As the staff in the Judge Advocate General's office at Canadian Headquarters enjoyed the news of the war's end, they began reviewing Pringle's petition. Officers were asked to report on the legality of the finding and also on the facts of the case.

Colonel W. A. I. Anglin submitted an exhaustive, twenty-page document that laid out all the pertinent facts and issues in Pringle's case. There were two questions that the authorities in England needed to answer: Was there ground for revision of the finding of the sentence or for refusal of confirmation? If no such ground existed, would the overseas authority commute the sentence? It was a complex case. The trial's review sheet, which had been completed on March 26, 1945, concluded, rather ambiguously, that there had been "no substantial injustice to the accused."[22]

Anglin reported that he found no illegalities or irregularities in Pringle's trial that required overturning the verdict or sentence. He referred to reports by three other officers, among them Lieutenant Colonel K. G. Morden, who on April 9 submitted a two-page review that concluded Harold Pringle's shot was fired "either with the intention of killing Lucky or making doubly sure he was dead." Morden saw only one difficult point: the question of whether Lucky was alive at the time of Harold Pringle's shot. He judged the court's verdict to be sound and maintained, "there is more than a scintilla of evidence that Lucky was alive at the material time. I do not see how we can, on review, advise that the court erred." Morden's opinion was supported by other officers, such as Lieutenant Colonel L. R. McDonald, who found "no adequate reason for withholding confirmation of the finding and sentence." In his report, Anglin summarized the events of November 1 and the activities of the Sailor Gang, and explained the chronology of the shootings and the testimony by the two pathologists. As far as commuting the sentence from death to another was concerned, Anglin wrote that there were "no purely legal grounds for commutation in the case in hand."[23]

In his final entry, however, Anglin made an important assertion. It was on a point of fact, rather than of law. Anglin listed it under the heading, "My Personal Doubt as to 'Lucky' Being Alive at the Time of Shot 2":

"The foregoing is submitted in my function as DJAG, but as any conviction for murder with a death sentence is a most serious matter I take the liberty of adding my personal reaction to the case for what it may be worth to others concerned. I doubt that Lucky was alive at the time of Shot 2."[24]

Anglin wrote that he did not give weight to Pringle's and Croft's testimonies. Instead, he based his doubt on that fact that "evidence that Lucky was still alive is inconclusive." Even if Pringle and Croft thought Lucky was alive when they shot him, if he was dead there was no murder. Anglin said that he was more impressed with the defence medical expert than with the expert for the prosecution and noted that even if the Canadian authorities agreed with him, they did not have to commute the sentence. He suggested that if the finding was commuted, the Canadians could order a retrial on a charge of accessory after the fact. The penalty for that crime was life in prison. Anglin chose his words carefully. His findings were presented as observations, not suggestions. "I am sure it will be appreciated that I am not suggesting that the sentence should be commuted or the accused re-tried," he wrote in conclusion.[25] The inference, however, was clear: there was reasonable doubt.

The officers at Canadian Headquarters in London, however, had their own opinion of Harold Pringle. This opinion had been delivered by mail during 1944 and 1945, courtesy of Pringle's unhappy ex-lover from Portsmouth. Thanks to Esmee's correspondence, the highest officers in the Canadian army were aware of Pringle's desertion and of his debt to her. On February 6, 1945, eight days before Pringle's court martial had begun, Esmee once again sent a letter demanding the twenty-one pounds Pringle owed her. Major General E. G. Weeks replied to her query, explaining that Pringle was facing "a very serious civilian charge....In view of the circumstances, it is very doubtful if he will ever be in a position to effect payment." Nothing, however, was going to keep Esmee from her money. She continued writing the Canadian authorities and threatened to take the army to civil court.[26]

Anglin's report was not given a favourable reception by the upper echelons at the JAG. Brigadier Beverley Matthews dismissed Anglin's finding and was vehement in his belief that the verdict was right and the penalty deserved. In a two-page memo, he stated that "our man Pringle" had delivered "perjured evidence." He maintained that the fact that the court chose to believe the evidence of the prosecutor's pathologist demonstrated that the pathologist's testimony must have been right. The guilty verdict of the British court also held great weight. "What we have, in effect, are the decisions of two Courts agreeing that Lucky was alive at the time of the second shot, and if this is accepted as a fact, there is nothing on the merits of the case to disturb the finding of guilty, nor ipso facto, the sentence of death." Yet Matthews revealed an eye for the political reality an execution might have after victory had been declared: "So far as I know, there have been no executions as a result of military trials within the Canadian army during the course of the war, and this would be the first one coming within a short time after the cessation of hostilities."[27] Nonetheless, Matthews recommended that the army confirm the sentence and verdict.

The decision rested finally with General P. J. Montague, the man who in 1943 had begun to create the legal framework for military executions in the Canadian army. Montague, who had sent a number of personal letters to Esmee, was well aware of Harold Pringle. He read the reports on the case and paid particular attention to the secret medical report filed by Sir Bernard Spilsbury. On May 12, Montague sent a two-page report to the Department of National Defence in Ottawa. Montague found no reason to commute the sentence or to reverse the court's finding. He was therefore submitting the evidence to the governor general for final confirmation.

"It is my firm recommendation that the finding and sentence should be confirmed," he wrote.

> I desire to point out further that the conviction is a conviction of
> murder, and the case must be considered as a civil offence. If I
> were a member of a Court of Appeal reviewing the findings of the
> Jury on the evidence in this case, I would find no reason for inter-
> fering with a finding of guilty. The fact that the accused and the
> victim were both members of the Canadian Army, and that the
> trial was by a Canadian Court Martial, is not, in my view, the

controlling feature of this case. In essence, this is a case which
arises out of the shooting of one Canadian citizen by another
Canadian citizen. Considering the matter in this way, I have come
to the opinion that the fact that the war is now over and won
should not influence me to treat the matter otherwise than simply
as a case of murder.[28]

The comparison to a civil—that is, non-military—case had certain
flaws. If Pringle had been tried in a civilian court, a lawyer who had never
tried a case before and who only had six days to prepare his case would
never have been allowed to defend him. A civilian court would not have
permitted a doctor on the jury, especially a doctor who worked at the
same hospital as the expert witness for the defence. If Pringle had been
tried in a civilian court, his jury and those who judged his appeal would
not have been told that he was suspected of committing other crimes
(none of which he had been charged with)—all that would have been
inadmissable.

After the war, Michael Cloney always wondered if he could have
saved Harold Pringle. The man originally selected to defend Pringle
obtained a copy of the court martial and the JAG's reviews; for fifty-five
years he kept them at his home. Occasionally he would pore over the
proceedings, wondering if he could have done better for the soldier from
Flinton. In the 1950s, Cloney would try the army's only other capital
case—and keep his client from being executed. In 2000, the retired judge
and former military lawyer added his own opinion of the case against
Harold Pringle in vernacular terms: "I can't believe they found him
guilty. There was reasonable doubt a mile wide."[29]

16.

AVELLINO

In May 1945, Captain Ramsay Park was finishing his seventeenth month at Avellino. The town remained what it had been for the duration of the war, the sleepy location of the Canadian army's reinforcement base and 2 Echelon Canadian Military Headquarters. Avellino was an ancient place that, thanks to its mountains and pine trees, reminded the Canadians of home. It lay in a small valley that stretched along the foot of the Apennines, and it was the largest producer of pine nuts in Italy. In fact, its name was said to mean "nut" in some forgotten language. Avellino had a quaint town square, a number of churches and a few prominent families. Atop the valley's highest peak sat the monastery of Montevergine, which had a reputation for curing human maladies. The church was filled with crutches and other supports that grateful patients had left there following their healing; the bones of many saints were on display in caskets in the monastery's small chapel. The most prized item was a very small piece of wood that was said to be from the cross on which Christ was crucified. The monastery also had a wine bar, which Canadian officers frequented. The entire Avellino area was famous for the production of robust wines, such as the white Fiano di Avellino and the red Taurasi.

Life for officers stationed there was a steady flow of bureaucracy. On May 7, the Canadian headquarters in Rome was closed and its staff sent to Avellino for a stopover before their eventual return to England and then Canada. Now that the war was over, censorship by unit commanders was discontinued, although letters would still be censored by the commandant at the base. Orders were issued each day. These covered everything from the most banal matters to the most crucial. In May 1945, for example, the army declared sunstroke to be a self-inflicted wound; soldiers were warned to take precautions as Avellino was malarious; they were warned not to eat Italian ice cream as it was suspected that it caused diarrhea. The bishop of Avellino held a mass for the Allied soldiers who had lost their lives fighting in Italy and for the civilians who had died as a result of enemy action.[1]

The war had first arrived at Avellino by air. On September 20, 1943, a Sunday afternoon, American war planes dropped bombs. They targeted Avellino's farmers' market, which was located on a small square at the crest of a hill near the town's centre. On that morning, Avellino had thirty thousand inhabitants; after the bombing, three thousand were dead, most of them women and children. Benito Scopa, who was five years old on that day, was shopping with his mother at the market for the family's lunch. When the bombs struck, the explosions brought down a giant awning. The *baldacchino* collapsed, covering Benito and his mother; for the rest of his life he would credit his survival to it. At first, as panic ensued, people wanted to believe that the bombing had been an accident. But this hope was extinguished once the American fighters began strafing the crowd. "They flew low and fired right at the women and the children," recalled Benito. In a matter of minutes, ten per cent of Avellino's population was gone. The bodies carpeted the ground, piled two and three feet high in many places. Those who survived carry souvenirs of that afternoon. Benito still cannot stand being in a crowd and faints at the sight of the smallest amount of blood.[2]

Three weeks later, a fifteen-year-old girl was playing in the forest near the outskirts of Avellino. She and her family were living in a makeshift tent in the woods, having fled the town. As she was playing, she noticed a figure emerge, "as if appearing from thin air." He was crouched close to the ground and he was wearing a round helmet and a green uniform she did not recognize. He beckoned to her and asked her in Italian,

"Dove sono i Tedeschi?"—where are the Germans? She told him the Germans had gone. The soldier gave her some presents and told her not to worry; "*Siamo Americani. Siamo amici*"—we are your friends. An hour later, the girl returned to her family and told them the Americans had arrived. You're crazy, her father told her, they can't have. "Look," she said, "*look*, look what they gave to me." Then she lowered the lip of her skirt, which she had used as an impromptu basket; nestled in the folds were dozens of candies and chocolate bars.[3]

The Canadian army entered Avellino after the Americans liberated the town, on November 22, 1943. In *Avellino e l'irpinia nella tragedia del 1943–44*, local historian Vincenzo Cannaviello describes the effect the Canadians had on the small city. They chose Avellino because it was ideally situated between four strategic cities. To the west lay Naples and Rome; to the east lay Bari and Ortona. From Avellino the Canadians could supply all four destinations. Immediately after taking control of Avellino, the army commandeered every inhabitable house, school and villa and gave the civilians forty-eight hours to vacate the premises. A nunnery became the Canadian Military Hospital. Left without homes, people went crazy, wrote Cannaviello, "wild like plants in the desert." They lived in the woods and earned money by begging at the side of the road, saying, "We are human, we are not animals."[4] To make the city easier for English-speakers to navigate, the Canadians renamed major streets. Via Fratelli Del Gaudio became Fraser Avenue. Via Mancini became Saskatchewan Road. Corso Littorio became Queen Street. The clerks at headquarters began publishing a weekly newsletter entitled *Echelon Etchings*. The Canadians opened an officers' mess and christened it Maple Leaf Gardens.

The tone of Cannaviello's book is bitter. While he admits that the Canadians were handsome, "*tutti belli*," and their tobacco gave the air an exciting aroma, he criticizes their treatment of the citizens of Avellino. Canadians were less respectable and less dignified than the Italians. They were also "*troppa devota a Bacco*," badly devoted to alcohol.[5] Soldiers were often seen weaving about in public, and the military police were routinely called in to pick them up. One drunken sergeant en route back to camp from Salerno froze to death after passing out by the road; Captain Norman S. Bergman had presided over the court of inquiry.

Italians stayed on their guard, particularly after dark, since a soldier "carrying a gun could kill as many as he wanted."[6] Canadians loved to fight. One word, Cannaviello maintains, and they would put up their fists. In 1943, four Canadian soldiers beat a farmer named Mario Grado to death. The Canadians' taste for pugilism can be attributed in part to their experience at the front. "When the soldiers returned from fighting they changed completely," remembered Teresa Preziuso, who was sixteen years old when the Canadians arrived in Avellino. "They were joyless. Their eyes were dull. They drank and they fought with each other. They even changed in how they looked. We had a couple of Canadians who would sometimes eat supper with my family. They went away to fight at Cassino. When they came back they knocked at the door. My mother couldn't recognize them. They had changed that much. I remember them saying, 'Mother, don't you recognize me?'"[7]

Cannaviello accuses the Canadians of being a corrupting influence on the town's female population. They "put a new fantasy in the minds of women."[8] At night teenaged girls could be seen walking with Canadians. Parties were held at the Canadian officers' mess to which only the young, pretty women of Avellino were invited. A soiree held on February 12, 1944, Cannaviello writes, was more like an orgy than a social gathering. On another occasion, Cannaviello describes seeing a girl dressing as she left a truck filled with twelve soldiers. Other older citizens of Avellino confirm his assertions. Avellino historian Andrea Massaro says that in the black market section of Avellino, working-class women had sex with soldiers in exchange for food. At the town's fountain, down by the river where the women did the washing, they would stop their duties and casually provide gratification.[9] One Avellino woman recalls how three soldiers came to her asking where they could find *ficky, fick* (the Italian slang for a woman's genitals). The woman, who was then only twelve years old, thought the men were asking for figs, *fici*, and told them to go down the street to a nearby shop. When they arrived at the establishment, the Canadians thought they had hit the jackpot: the shop's owner had three beautiful young daughters. He was not impressed, however, with their intentions, and he ran them out with a broom.[10] When not driven by financial need, many young women were watched closely by their families. A writer for *Echelon Etchings* lamented that his Italian sweetheart had a father who "kept the shot-gun behind the door and the wedding bells under the bed."[11]

Still, not all Canadians were bad, Cannaviello admits. When they weren't drinking they were very affectionate. They would embrace you and joke. They gave gifts. Here, he echoes British officer Norman Lewis's description of Canadian soldiers: "They give candy to every child in sight, shove all male Italians off the pavement and make an instant sexual advance to every woman of child-bearing age they encounter."[12] Many Canadians adopted local families and gave them supplies and food. In Avellino, if you walked down the street at dusk, you would see Italian women wearing dresses made from Canadian uniforms and their children running about in outfits sewn together from Canadian blankets. Serious love affairs developed. One elderly Avellino resident remembers a young French Canadian soldier who fell in love with her and sent dozens of love letters. She never saw him again: he was killed fighting north of Florence.[13] A number of Canadian soldiers married local women, although the archbishop of Avellino refused to grant them marriage licences.

Avellino was also home to Number 2 Canadian Field Punishment Camp, which by May 1945 was the last Canadian military prison in Italy. There were 143 soldiers there under sentence, states its war diary, with 4 in hospital and another 178 in the "concentration camp." All these men required transport back to Canada, even those the army deemed "incorrigible." Prisoners the army thought were good soldiers who had fallen on the wrong side of military order would be released and transported back to Canada as free men. The incorrigible would be transported as prisoners and confined in military prison once they returned to Canada. Even now that the war in Italy was officially over, crimes were still being committed. In May, 11 Canadian soldiers were sentenced to terms over six months, and another 18 were given sentences under six months. One soldier was convicted of manslaughter. On May 17, after reviewing the service records of those in prison, the army released 178 of the 325 men in prison. They were sent to Naples, where they boarded a ship and sailed for England. On May 25, another 104 were released and sent off. Meanwhile, arrangements were made for the eventual apprehension of the hundreds of Canadian deserters who remained at large in Italy. The Canadian authorities decreed that deserters who were arrested after the Canadian army had left Italy would be sent to the British for processing. The British would transport the offenders to England, where the Canadian army would take over.[14]

By May, the tale of the Lane Gang had been reported to the army at large. The British army newspaper, *The Crusader*, recounted the exploits in a two-page tabloid-style article. While in hospital, Canadian private Stanley Scislowski read the story and was so fascinated by it that he kept a copy for decades after the war until, he said, it "finally crumbled to the point where I couldn't read it anymore." Scislowski went on to write a memoir of his time in Italy, *Not All of Us Were Brave*. In an effort to preserve the tale, he wrote a brief description of the *Crusader* article and passed it on to me. There was no mention of Scarface or Gunner Ceccacci or any other member of the real Lane Gang. Instead the article focused on two Canadian soldiers.

> Both were deserters from their infantry battalions. One was from the 1st Division and one from the 5th Armoured Division. In Rome, they got mixed up with as tough a gang of multinational cut-throats and criminals as ever walked the face of this earth. It was likely the two joined up with what was known by the Criminal Investigation Division of the American Military Police as the Lane Gang, a notorious heterogeneous mixture of deserters from practically every Allied formation in Italy. There were quite a few racial types involved in it, as well as German deserters and Italian criminal elements. They did everything you could name in the black book of crime. They hijacked lone vehicles driving along the highways. They murdered. They were into dope dealing and prostitution. And they were involved also in a big way in counterfeiting. They ruled underworld Rome with an iron hand and they even had the armies nervous, what with their seizures of

supply-laden trucks on the roads and highways, killing the crews if they gave any opposition. They grew outrageously rich from revenues accrued through the sale of the stolen goods.

Eventually the Criminal Investigation Division got wind of a meeting or party going on by the criminals in a building tucked away in a backwater section of the city and raided it. As the hoods took off in a running gunfight with the MPs, one of the Canadians was seriously wounded. Rather than leave him behind alive for interrogation, his buddy from the 1st Division cold-bloodedly shot and killed him. Within minutes, the killer was apprehended and after a long period spent in a prison com-pound, was found guilty of the crime and sentenced to death by a firing-squad.[15]

This version of events became the official story, and it is the same story that Colin McDougall uses in *Execution*. McDougall has Fraser, the character with Harold Pringle's fierceness and outlaw behaviour, desert and escape to Rome, where he joins up with a black market gang, "the worst kind of scum and cut-throats."[16] While on leave, Jonesy, the char-acter with Harold Pringle's more innocent traits, meets Fraser, who after a night of drinking brings Jonesy back to the gang's hideout. Jonesy over-stays his leave, and one morning the US Military Police close in: "There was a lot of gun play, several of the gang were killed, a few escaped, and two were taken prisoner—Jonesy and a G.I. deserter. A U.S. Policeman was killed. Frazer, Jones and a couple of others tried to break out through the back. Someone had shoved a Colt .45 in Jonesy's hand, he came run-ning out trying to cock it and two rounds actually went off. Not that he hit anyone, it was one of the others who killed the M.P."[17]

This fraudulent tale of the Lane Gang allowed the Allied public rela-tions machine to change Harold Pringle into a hardened master criminal. Instead of turkey thefts, drunken fights and a long drive into the countryside, Lucky's murder became a cool homicide. Obviously, the military police knew that the Sailor Gang was a separate entity and that the Lane Gang was the larger, more organized operation. After all, it was the SIB who investigated and arrested both groups. All that did not matter. The creation by the military press of a large, sophisticated organization allowed the Allies to attribute unsolved crimes to the legendary Lane Gang. That was the story's most attractive feature. As far as the Allies and the Italian civilian authorities were concerned, it was a happy ending. The surviving members of the "Lane Gang" were to be shot. Justice would be served.

The Canadian officers in Avellino did not know much about the Lane Gang, but they knew a Canadian was being held in a British prison near Rome and they knew there was a good chance that there would be a firing squad. In May, Captain Ramsay Park, who was recovering from a bout of malaria, paid little attention to such matters. He was busy organizing the polling for the federal election that was to take place in June.

Park was billeted in the villa of the principessa di Marzo, of the aristocratic Marzo family, the most respected in Avellino. The Marzos owned vineyards, and their villa was set in the heart of the town on a few acres of well-groomed gardens. Tall trees and rose bushes sat by sculpted pools of water and Renaissance statues. The Canadians occupied the villa's lower floors, while the principessa, who was in her late forties, lived on the top floor with her daughter. The principessa was a beautiful woman, with straight black hair and an elegant face that delicately combined strength and grace. Her husband was missing; the principessa believed that he had been killed sometime during 1943. Her daughter, Alina, was in her early twenties and was, remembers Park, also very beautiful, possessing a luminous unadorned glow. Alina taught him and some of the other officers Italian, but though he would have liked the opportunity, Park was never able to strike up a romance. "Her mother kept her under close watch," he said. "I guess she didn't want her having some Canadian's baby."[18]

Also billeted at the Villa di Marzo was Lieutenant Michael Cloney, who had been married shortly before going overseas and had a young son he had never seen waiting for him in Canada. The war had been lonely for Cloney but relatively uneventful. In early April 1944, he had defended Captain Norman S. Bergman. Bergman, who had unsuccessfully defended Harold Pringle, had been accused of stealing his regiment's petty cash, a sum of almost one thousand dollars. Cloney

COURTESY OF MICHAEL CLONEY

Michael Cloney, left, and H. Ramsay Park in England following
Pringle's execution, 1945.

—

worked hard on the case and noticed that Bergman, who faced imprisonment, was not very concerned. One night when Cloney was working
late, Bergman happened by his tent on his way to the officers' mess; he
had laughed, telling him, "Don't worry, Cloney, it'll be all right," as if
some kind of fix were in. Bergman's prediction proved prophetic. On
April 21, the legal proceedings for that week were reported. There had
been twenty-five courts martial and only one acquittal: Captain Norman
S. Bergman.

Shortly after the case, Cloney was given a plum assignment: turning a nurses' leave centre on the Amalfi Coast into a retreat for Canadian officers on leave. It became a popular spot and won the nickname Cloney's Cloisters. Along with this duty, Cloney made frequent trips to and from Avellino. He would visit with his casual acquaintance Captain Park, whom he found mild-mannered: "Park had a very characteristic laugh. It was a kind of chortle that bubbled up in the middle of sentences. He would be describing something very serious and this laugh would break out."[19]

An average day in Avellino consisted of military administration, followed by recreation. Liquor and cigarettes were available at the Canadians officers' mess, which was located off the main town square. Men dined at the Ristorante Rossetta, and both officers and enlisted men often ate with Italian families. "If you could provide meat, you were welcome anywhere," recalled Park. Companionship was also available, and some Canadian officers had regular girlfriends. The district area provost marshall, H. F. Law, fell in love and was engaged to an Italian. In May, the pair married in a service at the Villa di Marzo. Park, Cloney and the other officers were there. The festivities were presided over by the officer in charge, Brigadier J. C. Stewart. Park was more solitary than most. He did not have a steady girlfriend, or at least "nothing you would describe as a girlfriend."[20]

Along with permanent staff, there were also Canadian officers who were being routed home through Avellino. While most of the Canadians had been sent up to Holland and France in February 1945, a few were still left in Italy. Among those sent to Avellino in May 1945 was Captain Thomas Jamieson. After taking part in the January 1945 Po Valley offensive, Jamieson had been kept at Canadian Headquarters in Rome and then sent briefly to Greece, where he and the British contingent had put down a rebellion led by the Greek Communist partisans. The partisans had been allied with the British during the war and had proven more effective at fighting the Germans than the right-wing royalists. But the partisans were Communists, and now that the war was being won, they had to be stopped. So Jamieson found himself fighting the same army he had been supplying a year earlier. The British intervention was not enough to neutralize the Communists. It was not until the Civil War of 1946, with massive amounts of American support, that the royalists were able to defeat them.

Jamieson was familiar with the circumstances surrounding Harold Pringle's arrest. In November 1944, he had been stationed at Canadian Headquarters in Rome and had learned about the Sailor Gang, about the multiple shooting, about the international character of the gang; he knew that Harold Pringle had been found guilty and sentenced to die. Jamieson was a good shot, and thanks to this skill and his knowledge of Pringle's case, he was assigned the task of canvassing Avellino for prospective marksmen. He was told to casually make his way through the base and bring soldiers up to the camp's firing range. There, he had the men shoot target practice and made note of how each fared. Jamieson brought cooks and drivers, men who had not fired a rifle since basic training, and tried to teach them how to shoot straight. If these men failed, there were the soldiers of Avellino's Special Employment Company, but they were not a preferred choice. The Special Employment Company was composed of shell-shocked soldiers whom the army deemed unfit for front-line duty. These men were kept behind the lines doing menial labour. Many had been labelled by army psychiatrists as unfit "for duties within sound of gun-fire." Half a dozen men from the Special Employment Companies had been reported drowned in the Liri River following the Cassino fight. It was not lost on Jamieson that the Liri was a slow-moving river not more than five feet deep. A firing squad of such men was unlikely to be very effective.

As the first sunny, warm weeks of May passed, Jamieson became nervous. He heard word from his friends at British Headquarters in Rome that the Canadian upper echelons in London, England, were ready, in the event that Ottawa disallowed Pringle's petition, to choose an officer to lead the firing squad. You did not have to be clairvoyant to see the way matters might turn. Jamieson was already picking the men, and the odds were that he would be asked to lead the final assignment. The idea terrified him. Jamieson had seen action and he knew what it meant to fire a weapon with the intent to kill. He even knew what it meant to watch someone be executed. While in hospital with a head wound,

Jamieson had been in a bed near a wounded German who kept screaming out in pain. The screams were continuous and eventually they
annoyed a nearby British officer, who instructed the orderlies to take the
German out. They did. He never came back. Lining up ten feet before a
Canadian and shooting him in cold blood was unimaginable. It was
around this time that Tom Jamieson began suffering from insomnia.

IN MID-MAY, PETTY OFFICER BILL CROFT was in his third month at
the Royal Navy Provost Centre in Santa Lucia, a suburb of Naples. Croft
lived in a small, bare cell, according to Babington and Gardner, where he
spent his time reading thrillers and doing crossword puzzles. Croft kept
his sense of humour and spent many hours chatting with his jailers, who
played cards with him and talked with him about the war. Maria was now
living in Naples; she and her baby visited Croft twice a week. Bill and
Maria remained passionately in love. Shortly after his trial, Croft asked
the navy for permission to marry his Italian sweetheart. "The prison
chaplain objected," wrote Babington and Gardner. "But the Royal Navy
captain in charge took a more sympathetic view."[21] Maria and Bill were
married in the officers' quarters. A local priest stood in for the army
chaplain.

Bill Croft held out hope that he would be spared, and he spoke with
Maria about the life they would lead once he was free again. Now that the
war was over it would not be necessary to live outside the law and they
could settle in Naples. He could find work as a sailor. Yet it is likely that
somewhere in his heart, Croft, a sharp and cynical man, must have
known that his chances were slim. On May 15, the commandant of the
prison sent a message to the Admiralty stating that "the circumstances of
his custody is having an adverse effect on the men's morale."[22] The Royal
Navy acted quickly. On May 22, it sent its confirmation of Bill Croft's
death sentence. The prison commandant promulgated the sentence. Bill
Croft had one last request.

That afternoon two corporals visited Maria at her apartment. They
informed her, wrote Babington and Gardner, that there had been a
change in orders. From now on, she would be allowed to visit Bill each
day. In fact, they were on their way back to the prison and wanted to

know if she cared to join them. Maria gathered up her baby daughter, and the corporals drove her to the prison in their jeep. Bill Croft was "the same as ever when she saw him," wrote Babington and Gardner.[23] He and Maria spent half an hour together. He played with his daughter and chatted with Maria in Italian. They laughed, and Croft was delighted to see how happy Maria was at the prospect of seeing him each day. When their meeting was done, Bill Croft told Maria he would see her the next day. Nothing he said or did, Babington and Gardner wrote, gave her any hint that he was about to die.

Croft was brought to Number 55 British Military Prison, which was located on the island of Nisida, a small volcanic outcropping in Naples' harbour. The island had first been discovered by Greek navigators in 700 BC and had since been home to strange occurrences. "The island," Oreste Schiano di Zenise told me, "has a somewhat sinister aura to it."[24] The Romans used Nisida as an aristocratic playground. The Roman consul Luculus had built a lavish palace there, and it was in this palace that Brutus, Cassius and the other conspirators are said to have plotted Julius Caesar's assassination in 44 BC. After the murder, Brutus and his wife Portia fled to Nisida. There, unable to endure the shame of her husband's crime, Portia killed herself by swallowing burning coals.

Under Constantine the Great, Nisida was granted to a religious order. Luculus' palace was destroyed and a small castle erected from its ruins. A prominent family, the Carafa, built a warning tower that allowed them to alert islanders to the approach of the Moorish pirates who regularly attacked the Italian coastline. Throughout the Middle Ages, Nisida was owned by private families. In the seventeenth century, it was returned to the Neapolitan Crown. During this time, two monks and a woman ran a counterfeiting operation on Nisida, minting their own false coins. Those who happened upon their secret operation did not live to speak of it. The trio was eventually discovered. In 1632, during Holy Week, all three were hanged.

The Neapolitan government began construction of a plague hospital on Nisida, but it was never completed, and in the late seventeenth century the hospital was converted into a holding pen for "undesirables" who arrived by ship. It was also around this time that Nisida became known for its asparagus and grapes. It once again became a place for rest and relaxation; on the gates of Nisida were written, in Latin, the words "Seaman, snub the boat and furl the sail. Here is the aim of your work. Happily calm your soul." During the Second World War, the Italians, the Germans and finally the Allies all occupied Nisida. The British adapted the old hospital and turned it into a military prison.

It was in this prison that Bill Croft spent his last night playing cards and conversing with his jailers. According to Babington and Gardner, on May 23, just before dawn, Croft was taken from his cell and marched to a quarry near the prison yard. A warm day was beginning, and the heat began to burn through the few trees and shrubs that dotted the barren plot of land. Three posts were fixed to the ground, each six or seven feet high. Bill Croft was tied to the middle post. He asked not to be blindfolded, but the request was not granted. A small white disc was pinned to his heart. Two American officers and a military doctor were on hand.

The firing squad consisted of twelve Royal Marines commanded by a non-commissioned officer who had been given special training for his unsavoury task. The men were provided with one bullet each; in keeping with tradition, one of the rounds was a blank. The firing squad was given the order to fire, and the "noise of a ragged volley filled the air."[25] Croft was cut down from the stake and examined by the doctor.

The Sailor was still alive and fully conscious.

The doctor turned to Captain Barnes, the officer in charge of the firing squad, whose responsibility it was, in the event of a botched execution, to deliver the *coup de grâce*. Reluctantly, the doctor pointed to Croft's heart. Numb, Barnes knelt, aimed his pistol and fired. There was a moment of stillness. Bill Croft's chest heaved; somehow, he was still alive. To Captain Barnes he whispered, "Bad shot." The doctor pointed to Croft's temple. Again, Barnes aimed his pistol. That shot did the job. Bill Croft was dead, like Lucky, of multiple gunshots, the last two to the chest and head.

The Royal Navy was embarrassed by the bungled execution. A naval legal officer sent a letter to headquarters. "It has been suggested to the Admiralty," he wrote, "that the use of a firing party might perhaps be discontinued in favour of execution by a clamped and fixed Bren gun firing a limited number of shots in automatic mode, or of execution by a revolver at close range....I think it is desirable to investigate this question with a view to avoiding a recurrence of the unfortunate incident at Naples."[26]

When Maria learned that Bill Croft was dead, she was, wrote Babington and Gardner, "reduced to hysterics."[27] Years later, after rebuilding her life, Maria moved to England, to Bill Croft's home town of Grimsby. She remarried and raised her daughter, refusing to discuss her lost love or the exploits of the Sailor Gang.

On the day of Bill Croft's execution, Harold was unaware that his friend had been killed. He was still serving time in the prison near Rome and receiving his calls from Father Farrell. While waiting for a visit, he wrote home to his parents. After his usual inquiries regarding everyone's health, Harold mentioned his case:

> Say Mother Dear I still havent heard more yet about my trial. But I dont think it will be much longer now. And I sure hope that you are not worrying about it please dont *for me*. What is Dear Dad working at now. I sure hope he is in good health. And how are all my Sweet Brothers + Sisters. I sure hope they are in the very best of health. And has there been any more of the Boys home yet. If so give them all my best regards. I was to Holy Communion again Sunday and always three or four times aweek. So that isnt to bad is it? I think Father Farrell will be in to-night I havent seen him since Sunday at mass But I guess they keep him on the go most of the time. I think he looks after about three places altogether now.
>
> Well my Darling Mother I guess I will ring off for to night. But I will write again real soon don't forget to give everyone my best regards. Say Mother has Father Kinlin been up to see you if so please dont worry. To My Darling Mother + Dad + b + s. With all the best of luck in the world God Bless you all.[28]

HAROLD PRINGLE MIGHT HAVE been better served keeping any spare luck for himself. Now that both Charlie Honess and Bill Croft had been executed, the chances of the Canadian authorities reversing his sentence were growing slim. In early May, the Canadian Judge Advocate General in London had been busy investigating Harold's petition. The JAG determined that there was no American hospital in the vicinity when Lucky had been transported on November 1. But they did not investigate temporary hospitals. If they had, they would have learned that there had been a casualty dressing station in Ceprano, a town down the highway from where the Sailor Gang had stopped on November 1. They would have learned that it was at this hospital, shortly after the Hitler Line, that Harold Pringle said he had been treated for minor wounds.

On May 17, the Canadians had received a cable from the Royal Navy: "Findings and sentence on Croft confirmed by Admiralty. Navy expects to execute Croft on 21 May 45." The cable was passed on directly to Montague, with a note, "Sir I thought you might be interested to see this," tacked on by Brigadier Beverley Matthews. The news must have excited Montague. He sent a cable telling the British to "ensure that I am advised immediately [when the] execution has taken place." On May 23, at 9:15 a.m., one hour and fifteen minutes after Croft was killed, Montague had received a cable from the Canadian commander at Avellino, Brigadier J. C. Stewart: "Execution took place at 08:00 hrs today."[29]

Meanwhile, the Canadian Provost Corps planned on transporting Harold to England from Italy. Brigadier Stewart reported that Harold was being held in Rome, would be sent to Avellino and then would be "moved under arrangements Candex" on one of the embarkation drafts that were being sent to the United Kingdom: "Propose dispatching C-5292 Pte. Pringle Harold Joseph to UK on MKF 45 29 May. Pringle is awaiting promulgation of sentence on murder charge. Captain HF Law DAPM proceeding MKF 45 in charge of Suspect."[30]

So at the end of May, Harold was brought down south. He was placed in No. 2 Detention and Field Punishment Camp in Portici, a small town at the foot of Mount Vesuvius. Father Farrell was encouraged by the move. After all, if the army intended to kill Harold, why would it go to the trouble of moving him and then transporting him to England? Surely they would have shot him in Rome. And there were other, more superstitious reasons to be optimistic. When Vesuvius had erupted in 1944, the lava and dust had rolled down the side opposite Portici. The town had been spared.

Major General Montague and the rest of the JAG were not following Father Farrell's logic. Now that Croft had been executed, it made no sense to move Pringle to England. Executing Harold Pringle immediately, however, might be risky. A federal election was being held on June 20, and the execution of a Canadian private months after the war was over, whether on British or Italian soil, would not help a prime minister who was already vilified by men who served overseas. "All the officers at Avellino always assumed the government held off executing Pringle until after the election," Michael Cloney recalled. "They did not want the bad publicity."[31]

Meanwhile, the Judge Advocate General in Ottawa, which was reviewing Pringle's case, was concerned by what it perceived to be flaws in the proceedings. It sent a cable asking why a medical officer had been allowed to be president of a general court martial panel; only combatant officers were eligible to serve. Also, was not this officer a co-worker of one of the witnesses for the defence? Wouldn't his personal connections cause prejudice? This was not an issue, replied Montague. By strict legal definition, all officers in the Canadian army were considered combatant officers, except for those granted honorary commissions.

On May 28, Montague sent a cable to Brigadier Stewart in Avellino. Along with it was enclosed a three-page set of instructions. "You are directed to retain Pringle in Italy until final decision on confirmation is made," the cable read. "Captain Law DAPM will also be retained. See instructions for carrying out judicial executions."[32]

17.

VESUVIUS

Harold's window in Number 33 British Military Prison looked east, away from the Gulf of Naples. The makeshift compound was located near Portici, a small, ancient town five miles outside Naples that the Romans had believed had been built near the Gates of Hell. In 1737, Charles of Bourbon and Maria Amalia of Saxony sought refuge at Portici, where they built a palace. In the nineteenth century, that palace was turned into an agricultural school and an elaborate set of botanical gardens were planted. In 1943, the Allies occupied the gardens and turned them into a vehicle compound and military prison.[1]

On June 5, 1945, Harold sat on his cot, leaning back against the wall. Before him lay an immaculately kept cell that contained a cot, a table and a chair. Harold had folded the sheet on his bed back over his army blanket and creased it. On the table sat a pencil, cut short, and three books: the Bible, *The Song of Bernadette* and *True Devotion to the Blessed Virgin Mary*. There were also two tin boxes, each containing a rosary. The larger of the two held a pair of medals and one coin medallion.

Outside, diesel fuel choked the scent of palm trees and exotic Italian plants. Trucks rumbled by, their wheels crushing pavement and dirt beneath them. As he listened to them grind, Harold let his legs go limp off the bed and shrugged his head slightly to the left so that it rested on the wall's cool concrete. In his left hand he held a deck of worn playing cards. It was two in the afternoon and already he had played over twenty hands of solitaire. He could not face another game. Instead, he looked out from his cell toward Mount Vesuvius, letting his imagination and memory—all he had left—begin their work. Harold imagined soldiers scaling up Vesuvius. He remembered Tony Basciano giving orders at the Hitler Line. He saw his Roman girlfriend and remembered the apartment on Via Cesena and how it had been the first time he had lived in a place that had electricity and running water. He recalled her telling him not to think about the war. The war was over. Harold imagined his father with a rifle, dressed for a fall hunt, emerging from a bush. He remembered his mother in her small garden in Flinton. He remembered being nine years old and carrying a can full of summer strawberries to his mother, who poured a little water on them, placed the can on the stove and brewed the strawberries up into a succulent jam. Then Harold Pringle thought of snow. Outside it was hot—ninety degrees Fahrenheit—but in his mind he saw cold, quiet snow covering everything. He thought of making tracks in new-fallen snow.

The memories proved a little too much, and Harold broke off his stare, finding himself back in his cell. Outside sat two British sentries. The Brits liked their cheerful prisoner—they sometimes even played gin with him—but they noticed that time was eating away at Harold's disposition. Since his conviction, Harold had heard nothing from Canadian authorities, and Captain Bergman, the lawyer who had prepared and filed his petition, had gone back to Canada. Father Farrell was in Rome, and he sent regular letters. Captain Law, the officer who had gone to Rome and brought Harold down to Naples, said he was going home. That was why Harold had been brought to Naples. Yet this logical assertion—that it would be easier to shoot him in Rome than move him to Naples and shoot him—was not providing much comfort. Harold tried not to think about the fact that he went to bed every night with the possibility that the following morning might be the morning they would wake him up and tell him that he was finished.

Harold lit a cigarette. After spending six months in jail in England and another six months in prison in Italy, he was now an avid smoker. He inhaled and felt the warm smoke burn down his throat. Harold had begun trying to extend his life by becoming more conscious of his actions. He stretched experiences—eating, smoking, playing cards, reading, praying, breathing—and tried to make them last. When he looked out the window, he really looked. When he prayed, he really prayed. When he ate, he tried to savour every bite. In this way, he thought, he was making his life longer.

Harold rose, walked a few steps to his desk and picked up *True Devotion to the Blessed Virgin Mary* with both hands. He began reading from where he had stopped that morning.

Chapter V: Mary Our Mediatrix
We need Mary in order to die to ourselves.

Our best deeds are ordinarily soiled and corrupted by the evil that taints our humanness. When one pours clear pure water into a dirty and foul-smelling container, or wine into a cask spoiled by the vintage it held before, the good water and the good wine suffer contamination.

When God pours His grace into the vessel of the human soul—the heavenly dew, the pure living water, or the delicious wine of His love—His gifts are sometimes corrupted by the bad odor that original and actual sins have left within it; or by the bad leaven and the evil dispositions which are the sediment of sin. Our actions, even those born of the most sublime virtues, are affected by the dregs of sin.[2]

Ever since joining the army, Harold had seen and taken his fill of the dregs. Prison. Combat. Rome. After a while a man got so used to it that sin became like a suit of clothes he wore. During war it was the uniform, and everyone around knew the feel of the fabric. It got so you couldn't recognize a man unless he was covered in it. Harold looked out toward Vesuvius and wondered where the C Ration Kid had gone. While he was locked up in Rome, Harold had learned that C Ration had been put in an American military prison in the spring of 1945 while Harold had been awaiting his murder trial. AWOL or not, however, the C Ration Kid was still a Ranger. He wasn't locked up long. C Ration told the SIB detectives that he wouldn't testify, and then he busted out. So, thought Harold, maybe C Ration was sitting at the foot of Mount Vesuvius right now smoking a cigarette. Maybe he was back in Rome. Maybe he and his scar and his blond hair were back in Nebraska. Maybe. Either way, Harold figured Staff Sergeant Williams was always going to be out there somewhere. He was going to be AWOL forever, but he was never going to leave the war.

As his thoughts of the C Ration Kid faded, Harold returned to his reading.

> We have, for our own, nothing but pride and blindness in the mind, weakness and inconstancy in the heart, lust and passion and diseases in the body. We are by nature more proud than peacocks, more attached to the earth than toads, more ugly than goats, more envious than snakes, more gluttonous than pigs, more quick than tigers to red anger, more lazy than turtles, more weak than any reed, more inconstant than any weathercock. We have within ourselves only nothingness and sin; and we deserve only the wrath of God and everlasting Hell!
>
> Considering this, is it any wonder that Our Lord bade His would-be followers to renounce themselves and hate their lives— that he who loved his life would lose it, and that he who hated his life would save it?[3]

Across the yard at Number 33, a priest dressed in a British army uniform walked toward the jail. Chaplain Thomas Lenane—Father Tom, as he liked to be called—was on his way to meet a new prisoner. The commandant of Number 33 told Father Tom that the man, a Canadian named Harold Pringle, was the subject of a death watch. He was a deserter and a black marketeer, and he had killed another Canadian the previous November. There had been two other deserters in on the murder, the commandant told him; both were British, and both were now dead. The Canadian was being kept around until his papers came back from Canada, but either way, the officer assured Father Tom, it was up to the Canadians, not the British, to shoot him, if that was what they eventually decided to do. That was just fine with the British commandant. He had seen an execution during the First World War and he did not want to see another.

As he walked toward his first meeting with a condemned man, it is likely that Father Tom wondered to himself what God wished from him. Father Tom had spent the year and a half since the liberation of Rome travelling with the Eighth Army as it swept north. He was there for the smashing of the Gothic Line and the assault on the Po Valley, and it had all been murder on a grand scale. To a soldier, the priest's lot looked pretty cushy. Some privates and officers, such as Captain Tom Jamieson, referred to the priests derisively as "sky pilots." All they had to do was say a few psalms, marry a few fellows to a few Italians and hear a few confessions. The average soldier, however, missed the truth. An army chaplain serving in the field spent his days and nights witnessing death after death. He was the man who was required when a dying man was coughing out his last breaths. The chaplain was the harbinger. He was not the man a soldier wanted to see coming at him if he had been hit—they only sent for the priest so he could send you off. In combat, some soldiers would recoil at the sight of a chaplain because it meant that the medics had given up hope.

Father Tom learned that when soldiers felt their souls slipping out of their bodies, they all loved their mothers and fathers and wives and children or whoever it was that made them want to stay down on earth. War was death piled on death, each one a personal experience. Like many chaplains, Father Tom found himself mentally wiped out by the experience of watching people die, and in the spring of 1945, he was sent back to the rear to become chaplain at Number 33 Military Prison and Detention Barracks. His nerve may have been shaken, but his faith, the faith that had kept him going during the Nazi occupation and the campaigns of 1944 and 1945, was as solid as ever. His faith was the only thing that brought reason to a wild, murderous farce, and he was sustained by the knowledge that all the soldiers who left this life could be sent to a better one if they could open their hearts to God. One could not make a mistake following in the footsteps of Christ. It was a path covered in grace and perfumed by the Holy Ghost. It led to Jesus Christ. It was a perfect way, without mud or dust. It led straight and safely to God and to eternal life. It did not lead

The Villa Marzo in Avellino, where Ramsay Park was billeted, 1945.

—

to the left or right. It was the road Father Tom walked day and night. It was the road that, on June 5, 1945, brought him to Harold Pringle.

IN AVELLINO, Captain Ramsay Park sat in the garden of the Villa Marzo with Alina di Marzo by a small coppice nestled in roses and chrysanthemums. The beautiful aristocrat was teaching him Italian, and the Canadian officer tried to recite plain phrases. It was frustrating. Normally, Park had a facility for languages. He had learned French in school and even a little German, but Italian was proving a tough one to crack. Perhaps, on some secret level, he wanted it to remain a mystery. Perhaps he wanted to simply listen to his young teacher's melodic singsong Italian and convince himself she was telling him to kiss her.

Then again, he was becoming absent-minded; concentration was becoming a problem. A shadow loomed over what was left of the Canadian army in Italy, and Captain Ramsay Park was slowly realizing that this shadow was positioned right above his head. Since April, the army had been emptying out of the country. Both Canadian headquarters had been closed on April 6, along with all the hospitals, the tobacco depot, the graves registration unit, the wounded rest home and the reinforcement depot. Since April 9, 1945, 550 officers and 5,573 men of other ranks had been shipped out.[4] Park might have seen the look of profound cynical relief on the face of Captain Jamieson who, because he had a family waiting for him in Canada, had been shipped home at the end of May. Those few left in Avellino were feeling increasingly restless. The Italians were taking their country back, and they neither wanted nor needed any help from the Allies. The Canadians were left marching aimlessly on parade grounds, drinking wine on their off hours, walking the countryside near Avellino dreaming of home. The days of cheap, desperate sex were gone. The economy had bounced back, and thanks to the surplus of potatoes the civilians were no longer starving.

The black market continued to buzz along, despite the army's declaration that it had been smashed with the apprehension and execution of the "Lane Gang." The Central Intelligence Division reported that a criminal ring was stealing American tires from parked jeeps and selling them on the black market. There was a report that the French army was purchasing black market goods directly from the criminals. Thirty-five Allied trucks were found carrying black market olive oil between Avellino and Foggia and Bari. In fact, millions of dollars in military goods were going missing. In Northern Europe, Canadian officers from the Judge Advocate General were also busy. That spring, a Canadian legal officer had sent a request to Colonel Anglin asking for more lawyers. "Every day it becomes more apparent that the burden of disciplinary work is going to increase," wrote Captain T. G. Norris.

> I had to send Mordent to Paris in connection with an involved Black Market case. We had to send two officers to prosecute in Black Market cases at Army. I have had to detail one officer in a spy prosecution. There are two very heavy and important special prosecutions in Antwerp, involving a gang of hold-up men (Cdn. Soldiers) who have been operating for a considerable length of time. There is also a difficult SIW [self-inflicted wound] case involving an RSM. Tritschler has recently completed as Judge Advocate three cases involving a charge of murder (reduced to manslaughter) in Brussels.

In all, Norris reported he had 150 cases to prosecute, with more soldiers being picked up daily in "sweeps in the larger cities."[5]

And Park, a lawyer, was taking Italian lessons.

He sat beside the principessa's daughter and said, "*Buon giorno.*" She reminded him of previous lessons and how in Italian one broke words into genders. A *ragazza* is a girl. A *ragazzo* is a boy. A *bella ragazza.* A beautiful girl. A *bello ragazzo.* A beautiful boy. You understand?

Park nodded. A *bella ragazza.* A beautiful girl. Park wished her words would course through his ears and explode in his eyes. He wished he could pour her words onto his eyes and have them wash away the pictures that appeared there when he slept. He was now having nightmares, harrowing dreams of hands holding guns. His hand, his gun, pointing toward the temple of a fellow he has never met who is tied to a post stuck in the ground. He saw pictures of twitching soldiers convulsing uncontrollably, pictures of Captain Hugh Ramsay Park standing there issuing the *coup de grâce.*

"*Capisce tenente?*"

"*Si,*" said Park. "*Si, ho capito.*" The sunlight exploded around them and he looked into her eyes. Then a strange sight: Park saw her head move over just four inches, as if it were growing out of her shoulder. He wondered—if they finally picked him, how in Christ's sake he was going to do it?

IN FLINTON, ONTARIO, Mary Ellen Pringle opened a letter.

> My Darling Mother + Dad.
> Just a few lines in answer to your kind and welcome letter which Ive just received. and I sure really glad to hear from you again But very sorry to hear you have all been sick. I sure hope and pray this few lines fine you all in the very best of health now. For myself Im in the very best of health. Say Im sure Father Kinlin got Father Farrells letter as he had an answer from Father Kinlin. Well Mother Im at another place now in Italy. Well that is to say just another camp. And I sure miss Father Farrell. But the Catholic at this camp is all so very good he is a friend to Father Farrell. He

was in this morning awhile and I still go to Holy Communion
nearly every morning so please dont worry please. I also had a
lovely letter from Veronica to day. She sure writes a very nice letter doesnt she. I guess does most of the writing doesnt she. I will
answer her letter to night. And also have to answer one to Father
Farrell tonight.

Well Mother Darling how is everyone around Flinton. I sure
hope they are all well and in the very best of health also give them
all my best regards wont you. Say I sure hope Charlie doesnt have
to go overseas anywhere. At least I hope doesnt have to go to the
Burma Front. And how does he like army life. Say Mother Darling
I sure hope you are feeling better now. And how is uncle Leos
wife now. I sure hope okay. Say it sure is hard to find anything to
write about now that the war is over isnt it. But I guess every one
is very glad it is over. Myself I dont think it will last long with
Japan What is Dad working at now. He sure doesnt write very
often. I sure hope he well. And how is all my sweet Brothers +
Sisters.

It sure will be wonderful when the time comes so we can all
see each other wont it Mother I know I sure am awful lonesome
for you and everyone from Flinton. Well Mother they have just
gave me two more letters. But I dont know who they are from yet
So I'll just have a look and see who they are from. Well Mother I
have just received a letter from my Darling little Doreen Woods.
Also a picture the letter had about 12 pages it is really wonderful
letter she tells me she is engaged to Doug Davison from Flinton.
But she said she didnt think it would last though.

And the other one was from Mildred Southen. She was
telling me she was down home some time ago. I sure surprised to
hear from her. So I will have some more to answer tonight. But
believe me I dont mind answering them when I get them. Say is
Doreen ever a wonderful looking girl now. Her Boyfriend better
hurry up or he may lose her.

I sure thought a lot of Doreen.

But I guess it is a bit to late now.

But the old saying never give up.

Well My Darling Mother + Dad I guess Ill ring off for now.
But will write again real soon. So wish you all the very best of
luck in the world And May Good Lord Bless and keep you all in
the very best of health. With love from your lonesome son
Harold.

Answer real soon.[6]

AT THE BEGINNING OF JUNE, Captain Ramsay Park was ordered to
keep the war diary for Canadian Section 1 Echelon Allied Field
Headquarters. On June 3, he reported that seventeen soldiers were evacuated on the hospital ship *Oranje*. On June 6, arrangements were finalized
for the apprehension of Canadian deserters. Military intelligence estimated that there were fifty at large, but the figure was low. Five years later,
when an official pardon was issued, there were over one hundred still at
large in Italy. Meanwhile, only twenty-one Canadian soldiers were still
serving sentences in Italy. Fourteen were awaiting transfer to England, five
were awaiting trial, one was in hospital and one was awaiting confirmation of a death sentence. On June 10, it was announced that the remainder
of the Canadian army in Italy would be shipped back to England.
However, Park wrote, "A small rear party of seven officers and 24 other
ranks [would be] remaining to deal with the case of C-5292 Pte. Pringle,
H. J., sentenced to die by being shot, on a charge of murder."[7] These
thirty-one men would stay in Italy until Harold Pringle was either shot or
shipped back to Canada to serve a prison term. The next day, the firing
squad was chosen and Park, as he had feared, was selected to lead it. "Since
the army's lawyers want Pringle shot," Park recalled his commanding officer telling him, "I think a lawyer should lead the firing party."[8]

The firing party was ultimately chosen from the ranks of the Special
Employment Company. Military authorities believed, apparently, that
front-line soldiers with psychiatric trouble would be more efficient than
the cooks and clerks Captain Jamieson had trained. Fifty-five years later,
Park would recall, "It was not much of a firing squad. As far as I knew it,
they were all shell-shocked like me. They had seen combat but had had
enough of it and had been sent back."[9]

After being placed in charge of the firing squad, Park began keeping to himself. The officers avoided him. His nightmares worsened. The dreams were always the same. The firing squad would fail to kill Pringle, and Ramsay Park would walk up to the wounded prisoner and fire two shots point-blank into his head. During the day, Park began worrying: "I began wondering if I could do it."[10]

There were five other Canadian officers left in Italy. The commanding officer was Brigadier J. C. Stewart, a thin, handsome veteran who had won the Distinguished Service Order in the First World War. There was Adjutant Major R. G. M. Gammell, a well-educated, self-possessed, private man from Montreal. The medical officer was Doctor J. E. Cowle, a fellow with a good sense of humour. Cowle once placated a private who kept bothering him for a health record by signing "VD Control Office" on the soldier's sheet. The Protestant chaplain was H. Gehl, a minister from southern Ontario. There was also the district area provost marshal, Captain Henry Law, who had brought Harold Pringle down from Rome and who had been married to an Italian woman in May.

On June 10, Harold received a letter from Father Farrell:

My Dear Harold,

Thank you very much indeed for your long and cheery letter which I was very pleased to receive. I am going to find it hard to compete with you as regards to the length of your letter, but as my handwriting is larger than yours, maybe my letter will appear as long as yours even though it isn't.

I was wondering what was happening to you and now I see you have landed at No. 33. I am glad they are looking after you and pleased that you like the change. Even the change of scenery will help stem the boredom of your waiting. You seem to have quite a lot of Catholic chaplains looking after you and it is a wonderful consolation for me to know that you are receiving our Lord in Holy Communion every morning. Nobody could have a greater privilege than that and coupled with the excellent books you have read—the Rosaries you have said, you must feel that our Lord is very much nearer to you than ever before in your life.

We all come into the world to try and love Him—if we achieve that, we need not have a worry in the whole world. Your hand in the hand of Christ—marching along the road He wants you to walk along. So don't worry about anything—you and He are the greatest of pals—that is all that matters—offer yourself to Him—offer Him everything—your anxieties about those at home—your long weary hours in your room—your worries about your own fate. No harm can come to you now—you are going with Him wherever He leads. Even if He wants your life— let Him have it—when He wants it. He gave His Life to buy your ticket to Heaven—offer Him your own whenever He wants to take it.

I haven't seen Staff Sergeant Murphy for ages. I think he must have gone to bed for a few weeks after his hard work looking after you. You probably kept him talking till all hours in the mornings. I will remember you to him if and when he gets out of bed. Your pal the RSM had gone back to England. Lucky man! Anyhow I hope to finish up here at the end of the month and expect to be in England in July.

Are you still playing cards all day? I don't suppose you have got out of that game of patience yet. Probably you never shall— the trouble with you is that your Mother never taught you how to shuffle properly.

I was so glad to hear that you were getting plenty of letters from Canada. That will cheer you up. You can rest assured that I will most certainly write to your Mother. That is a promise.

I haven't any more news and so I will close.

May our Lord and His Mother bless and protect you always.

Yours sincerely in Christ

BS Farrell CF.[11]

Harold folded the letter and placed it on one of the well-ordered piles he had arranged on his desk. There were three piles, sorted according to authorship. Letters from home were on a pile to the left, letters from priests in the middle and letters from old girlfriends on the right.

The right-hand pile was high. Harold had sent letters to old flames and some had replied. Doreen Woods from Northbrooke, the small village up Highway 41 from Flinton, had written him, as had Geraldine Andrews. Harold had had no word from his Italian girlfriend. After his capture, he assumed, she must have drifted back into Rome.

The letters from girls in Canada were filled with gossip and talk of the future. When he read them, Harold could see the future laid before him when he enlisted in 1940. He would fight bravely and come back a hero, like his father, and find a girl just like his mother, and be happy back in Flinton, because he had seen the world and was glad just to be back there alive. That story, however, had gone awry. A series of poor judgments and bad accidents had steered him through the army's treatment of his shell-shocked father, through alcohol, which he never touched before going overseas, and through women, so unlike those he knew back in Flinton. All that was an invention of the war. Another of Harold's former loves was also been busy writing, but her concerns were fiscal. Since January 1945, Esmee from Portsmouth had sent one dozen letters to the Canadian Military Headquarters in London demanding that the army reimburse her twenty-one pounds. This Harold did not know. To him she was a phantom, the English girl he had once wanted to marry.

After finishing his reading, Harold remembered he had one more letter to write. Lights out would be called shortly, and the opportunity would be lost. He had to keep writing, to let everyone know that he was all right and still there. Besides, his mother was sick, and sick because of him. She wanted to know what would become of him and why they had charged him with what they did. He balanced the pencil delicately on the paper to preserve its tip.

June 11, 1945, Time 22:00 hrs
My Darling Mother + Dad,
Well Mother Darling its sure hard to find anything To write about now days there just doesn't seem To any news atall. But just the same I keep writing quite often. But the same old thing over and over you must get sick of reading it dont you. How are all the

children I sure hope all in good health. I still havent heard from
Marion I sure hope she received my letter all right. And has she
been up home yet. I think you said in one of your letters some
time back that she was coming out home for afew days.

I sure hope her and husband and children are in good
health. And what is Clinton doing now. Is he still in the army yet.
And where is Charlie I sure hope he's still in good old Canada
and doesnt have to leave either.

Well Mother Darling I still havent heard anything yet. But as
soon as I find out I will write and let you know I sure hope and
pray your not worrying. As you will only make yourself sick. So
please dont worry will you.

As the good Lord knows everything and the truth and also
knows that the petty officer and myself was really taking the Chap
to hospital. I sure would like to tell you everything. But I say this
much and that is I really wasnt guilty of what I was charge with.
So please dont think any more of it (please).

How are all Grandmas I sure hope they are well and in the
very best of health. I used to hear from Aunt Ida quite often But I
guess they have forgotten me. But just the same give them all my
Best regards. To one and all.

And how is uncle Leos wife Eileen I sure hope she is out of
hospital now. And how is every one down the old road Well
Mother Darling I dont know if youll be able to make out this or
not as Im hurrying.

Well Mother I went to Holy Communion yesterday And
again to day. They sure are really wonderful hear. And they all
seem to like me. We get along very good together. I think I will be
going to England soon. Which will be much better.

Well Mother Ive just wrote a letter to Doreen Woods. I had a
wonderful letter from her a few days ago. Well Mother I guess I
will say good night for now But try and write more in the next
letter. And sure hope to hear from you again real soon. So ontil I
wish you all the very best of luck and every thing else. And may
the good Lord keep yous in the very best of health. Good night

Darling Mother + Dad + B + Sisters. Answer Real Soon. From
your Lonesome Son Harold. Lots of Love to all.[12]

THE MEN SELECTED TO SERVE on the firing squad were not thrilled with
the assignment. Captain Law, who had spent two days with Pringle when
bringing him down to Naples from Rome, was also depressed. He had desperately wanted to put the cheerful lad from Flinton on a ship and send
him off to England where he could be someone else's problem. Though he
would not have to lead the firing squad, it was his responsibility to rehearse
it, and so Captain Law stood out in a field on the lower hills surrounding
Avellino and watched his sergeant take the men through practice. Were the
reality not so dark, the exercise would have been comic. Some of the men
grew anxious around gunfire and recoiled uncontrollably at the sound of
rifles chattering. Some sweated profusely and breathed heavily. These soldiers, who had once carried rifles in combat, began reacquainting
themselves with the feel of their guns. Some held them as one might hold
a writhing snake. Some wondered why they were shooting a Canadian now
that the war had finished. These men were told that it was none of their
business, but if they did have to know, then they should know that
Canadian Headquarters in London was sure that Private Harold Pringle
was a cold-blooded killer who had murdered a comrade who had been trying to return to his regiment. The men on the firing squad were told
emphatically that there was absolutely no doubt as to Pringle's guilt.

Law comforted himself with the knowledge that the execution, while
likely, was still not yet a certainty. The official word from London was to
prepare in case the sentence was confirmed. Still, Captain Law thought,
it was a bum assignment, and as he thought this he looked up just in time
to see one of his squad pass out in a dead faint. He braced himself for the
worst. Meanwhile, the other Canadians in Avellino tidied up other loose
ends. Files were stripped and pertinent bulk files were prepared for ship-
ment to Britain.

In London, the Canadian chief of staff, P. J. Montague, was growing
weary. Political procrastination was harming his men and he did not like
it. There was no question in Montague's mind that Harold Pringle
should be executed; in fact, as far as he was concerned, the execution

should have occurred long ago. The delay was unfair even to the man who was to be shot. There was no reason to make the boy wait. Private Harold Pringle was still a Canadian soldier, and he deserved the courtesy of a swift end. And what of the other soldiers stationed in Avellino, men who had done their duty, who were being left to rot while waiting to perform a very unpleasant task? They deserved a speedy resolution.

Of course, to Canadian politicians, soldiers were meant to sit in far-off places while waiting for orders. They did not understand, as Montague did, that there was a limit. By June 12, the general was fed up. "While I appreciate fully the need for most careful pre-confirmation consideration in this case," he wrote the Privy Council, "it is advisable that residue Canadian element in Italy be withdrawn earliest possible. Officer in charge and DAPM and detail of personnel must remain there until final disposal Pringle. Can you forecast for me the date of decision of Governor General in Council." The clerk of the Privy Council replied that the decision would be rendered in approximately ten days: "Will inform you by cable at earliest possible." Montague sent word to Stewart in Avellino, telling him not to expect any information regarding Harold Pringle's execution until June 26.[13]

On June 10, Father Tom was on his way for his daily two- to three-hour visit with Harold. The lengthy stays were possible because there were so few prisoners left in Number 33 to look after. Harold was among a handful. The priest and the private had become friends, and they passed the time by playing cards. Father Tom learned about Harold's life back in Flinton. The boy was strangely congenial for someone who sat on the verge of his own execution. Father Tom began to see that the possibility of this event seemed, for the most part, incomprehensible to Harold. Harold talked of what he would do once he returned to Canada. He even spoke of re-enlisting and volunteering to go to the Burma Front. He was innocent, he told Father Tom, and there was no way they could execute him once they knew all the facts, as they did now.

Father Tom was not so sure, although he never let Harold see his doubts. When Father Tom came to visit Harold, he saw that the Canadian army viewed the young man as a discard. The Canadians had gone to great trouble to bring home all sorts of used machinery—tanks, lamps, trunks—but they did not seem interested in retrieving Harold Pringle. He was a soldier who had malfunctioned, and as there was no longer a reinforcement crisis, he was not worth rehabilitating.

Father Tom wrote Father Farrell in Rome and learned more about Harold's case, and what he learned deepened his resolve to save him. This was a good soul who had wandered from the proper path, and he was salvageable. Why sacrifice him, he thought, when there were so many thousands of unsalvageable men buried all over Italy? Father Tom's memory was filled with faces—faces of the young soldiers he had watched drift from this world of sorrow and pain. For these men, all Father Tom gave was passage into the hands of Christ. Harold Pringle, however, was a young face he could save for *this* world. So Father Tom began agitating. In his novel *Execution*, Colin McDougall created a character named Father Doorn who was an "avenging prophet" set on saving Jonesy's life.[14] This character appears to have been modelled on Father Tom, who in mid-June began navigating the remnants of the victorious Allied army, trying to convince those in charge that there was one more life worth saving.

On the evening of June 15, Harold sat before his window and stared out at Mount Vesuvius. It was hot again—well over eighty degrees Fahrenheit—but Harold was deep in what had become a daily ritual: he closed his eyes and tried to imagine snow. He saw a winter night lit by a full moon and soft white snow covering a clearing in a far-off wood. Long grass, yellow-grey from the autumn, peaked through the smooth drifts that covered everything. There was stillness and peace and a cold that caressed the cheek, cooling it and bringing life to tired breath. He was coming back from a hunt, and he knew where he was going. Home. Home to a small house warmed by a single stove. He walked and the snow nestled down on him, building into small mounds on his shoulders and clinging to the front of his jacket. True, honest snow pouring down from heaven, soothing a world that had overheated. Every sore, red wound was healed. He felt cold grip him. It pulled the sin from him. It cleansed him. It carried him home.

Harold opened his eyes. He was seated at his desk, with a short pencil in his hand and a blank sheet before him. He examined the point. Flat.

Harold called to the guard and asked him, "Will you sharpen it for me, buddy?" The British soldier carved a tip with a penknife. "There you go, mate," he told Harold. "Back to the opus."

Harold began writing:

June 15, 1945, Time 18:35 hrs.

My Darling Mother and + Dad:

Just a few lines again To say Im well and in the very best of health. I sure hope and pray this few lines find you all in the very best of health.

Well Mother Darling I havent heard from you for about a week or more. But hoping to hear from you all again real soon. It is extraordinary difficult to find any thing write about now. As there isnt any news atall. But keep writing most of the time. I guess its not much to read But atleast youll know Im well and in good health. Well Mother how are the folks around Flinton I sure hope they are all well and in good health. Also give them all my best regards wont you.

Father Farrell came down to see me yesterday from Rome and he said to give you all his best regards. And he said he would write to you just as soon as he heard any thing. For myself I havent heard anything more yet. But still hoping it wont be much longer. I just cant make it out, also, great many others cant. Its over four months now that I havent heard anything. Have you heard anything about it yet. I sure will be glad when they make up there mind.

Say Mother Dear I going to Holy Communion every day again and the English priest hear is sure awful good and kind to me. There sure quite different from the Canadian Priest, and how, after what the Canadian army did to me and how that they did it. Well to speak the truth I dont think much of them. That is to say on the army side of it anyway. If ever I get out of this, well that is to say what they charge me with, and the good Lord knows that I wasnt guilty of well I just don't think I will stay in Canada. Im very sorry for speaking like this Mother darling But I'm sure youll

like it best for me speaking my mind. Thats much more than alot
of other people can do anyway. Well Mother Darling I sure hope
this awful letter hasnt upset you to much.

And again please dont worry as I said before that the good
Lord knows Im not guilty of my charge so please don't worry
about it will you (please). And please write often. Say you saw
Father Kinlin lately if not when you do see him give him best
regards. Also I will write to him right away. How are all grandmas
I sure hope they are well and in the very best of health. Also give
them all my best regards. Say how is Charlie getting on in the
army. I sure hope he doesnt have to go overseas. And is he still in
the same place yet. Well Darling how are the rest of my sweet
Brothers and Sisters I sure hope all in the very best of health and
what is Dear Dad working at now he sure doesnt write very often
anyway. I havent had a letter from him for about two months
now. But hoping to hear from him real soon. Well Darling
Mother I guess I will say good night for this time. But Ill write
again real Soon. So cheerio for now with lots of love xxxx for
now. And the very best of luck to everyone. And may the good
Lord keep you all in the very best of health. God Bless you all and
everyone. From your lonesome Son Harold answer real soon
soon, with lots of love to all Harold.[15]

By June 19, Brigadier J. C. Stewart, the commander of the thirty-one
men left in Avellino, was reaching a fevered frustration. At the present
rate, he estimated that they might see Canada by 1946. His men, some of
whom had not been home since 1940, were sullen, and discipline was a
concern. Canadian soldiers had rioted in England while awaiting transport; although Stewart did not believe his men would go that far, he was
afraid they would refuse to shoot Harold Pringle. He tried to keep them
busy and focus their minds away from their task, but it was impossible
not to ignore the fact that the sole reason they were still in Italy was to
kill a Canadian. On June 14 the wet canteen had closed, taking with it the
final sale of beer and the distribution of free cigarettes and chocolate.
Now soldiers had to drink at Italian restaurants. Stewart cabled

Montague in London, begging for an embarkation date that he could promise his men. That would make it a concrete situation: execute one last military act and then go home. "Next sailing UK approximately 27 June and then NOT till 18 July. Necessary to advise movements of requirements for sailing some six days prior to embarkation. Your signal states information re Pringle should be here by 26 approx. May I make arrangements for departure of residue by sailing 27 June."[16]

Montague replied quickly: "Under no circumstances. You will therefore make no arrangements for departure from Italy on sailing schedule 27 June."[17]

CAPTAIN RAMSAY PARK CONTINUED his Italian lessons. He made a trip to Pompeii on leave. He tried to keep occupied. Each day he hoped for some word on whether the execution was going to go through, but he heard nothing. He had small discussions with Law and Cowle, which reinforced the notion that they were going to kill a hardened criminal. By now the stories were reaching epic proportions. Rumour had it that Pringle had led a gang of two hundred deserters drawn from all armies, including the Germans. He had shot two men in cold blood through the head when they had informed him that they wanted to rejoin their units.

One June 21, while he was working in the staff office, Park saw an English priest, along with a lawyer from the British Judge Advocate General's officer, arrive at Brigadier Stewart's office. They spent a half an hour with Stewart, and when Park saw them emerge, he noticed that his commanding officer looked pale.

THAT NIGHT HAROLD was writing again.

June 21, 1945 Time 18:45 hrs.
My Darling Mother and Dad.
Just a few lines again to say Im well and in the very best of health.
And I sure hope and pray this few lines find you all in the very
best of health.

    Well Mother Dear I sure hope you'll forgive me for not writ-
ing this last few days as Ive run out of news or anything to write
about. I havent heard from you now for about two weeks. So sure

hope your getting my letters ok. Well Im still in Italy yet and still havent heard anything more from Canada. My lawyer has gone back to Canada and I havent heard anything more about it. But the English Catholic priest of this camp is doing all he can for me. Say Mother he had the Holy Father from Rome say mass for me isnt that wonderful of him. I hardly ever see a Canadian priest atall. He also got me a English lawyer. He said he was going to wake the Canadians. I still receive holy Communion every day. But through the English priest not the Canadian. I dont know if I told you or not that Father Farrell came down to see me. And drove over two hundred miles to get hear. So I think thats quite wonderful. The Canadian camp is quite near hear and they havent been up atall. But this English lawyer and Father Lenane went down to see the head Canadian officer in Italy to day. And Father Lenane said if he didnt do something right away that he would write Mr King of Canada.

So I hope to have some news for you real soon. Well Mother Darling how is everyone around Flinton I sure hope all in the very best of health also give them my best regards. I suppose that most of the boys are all home now ain't they. And how are all my Sweet Brothers + Sisters. I sure hope all in the very best of health. And has Marion been up home yet and did she get my letter I havent heard from her yet. I sure hope they are all in good health and is my Brother Charlie still in Canada yet or has he gone over-seas. I sure hope not.

How are all the folks down at Grandmas I sure all in the best of health. Myself I dont know why I ask as they never write. But still hope they are well. And if everything turns out ok I think Ill ask to go to Burma front. Say Mother Dear how is Aunt Ida and Uncle Leo. I sure hope shes well now. Say why is it that Dad never writes, I have not had a letter from him for Months now. I sure hope he isnt sick. And how is Father Kinlin, I sure hope in good health also give him my best regards.

Well Mother Darling again please dont worry about this will you, as everything will be ok.

And Ill write again real soon. And I sure hope to hear from you again real soon. If only you knew just how happy your letters make me I think you all would write more (often).

Well Mother Darling I guess I'll ring of to-night. But will write again real soon So cheerio Dear Mother and all, with the very best of luck to all and may the good lord keep you all in good health. With all my Love and kisses answer real soon. From your Lonesome Son Harold. all so give my best regards to Mildred.

Harold.[18]

18.

BRECCIELLE

O n 20 June 1945, Prime Minister King had a meeting with A. M. Hill, the assistant clerk of the Privy Council.[1] It must have been a cheerful discussion, held in King's office on Parliament Hill. Thanks to the victorious conclusion of the Second World War, the prime minister had won himself another federal election—despite the conscription crisis, a disaster that would have felled most other politicians. King was victorious but not unscathed. While he carried the election, he had lost his own riding.[2]

Now that the election was over, Hill was meeting with King to refresh the prime minister's memory of a certain Canadian private named Harold Joseph Pringle. The man was a deserter who had been found guilty of murdering another Canadian soldier, also a deserter. Harold Pringle had first come to the attention of the Prime Minister's Office in March, but King and his staff had decided that nothing should be done until after the federal election. In the interim, as Hill informed King, the Judge Advocate General, under the direction of Major General P. J. Montague, gave the case close consideration and found no irregularities in the trial. Pringle had been sentenced to death. Thus far, Hill told King, the government had shown leniency to soldiers condemned to execution. A total of eight Canadians had been convicted of murder during the war; some had even killed their superior officers, yet none of these had been executed. It was important to note, he said, that Pringle had maintained his innocence throughout his trial.

But there was a catch.

Pringle, it seemed, had not acted alone. Two Brits were involved, one a naval petty officer and the other a sapper. These two men had already been executed, and if the Canadians did not execute their prisoner they might anger the British. Also, they would seem soft by comparison. Canada would appear to lack the force of will necessary to be a great power. Then again, the execution of a Canadian soldier months after the war had ended, and long after all the Canadian army had left Italy, would not play well at home. It is likely that King, an astute tactician, observed that executing Harold Pringle in England would be a public relations nightmare.

Hill had an answer. Anticipating the need to kill Harold Pringle, the army had not shipped him to England with all the other soldiers under sentence. Instead, the military had kept him in Italy with a residue of Canadian troops in a small town in the south called Avellino. This troop detail was being trained to run a firing squad, and once ready they could execute Pringle in complete secrecy. The government would not issue a press release about the execution, and the incident would not be included in official army reports of courts martial and sentences carried out. There were no Canadian journalists in Italy to discover it. The army would erase all evidence of the firing squad by sealing all records pertaining to Harold Pringle for forty years. The soldiers involved in the execution would be ordered never to discuss it. Harold Pringle's family would also be instructed to hide the details surrounding his death or forfeit his military pension.

It must have sounded like a reasonable solution. A pragmatic man when he wanted to be, King might have been curious about the actual machinations of the operation. Given the fact that the Canadians had never executed a soldier during the entire Second World War, how were they going to go about doing it?

This was not a problem, Hill answered; the British had already sent instructions.

Two days later Major General P. J. Montague received a cable from Ottawa, which in five brief paragraphs outlined the government's position. The findings and sentence of the court had been confirmed by the governor general. The findings and order were being sent by plane to London, but the army was not under any circumstances to execute Harold Pringle until the official papers had been received and sent to Avellino. In addition, Harold Pringle's petition was disallowed; at the time of the promulgation of his sentence, the accused should be informed of this disallowance. Lieutenant Colonel Anglin, who had filed a report stating that he thought Lucky was dead at the time of Pringle's shot, was summoned to Montague's office. "Chief of Staff would like to have a word with you re: this cable," wrote Brigadier Beverley Matthews.[3]

On June 27, Brigadier Stewart received a package from headquarters in London. It contained the official Privy Council decision to execute Pringle, along with instructions in ten steps, entitled "Procedure For Military Executions."[4]

Captain Henry Law sat in Avellino's Maple Leaf Gardens—which was no longer Maple Leaf Gardens but was once again an Italian restaurant—and poured himself a glass of red wine. Sitting on his table underneath a stack of provost marshal files lay two pages of instructions, but though Law had read them a dozen times, the directions still baffled him. They read like a script, complete with characters, blocking and plot. There was the prisoner, whose function was obvious, and there was a cast of supporting characters. These actors had more intricate roles to play. The commanding officer, for instance, would arrange for the "production of the prisoner" and was also responsible for the promulgation of the sentence. "Usually this is deferred until about an hour or two before the time fixed for the execution," the instructions read. "It must be remembered that the President of the Court-Martial will have already warned the prisoner in writing that the sentence of death has been passed. The promulgating officer should ask the prisoner whether he has any request to make and whether he wants food or drink. He should be allowed, if possible, any drink he asks for and, if desired, a sedative injection by a Medical Officer."

Dr. Joe Cowle, left, and fellow officers at the
Officers' Club in Naples, 1945.

—

The chaplain was to accompany the prisoner from his place of confinement to the place of execution. The instructions stated that it was "undesirable that he should wear vestments or that he should read portions of the burial service before the execution." The medical officer would examine the body immediately after the firing party had discharged its volley and before the body was unbound. As the "Officer of the Provost Service," it was Law's responsibility to find the place for the execution. He was also burdened with organizing the firing squad and making many of the tiny arrangements necessary when planning an execution. The number of small, unthinkable, problematic details was remarkable, but the instructions provided an answer for each one. For instance, what was the best time for an execution? "The best time is shortly after dawn." The best place for an execution—well, that was more open to interpretation: it "should be secluded and as near as possible to the place of confinement."[5]

Law's musing was interrupted by the arrival of Captain Cowle, the camp doctor, known as "Cowley" among his fellow officers. Cowle looked happy, which was typical for him. After pouring himself a glass of wine, he told Law that he might have a solution to the question of where the execution should be done. A local farmer had told him about a place not far from Avellino near the small village of Monte Forte; from this village a dirt road circled the hillsides that bordered both places. The Italians called it the *le Breccielle*, "broken ground." Off *le Breccielle*, there was a rifle range, which, before the war, the Mussolini Youth Party had used for target practice. Along with its Fascist legacy, the Breccielle rifle range had a history of executions. In 1918, at the end of the First World War, the Italians had shot an Austrian soldier there whom they suspected of spying. In 1943, two bandits had been executed there.

Cowle's news encouraged Law, and the two officers immediately left the restaurant and jumped into Law's jeep. They drove ten minutes out of Avellino and then turned up the small drive to Breccielle. The sight was as described. The rifle range was a long, narrow, dilapidated strip of barren land alongside the road. At the far end, to the east, there was a concrete wall about twelve feet high. Law and Cowle walked to the barrier and examined its surface; it was pocked with bullet holes.

Law turned away, looking out toward Avellino and then staring open-mouthed across the valley toward Monte Forte. A high mountain range loomed into the sky; midway up its slope, a small, ruined medieval castle sat on a foothill. Those ruins, Law recalled, had been used by the provosts as checkpoint for searching trucks going between Naples and Avellino. The castle still had a number of sound rooms, and it backed onto a sheer cliff, leaving no means of escape. It would be the perfect place to keep Harold Pringle the night before his execution, just a five-minute drive away when the time came to move him to Breccielle. There was not even that much preparation required at the site. Law could have a couple of privates dig a stake into the dirt in front of the wall.

FATHER TOM'S MEETING WITH the Canadian brigadier Stewart was disheartening. The man knew nothing except that Pringle had been found guilty of murder and that he and the rest of the Canadian detail were to wait in Avellino for the paperwork. Unofficially, the officer told Lenane, it was not a simple case. He had learned from Canadian Headquarters that two other soldiers were involved, both British, and they had been executed. In the spirit of fairness, it was likely that twenty-three-year-old Harold Pringle would join them. This was the unfortunate logic of war: because others had died, it would be necessary for more to die.

Father Tom visited Harold every day and found the lad buoyed by his rosaries and by his prayers. Harold continued playing cards with his guards. When he was alone he sometimes sang mournful Canadian folk songs. A smile would spread across Harold's face the instant Father Tom arrived at his cell, and he would talk speedily, on any subject. Harold spoke so much of home that Father Tom began to feel as if he too was a native-born son of Flinton, Ontario.

When Father Tom prayed, he asked God and Jesus to help him remain strong when Harold, who appeared convinced that he would not be executed, spoke of the things he was going to do after the war. He prayed that he would not give away the dire nature of Harold's situation. He was there to guide Harold on his most important journey, a journey out of prison, out of the chains that bound men to earth and into an ever-lasting freedom; a flash of the cruel truth might hamper that crossing. If Harold realized that he was never going home, if he sensed that the army was not going to spare him and that he was never going to see his mother or father or brothers or sisters again, he might fall prey to despair. That was not the future Father Tom wished for his young charge. Father Tom prayed to the Blessed Virgin Mary, asking her, when the time came, to carry Harold up to heaven like a sweet apple resting on a beautiful pillow.

So when Harold spoke of Flinton and life after the war, Father Tom smiled back.

AT NIGHT, AFTER THE GUARDS grew tired of playing gin, Harold would read from *True Devotion to Mary*. "It is difficult to persevere in sanctity," it said.

> That is because of the strange corruption of the world. The world is so filthy it seems to sully all of us. Even the hearts of the religious are smeared with dust, if not with mud and slime.
>
> It is something of a miracle if one stays firm in the torrent without being carried away; if one sails through a stormy pirate-ridden sea without being shipwrecked, drowned or attacked by corsairs; or if one walks safely through a countryside reeking with pestilence. And it is the Virgin Mary who works the miracle. She works it for those children who serve her the right way.
>
> This being clear, we must now, certainly, choose the right way, the true devotion, to her.[6]

When he grew tried of reading, Harold put out his light and looked out his window toward Vesuvius, silhouetted against the evening sky, while a hot wind blew into his cell from inland. What time is it back home, he wondered? On a night like this his mother would sometimes wait up for him as he walked home. On those nights, Harold would sing to let her know he was returning. He would sing out, and the whole family would hear him. They would listen as he sang and walked through the darkness along forests and streams filled with wild things and hidden creatures.

Harold closed his eyes and breathed in deeply. Then he sang and clenched his eyes shut and dreamt that they could hear him. He sent each note out and imagined the notes floating across wide oceans and valleys and forests and rivers and lakes and trees back to a small white farmhouse in the woods.

"You're pretty good, mate," a guard said when he was done. "Give us another."

TO ITS RESIDUE OF CANADIANS, Avellino, which had once seemed so small, now began to feel like an enormous urban colossus. When a soldier passed a comrade on its streets, it felt as if long-lost friends were being reunited. To the Canadians, it was obvious that the Italians were eagerly anticipating their departure and that the citizens of Avellino were already trying to forget them. The preparations for Pringle's execution, meanwhile, continued as the summer heat increased. To a soldier like Park who had fought in many battles, it seemed an extraordinary amount of effort and expense, all for one death; after all, only six months earlier armies in Italy were killing thousands. Now there was just one more death to register; the men charged with bringing it about told themselves that it was only one more life and that after so many millions had died it couldn't make much difference.

Captain Ramsay Park left his copy of the execution instructions in his room at the Villa di Marzo. Its contents stuck in his mind. "These notes are to serve as a guide to those who may have to arrange for executions by shooting," the instructions began. "The main object is to carry out the sentence as rapidly and humanely as possible."

As the officer commanding the firing party, it was Park's duty to give the final order. After the prisoner was tied to his stake, Park would stand by the firing party and watch while a sergeant delivered orders to the men by hand signal. Once the firing squad was ready, its rifles, loaded, cocked and aimed, it was Park's duty to utter the "only word spoken from the moment of the prisoner's arrival until his death." That was the word "Fire."[7]

On June 29, Law had the squad up at Breccielle where the Canadians were conducting daily rehearsals for the event. Brigadier Stewart sent word to Number 33 British Military Prison that they would soon be taking Private Harold Joseph Pringle, C-5292, off their hands. This news was not cause for celebration at Harold's prison. In his notes for *Execution*, Colin McDougall wrote that "those guarding Jonesy understood him and grew to like him, and even feel protective of about him. Nobody wishes to harm Jonesy the person, Jonesy the presumed gangster, however must be punished."[8]

Meanwhile, the paperwork made its way from Canada to London; from London it was sent by plane to Naples, and from Naples it was sent by truck to Avellino. On July 4, the orders arrived and Brigadier Stewart telephoned Number 33. The commandant of Number 33 told Father Tom, in confidence, that the word had come back from Canada and that Harold was shortly to be executed. Father Tom did not tell Harold but began to spend more time with him. He asked the Pope to say a special mass for Harold; the Pope obliged.

That day, Harold, with both hands and feet shackled, shuffled out the prison door toward the truck that sat idling on the compound driveway. Around him swirled the scent of flowers, planted over one hundred years earlier by eager scientists. Father Tom was at his side carrying a rucksack of Harold's belongings. Two guards marched beside Harold; another four waited on the truck. Harold had been told that he was being taken to the Canadians, and he interpreted this news as evidence that he was going to be shipped home. After all, if they were going to execute him, why go to the trouble of moving him? Harold did not understand that now that the war was over, only Canadians could kill a Canadian.

Harold was lifted into the truck and seated between two soldiers with Father Tom sitting opposite him. The truck shifted into gear and its wheels crunched along the crumbling asphalt. It pulled out of the prison compound and began to weave its way along narrow country roads. Harold cranked his neck, trying to peer through a thin crack in the truck's canvas. He could see nothing but could feel sunlight on his face. The guards noticed his effort. They traded a glance, and then the guard on Harold's left stuck a hand through the canvas and, with a strong yank, pulled it back. A triangle at least nine inches wide was cut open in the fabric.

"Don't get any ideas," the guard told Harold, who barely heard him. Harold pressed his face up against the opening and watched the countryside pass by. He gazed in wonder at orange groves, green fields, cows, farmers, cars, houses, trees; he smelled the scent of dirt and earth; he absorbed the expanding blueness of the sky. Harold saw the Apennines, the mountains he had marched along as the Hasty Ps pushed toward the Hitler Line. As the truck neared Avellino it drove through a deep valley. Pine trees lined the road. Harold drew a deep breath and felt the hot air. Off in the distance he heard the sound of children letting off firecrackers.

Harold spent the night in the ruined castle at Monte Forte, in a room that looked out over Avellino. In the early evening, he prayed and talked with Father Tom. They played cards and told stories about their families. Father Tom was from Wales, and Harold wondered what it was like there. Harold was preoccupied with his mother and father, and he made Father Tom promise to write them in the event that anything finally did happen to him. Together they read passages from *True Devotion to Mary*.

> If we are afraid of going directly to Jesus Christ, God, either
> because of His infinite grandeur, or because of the vileness of our
> sins, let us implore the help and intercession of our mother, and
> His Mother, Mary. She is good. She is tender. There is in her
> nothing austere, nothing forbidding, nothing too sublime, noth-
> ing too bright. Seeing her, we see our pure nature. She is not the
> sun that might dazzle us by its rays. She is more like the moon
> which receives and tempers the light of the sun and adjusts it to
> our dim perception.[9]

Later, after Father Tom left, Harold sat awake in the darkness of his cell. He could not sleep. Thoughts coursed through him. He thought of Doreen Woods and of the house they might have lived in. In the darkness he saw Charlie, Bill and Lucky. The Sailor Gang crouched in shadows in the corner and smiled. They leaned against the wall, relaxed. Harold thought of sunny days walking along the Via Appia, the park at Re di Roma, the fooling around. He saw Lucky lying on the floor of 28 Via Pistoia, and he heard him saying, "Why did you want to do that for, Charlie?" And Harold remembered saying, "That was a crazy thing to do." He remembered noc-turnal firefights in the Arielli Valley with flashing red bullets harrowing through the trees. He remembered the night in the house with Ivan Gunter, the night he had finally decided to run. Shells were crashing down, and he told Gunter, ten cents a day, that's how much he made. He would be goddamned if he was going to die for ten cents a day.

Harold turned to the shadows in his cell and saw the Sailor Gang. Bill was there in his white navy uniform. He smiled. "If you fire at a dead body it won't haunt you," Bill told him. Harold saw Charlie and Lucky smile.

"We really was taking you to a hospital, Lucky," Harold said. "We really was."

Lucky ran a hand along the back of his neck.

"Well, Joe," Charlie answered. "We're all learning to be nicer."

If he got out of this, maybe he'd volunteer to go to the Burma Front, Harold thought. Then again, maybe not.

Captain Ramsay Park stared into the bathroom mirror and finished shaving. It was five in the morning on July 5, 1945, and down the hall in his bedroom, his batman was preparing his uniform. Downstairs, the principessa's maid was making cappuccino. Park paused for a moment and reached for a cigarette that was burning in an ashtray balanced on a porcelain shelf by the sink. He drew deeply on it. Fifty-five years later, Park would remember that on this morning, he "knew what was on everybody's mind, including the men on the firing squad. They wanted to make sure he was killed the first time so that we would not have a wounded duck walking around."[10]

Down at the soldiers' barracks, Corporal John Churchward was waking his boys up. Although there were only ten men on the actual firing squad, the rest would be needed to close the roads leading up to the execution site in order to ensure secrecy. Churchward had already secured an issue of rum for the boys who would be firing. There would also be plenty of *vino* available after the event.

Brigadier Stewart was in his office talking with Captain Law, who assured his commanding officer that all the preparations had been made. What about Park, Stewart asked. "He'll be all right," Law replied. There was not much for him to do, just yell "Fire" at the right time. Stewart raised an eyebrow. "That is quite a bit of not much," he told Law, and lit himself a cigarette.

When they were done smoking, Law and Stewart, escorted by five privates, drove from their office to the castle at Monte Forte. There they found a Welsh priest who had spent the night sleeping in the same quarters as the sentries who guarded Harold Pringle's cell. It was five minutes to six in the morning. Stewart recognized the priest. "Father Lenane," he said.

"Brigadier Stewart."

"You know why we're here," Stewart said. "You can be on hand if you like."

The men then walked silently past the chaplain to the door of Harold's cell. Father Tom called out, "Harold. Harold, son. We are coming in."

Harold was lying on his cot, clothed, and he began to awaken. He thought, I must have finally fallen asleep. He saw the door open and Father Tom walk in, and then he realized that Father Tom was not alone. He saw an officer. And he saw Captain Law, the one who had brought him from Rome to Naples, the one who had said he was going to England. The officer Harold did not know began speaking.

"Private Harold Joseph Pringle His Excellency the Governor General in council…."

Harold's head swooned. He only made out bits and pieces of what the officer said.

"…when on active service, committing a civil offence, that is to say murder, in that he, in the Field, in Italy, on or about 1 November 1944, murdered Private McGillivray, otherwise known as Lucky."

Father Tom laid a hand on his shoulder.

"Therefore, His excellency the Governor General in Council, on the recommendation of the Minister of National Defence, is pleased to confirm and doth hereby confirm the said finding and sentence; the accused to suffer death by being shot."

Harold was offered his last requests. He asked for tea and cigarettes and strawberry jam. He refused the offer of morphine. On a sheet of YMCA foolscap, he began writing.

July 5th 1945
C5292 Pte Harold Pringle
My Darling Mother + Dad + Brothers + Sisters
Well Mother Darling this going to be an awful surprise to you all
and I sure hope and pray that you dont take it to hard. But the
papers have just come back from Canada and the army has found
me guilty so they say and I guess the good Lord wishes for me
and I sure will pray and do every thing in the world for you all.

Well Mother Darling I received a very nice letter from Marion yesterday. But I dont think I will have the time to answer it. I am sending this short note by Father Tom.

So again Dear Mother + Dad + Brothers + Sisters, May the Good Lord keep you all in the very best of health.

To My Darling Mother + Dad + Brothers + Sisters From your Lonesome Son Harold.

Good by My Darling

With lots of Love to all.

PS xxxxxxxxxxxxxxxxx

If you would Mother please let my Darling Doreen Woods know wont you. Also give her my love.[11]

BY SEVEN THIRTY, THE FIRING party was assembled at Breccielle. The squad of ten soldiers had been driven up by truck and was lined up ten yards from the concrete wall, in front of which a wooden post was fixed deep into the ground. Sergeant Hayden, the highest-ranking non-commissioned Canadian officer in Avellino, ordered his men to load one live round into their rifles and then to ground arms. Leaving their rifles resting on the ground, Sergeant Hayden then marched the firing party down the road away from Breccielle and out of sight of the firing range. Sergeant Hayden then reminded them that the best favour they could do for the prisoner was to shoot straight. He offered a shot of rum to those who needed it.

The mood among the firing party was one of resigned despondency. "They knew they had a job to do," recalled Park.[12] The men stood at attention, believing that this would be the last real order they would ever have to obey. Hands shook and minds teetered. The war had been a disaster beyond comprehension. People, countries, villages, families, cities, towns had been ruined. Billions of violent acts had been committed. Now all this suffering was going to be articulated in a final punitive act. War was simple: pull the trigger enough times, and eventually you got to go home.

While the firing squad was removed, Captain R. Gammell switched the rifles. He removed the live rounds from two guns and replaced them with blanks. Sergeant Hayden marched the firing squad back.

It was seven forty-five in the morning.

At Monte Forte, Harold asked Father Tom to write his mother and to send the letter he had written and his personal effects to her. When two soldiers fixed his arms behind his back and secured them with leather straps, Harold began to be overwhelmed. As he was marched past Father Tom, he told the chaplain, "Tell my mother I'm dead." Captain Law tried to place a cap over his face but Harold protested. Law said that he would compromise and use a blindfold and that they would tie it just before reaching the execution site. Law pinned a red scrap of cloth to Harold's uniform to mark his heart. Harold was led out of his cell at Monte Forte and escorted to a jeep that sat idling outside. The world exploded in colour. The sky's blue seemed to scream while the trees burst with green. Father Tom sat on the seat opposite him, and together they prayed. They are taking me for a ride, thought Harold, they are taking me for a ride. The jeep pulled out.

Meanwhile, a jeep left the Villa di Marzo. Captain Ramsay Park, clean-shaven and wearing his wire-rimmed spectacles, smoked furtively while he was driven to Breccielle. Beside him, a private kept his eyes on the road. There was no conversation. Park tried to stay calm. "By the time the actual date came I had it figured out that it was something that should be done," he would later remember. "I wasn't proud of the job, because what was worrying me was that if there was much advertising and the rest of it, I would be in the same position as a hangman, sort of a low-class citizen."[13]

Harold arrived at Breccielle at seven fifty. The way Tony Basciano later heard it, Harold was marched past the line of soldiers. He stared at the firing squad and said, "Come on, do what you have to do, let's get it over with."[14] The way Michael Cloney would later hear it, Harold told the squad, "I was never much good, and if I had gotten out of this, I would not have amounted to much good. So, go ahead, do your duty, do what you have to do. I don't blame you."[15] He was tied to the post at both his feet and his torso.

Park says that Harold Pringle was silent. He was peaceful. There were no last words. When Park arrived at seven fifty-eight, he found the squad at attention and Harold bound to the post. Behind the firing squad the rest of Avellino's officers were present—Gammell, Law, the Protestant chaplain Father Gehl and the commanding officer Brigadier Stewart. Cowle, the doctor, stood to the left of the line. Park took his place on the right, approximately two feet from the firing squad. Father Tom stood behind the line, praying. Sergeant Hayden ordered the firing party through its drill. Using hand signals, he had them shoulder arms, and aim. This was Park's cue.

Doctor Cowle could not look at Harold. Instead he watched Park, whose face was stiff, as if frozen by the task he was about to perform. Park's chest was heaving and sweat stained his shirt. There was a moment of perfect stillness as Park fixed his eyes on Harold. Another second passed. Then, barking the word, Park gave the order: "Fire."

The bullets struck Harold, and their force punched him back. His feet buckled and his body seemed to drain. He collapsed.

Each man in the firing party, as if performing a drill, turned his eyes away from the sight. Heads bowed, they gazed at the ground. Cowle rushed to Harold's body and found it laced with bullet wounds, all in the chest. He checked for a pulse. "The guy fell over," Park remembered. "The doctor was there immediately. It didn't take him long to determine he was dead."[16]

The shell-shocked men of the Special Employment Company had done their duty. Sergeant Hayden ordered the firing party to march back to the truck, but the men ignored him and walked to it in a chaotic mass. They slowly climbed in and were driven back to Avellino, where a large supply of alcohol and cigarettes awaited them. Father Tom approached Harold's body with tears in his eyes, while two soldiers freed Harold's arms from the straps that had held him to the stake and placed his body on a stretcher. The priest reached down and retrieved Harold's rosary from the dusty ground. He followed the stretcher, and as it was placed in the ambulance, he climbed inside with it. Park stood transfixed. After a few minutes, he stepped into his jeep. What he did or how he spent the remainder of July 5, Park would never know. The memory would be blacked out.

Half an hour later, in the British Military Cemetery in the town of Caserta, which means "City of Peace" in Italian, a small detail lowered Harold Joseph Pringle into the earth. Father Tom said a brief prayer and

thought of Harold's smile. When he returned to Portici, he telephoned
Father Farrell in Rome. The Canadian chaplain wrote a letter to Harold's
parents and also sent the news to Flinton's parish priest.

34 Special Training Barracks CMF July 5th 1945
Dear Fr. Kinlin,
In a letter dated April 9th which reached me quite safely, you
made the request that I should write to you as soon as I had more
information. You must have been wondering why I have not written to you for all this time and the reason is simply this, that there
has been no fresh information to give you. Only now is further
information available and it is with the very deepest regret that I
have to inform you that poor Harold Pringle was executed this
morning. May God have mercy on his soul.

It has been a most distressing period. I knew that you were
expecting to hear from me, and I knew also that Mrs. Pringle
made several requests that I should write to her; but the trouble
has been that with the uncertainty that has prevailed all these
months, I was simply afraid to write in case by the time the letter
reached you, it would contain information which was misleading
and painful. As time went on I naturally became more and more
hopeful that the case was being reconsidered, and that our long
wait would at least be rewarded by the news that at any rate
Harold's life would be spared even though there might be a
period of imprisonment to be done. On the one hand I could not
in conscience write to either you or Mrs. Pringle saying that it
was my confident opinion that Harold would not be executed if I
had to follow this letter up by another saying that the worst had
happened, nor on the other hand, did I feel justified in writing a
letter intimating that there was little hope for him and thus
upsetting you and Mrs. Pringle unnecessarily if things had gone
well. That was my predicament and it was difficult. Even Harold
could not understand why I kept putting off my letter to Canada
and I could not tell him my real reason because he himself was
very optimistic and cheerful and again I did not feel justified in

upsetting him unduly. It really has been a most difficult time for me and I do sincerely trust that both you and his mother will understand that in not writing, I was only trying on the one hand to avoid worrying you unduly and on the other hand, raising false hopes in your minds.

Let me give you a brief history of the case as I knew it. I am not concerned with the legal aspect, that is not my province, I am concerned merely with the human aspect and certainly from this point of view it makes a very sad story and a story which I think should be made more public. On Feb. 14th Harold was informed by his Court Martial that he had been condemned to death. He asked for an appeal to be made. It took his Defending Officer six weeks to frame that appeal and it was signed by Harold on March 30th. Straight away, it seemed to me an incredible long time to keep a man waiting who was under sentence of death. Then for two weary months the poor lad waited in solitary confinement for the appeal to go to Canada for a decision on his case to be finally made. I may add that at the time the appeal went up I myself drafted a letter pleading for mercy on the lines that the boy was in no sense a criminal and that he had had the misfortune to get mixed up with some very wicked people. But as I say we waited for two whole months and at times the boy's distress was pitiable although on the whole he was very optimistic and kept wonderfully cheerful. In fact, he was simply marvelous. At the end of May, the Canadian authorities (he had been detained all this time in a British Military Prison) came to take him to their own headquarters. We all thought this was a good sign as we felt that if he was to lose his life, the execution would have been done on the spot without further unnecessary delay. He was told by the Canadians (whether officially or otherwise I don't know) that he was to be shipped to Canada and this made it look all the more as if he was going to get away with his life. When he left my care at the end of May, I myself felt absolutely confident that things were going well with him and I almost ceased to worry about the case. Instead of being put on board ship by the

Canadians, he was put in another British Prison in Naples and there the waiting started all over again.

The Catholic priest in charge of this prison got in touch with me and gave me the impression that as far as he could judge the case was very black although nobody seemed to know anything definite. I went down to see Harold myself (I live just near Rome) and found him cheerful but getting very fed up with all these delays and changes of plans. I am leaving it to you as a human being to conjure up for yourself the mental torture of the poor lad who had been under sentence of death since Feb. 14th. I tried to get something moving through the British embassy in Rome but I met with no success. The trouble was that practically all Canadian troops had left this country and there was only a small rear party left at their headquarters; the Senior Canadian Officer there knew nothing except that he was to wait for Harold's papers to be returned from Canada. Finally the confirmation of sentence came through and as I have said the poor boy was executed this morning. It is my own personal opinion that on its merits there was every reason to hope that the case would have been dealt with more mercifully but unfortunately there were two other men involved, one a British soldier, another a British Naval man, and both their sentences had been confirmed the one by the British Army authorities, the other by the Admiralty, and this may, I say may, have proved an obstacle to the reconsideration of Harold's case. But my point all along has been that no matter what the circumstances are, it should not be tolerated that any man under sentence of death should have to spend five months in indescribable mental torture, and some adequate explanation should be forthcoming. You as a Canadian priest may be able to do more in this respect than I can. I feel confident that you will ventilate the matter in very high quarters.

But there is a distinctly consoling aspect to the very tragic case. Harold has died a wonderful death prepared in a way which I pray may be vouchsafed to me when my turn comes. For the last few months, he has led a wonderful Catholic Life. Since Easter he

has received Holy Communion every morning. Never a day
passed without his reading a portion of the New Testament and
saying his Rosary. He read some beautiful books during his
imprisonment including the *Song of Bernadette* which I lent him
and which he enjoyed very much and the last book I saw in his
possession was *True Devotion to the Blessed Virgin* by [Grignion]
de Montfort. I should have liked to have been with him at the end
but this unfortunately was not possible. But the British Chaplain
in Naples had taken him Holy Communion every morning since
he went down there. Perhaps it was God's way of making sure
that He got him and God's plan certainly worked. His was a wonderful death to be envied by us all.

I am sorry to write so distressingly to you and a lot of what I
have said had better not be passed on to his people; it is no use
increasing their sorrow. I said Mass for Harold this morning and
will say many more in the future and now of course I will write to
his mother but again I will wait a few days to make sure that the
news reaches her either through official channels or through you.
If there is anything else I can do just let me know. I got to love
that boy; he was really a lovely character and nothing I can do for
his family will ever be too much trouble.

With all good wishes,

Yours sincerely in Christ, B S Farrell.[17]

19.

CASERTA

On the early afternoon of July 11, 1945, a cloudy, humid summer day, Mary Ellen Pringle received a telegram from the director of records for the Adjutant General. Father Kinlin carried the telegram, but he had yet to receive Father Farrell's letter.

"Re: C5292 Private Joseph Pringle," the telegram began. "Dear Mrs. Pringle,"

"In connection with the regretted death of your"—here there was an enormous gap in the text and two lines beneath it was typed the word "son" and then "the soldier marginally named"—"I am directed to forward herewith for your retention a copy of 'Notes for the general information and guidance of the next of kin or other relatives of soldiers reported deceased' which no doubt will be of interest and assistance to you."[1]

Mary Ellen's daughter Teresa, who was eight years old at the time, recalls that when she saw her mother and Father Kinlin go into her family's small parlour, she immediately knew something was wrong. For a moment she heard the priest speaking in a hushed tone, and then she heard her mother let out an unearthly cry. Mary Ellen emerged from the room, with Father Kinlin by her side, and Teresa saw tears running down her cheeks. She took her daughter by the hand and called to her five-year-old son Cecil. The three left the small white house and began walking. All the while, Teresa remembers, her mother "cried and moaned." Mary Ellen walked the roads around Flinton for four or five hours. Her children trailed after her.

Finally they returned to the house. It was beginning to rain; Mary Ellen sent Teresa and Cecil inside, but she would not go back in. She stayed outside, by a rail fence, crying. Teresa watched from the window as the slight drizzle turned to a summer storm. She put on a jacket and ran out through the downpour to her mother.

"Mommy, you should come inside the house. You're going to get sick."

Then Teresa took her mother by the hand and led her back home.[2]

When William Pringle learned of his son's execution, he ran into Flinton clutching the telegram, screaming, "Look what they've done to my son!" That, at least, is the way the scene was described to Tony Basciano.[3]

Fifty-five years later, in October 2000, Teresa handed a letter to me and asked if I would place it in Harold's grave when I visited. It was a message for her brother, the one she never got to know, the one she remembered ironing his uniform. "Dig it into the earth, so that it won't be found," she told me, and she asked that a photograph be brought back to her. She and Veronica wanted to know how their brother had been laid to rest. A few weeks later I stood in a military cemetery in Caserta and stared at an ash that was nestled on the wet green grass before his gravestone.

This was tobacco residue, not burnt palm leaves sanctified by holy water, but its appearance before Harold's grave seemed to have some religious resonance. On Ash Wednesday, Roman Catholics receive a blessing in the form of a crucifix marked on their foreheads by a priest. As the mark is made, the clergyman says the words, "Remember man that thou art dust and unto dust thou shalt return." The moment marks the beginning of Lent, a time of fasting and penitence.

Who was this ash meant for? Who needed to atone? Who needed forgiveness?

First, I thought of Harold Pringle, who had been a far from model soldier, despite serving well while with the Hastings and Prince Edward

Regiment in Italy. Officially, the army executed him for murder, but the case against him was circumspect and thin and there was, as Michael Cloney had observed, "reasonable doubt a mile wide." There was every reason to find him innocent or at least commute his sentence. In hindsight, it is obvious that Harold was actually executed for desertion. The Canadian government decided to snuff him out, months after the war had ended, because the British had shot Honess and Croft and because the army, the Judge Advocate General and Prime Minister Mackenzie King and his staff did not think a deserter was worth saving.

A deserter was not worth saving because in a time of world war, a time in which people could either give everything they had or have it taken away from them, a deserter had exerted his right to say no. To a government, this was a weapon more lethal than any bomb and, as was often pointed out to me during the research of this book, we are lucky that everyone did not feel like Harold and the C Ration Kid. To which the reply was always, you're right, we are lucky. It was not a given. It should not be surprising that some front-line soldiers eventually refused to fight; rather, it is surprising that so many kept going despite the evidence that doing so would result in their own deaths.

It is ironic that the Canadian government would elect to execute Harold Pringle when there were hundreds of thousands of effective deserters, healthy men who refused to volunteer, walking freely about in Canada. In January 1945, for instance, graduates from the Osgoode Hall Law School, members of the Toronto Maple Leafs, university football players and a few well-known golfers were all declared unfit for service due to "mental instability." To the deputy minister of labour, it seemed "almost as though the thing had been planned by those examined."[4] Of course, Canada's greatest champion of contentious deserters was Prime Minister Mackenzie King himself. As a result of "home conscription," his state-sanctioned desertion, the combat soldiers who enlisted at the war's beginning were signed on for the duration. They would fight until they were killed or maimed, went mad or deserted. "Among the wounded we tended and the dead we buried were lads whose physique was not equal to war," wrote army chaplain William Smith in his 1953 book *What Time the Tempest*.

They had been urged into the army by the recruiting advertising
of which we saw some specimens in the newspapers from
Canada. This advertising worked upon fathers who should have
been kept at home. It worked on boys in their teens. It did not
work on thousands of able-bodied young men who might well
have gone into battle. Now we were burying lads who had the
stuff to go into battle but not the physical stamina to recover
from their wounds. And during these battles in the Gothic Line
we read in the Canadian papers about the Canadian hockey players and their well-fed and well-publicized summer training with
the reserve army. "O Canada we stand on guard for thee."
Presently in Canadian arenas crowds would cheer them as they
skated on the ice to play hockey under floodlights. In Europe
other Canadians went into battle and died in the darkness.[5]

Harold Pringle deserves some vindication. An official recognition
that he was not a cold-blooded killer but rather a young, rebellious, shell-
shocked rifleman would help heal his family, who were never free to
publicly mourn their son, even though he lies in a military cemetery. The
Canadian government could pardon Harold, or at least expunge some of
the stigma that surrounds him. It has done so in the cases of twenty-
three Canadian soldiers who were executed for desertion during the First
World War. It would be right to do it for Flinton's lonesome son.

Yet on another level, a government pardon or reversal would simply
be one more imperative, one more declaration, one more institutional
decree. Harold's execution order had been Privy Council 4418; his pardon would be Privy Council who-knows-what, and one wonders if it
would mean anything to him. If Harold's priests are to be believed, he
made his peace and asked for forgiveness. As far as Father Tom was concerned, Harold would always be up in heaven smiling down. "I have no
doubt as to his eternal destiny," he wrote Mary Ellen.[6] "Perhaps it was
God's way of making sure that He got him and God's plan certainly
worked," wrote Father Farrell. "His was a wonderful death to be envied
by us all."[7] An act of Parliament would never improve on that.

Meanwhile, Harold's earthly destiny will be to lie, like the other hundreds of thousands who died, forever at attention, in uniform even in death, names and numbers etched in marble, each grave the same as the next. He will remain there forever or until the cemeteries disappear and the Second World War becomes an ancient thing, like the Punic Wars or the siege of Troy. His is one of the countless "unlived lives" described in March 1945 by a Canadian private named Matthew Wherry in a short poem, "Ghosts of the Living," published in the *Maple Leaf*:

> In every haunted, tall fantastic city,
> In Prairie stillness by secluded streams,
> Beyond the sunset, strange to praise or pity,
> Unnumbered, unlived lives remain as dreams.[8]

During the writing of this book I began to feel like an agent for the unlived, an advocate for brief imperfect unlived lives, both noble and not, among which Harold Pringle's may have been the most expendable. All these unlived lives demand a final reckoning—or perhaps not a reckoning but an understanding, an understanding that beneath every grave lies the remnants of a life that once belonged to somebody. True, they fought together, but each one died separately, and while calling them heroes may assuage the burden of the generations that still benefit from their demise, it is a bittersweet homage. After all, heroes are supposed to die.

EACH MAN WHO RETURNED FROM overseas lost something there. It is equally fair to say that each man brought something home. The men who were involved in the execution of Harold Pringle brought home a secret. That secret affected them in different ways.

Tom Jamieson remained in the army until 1966, reaching the rank of major. He remained silent about his experiences overseas, although as he grew older little fragments seeped through. His daughter Ruth recalls, as a young girl, hearing him have nightmares in which he yelled out as if in the midst of battle. When his children refused to eat their supper, Jamieson told them how the children of Naples starved, subsisting only on orange peels.[9] Still, he kept his cynical sense of humour. It tempered an everlasting contempt for the Old World in which he had fought.

When asked about visiting Europe, he said he had no interest in returning to "that place."

Michael Cloney remained in the Canadian army's Judge Advocate General. He later became an Ontario Appeals Court judge. Norman Bergman, who defended Harold, returned from the war an alcoholic. He lived in Winnipeg, married and had two sons. Bergman went through what one son describes as "a difficult period,"[10] but he made a successful recovery from alcoholism and went on to be an extroverted participant in local politics. He died in 1984.

Joe Cowle, the doctor, became a prominent general practitioner in Toronto and later a chest specialist, developing expertise in respiratory diseases connected with mining. He worked as a referee on the Workman's Compensation Board and became chairman of the Ontario advisory committee on occupational diseases. He died at age fifty-eight in 1975.

Father Tom Lenane remained a Rosminian priest and ministered around the world. For the rest of his life he carried Harold Pringle's photograph with him and often drew on the memory of the young soldier's death as an inspiration for faith. Father Tom told his nephew, Father Bill Curran, that Harold's execution had been one of the most "harrowing and disturbing" incidents he had been forced to endure.[11] In fact, the Canadian private's execution troubled him more than any other event of the Second World War. He looked forward to the day when they would meet in heaven.

On September 20, 1945, the Canadian army deducted twenty-one pounds from Harold Pringle's estate and sent it to Esmee in Portsmouth. Evidently, Esmee was very pleased by the news of Harold's execution. "I fully appreciate the action taken by the Canadian Military Authorities," she wrote. "And tender my sincere thanks for your kind assistance in this matter."[12]

Lucky McGillivary's parents received a telegram in December: "The Minister of National Defence deeply regrets to inform you that F55044 Private John Norman McGillivary has been officially reported to have died approximately First November 1944."[13] They only learned of the circumstances of his death in January 1945. Their parish priest, Reverend

A. A. Johnston, reported to the Canadian army that he had informed Lucky's mother of his desertion and murder. "I asked her to tell the circumstances to nobody but her husband when he next comes home on pass. I suggested that if she were questioned by others she might answer that her son's death was 'caused by multiple wounds and that he died in 104 British General Hospital.'…Mrs. McGillivary took the sad news philosophically, and understands that her son 'forfeits all claim to pay, allowances, gratuity, and etc.,'" he wrote. "It seems too bad that such unfortunate information could not be mercifully buried with the deceased, but I suppose its divulgence would eventually become necessary if the family made a claim for pay or allowance."[14] Lucky's family was given the opportunity to have an inscription carved on his gravestone in Rome. It reads, "Gone but not forgotten. Dear to Our Hearts is the place where he sleeps."[15]

No one ever heard from the C Ration Kid. He may have melted back into America, or he may have remained in Italy. He may be there still, a naturalized Italian in his eighties, with an Italian name, wife and family, who harbours a secret about a soldier named Bobbie Williams from Nebraska and the streets of Rome. Then again, he may have fled to some new continent. In 1945, Mary Ellen Pringle began receiving letters from a Dominican nun stationed in South Africa who called herself Sister Mary Anselm, although there is no record of a Sister Mary Anselm in the Dominican registry. I cannot prove it, but it is my firm belief that this nun was in fact the C Ration Kid. There is a slyness in her tone, and she reports information that only those closely associated with the Sailor Gang could know. For instance, Sister Mary relays the exact date that Charlie Honess was executed, April 13. She also cites the day that Harold was transferred from prison in Rome to prison in Naples.

"No doubt you will be surprised to receive this letter, from one who is a complete stranger to you. But you are no stranger to me," read Sister Mary's first letter. "Well now, if as you say, Harold RIP was perfectly innocent, why, then, see what a glory is both yours and his for he is a true replica of Our Sweet Lord who was Innocence itself and yet was so unjustly sentenced to such a cruel death." She advised Mary Ellen, "for the sake of your children, do not speak of the circumstances of Harold's death, with neighbours or outsiders, for you know that the world is prone to be very hard and severe in its judgements."[16]

Sister Mary wrote that "Harold's last thoughts were of his own dear Mother, for when they were taking him away, he turned back to my brother, and handing your address, begged him to ask me to write to you. He met his death bravely and nobly, without the least sign of fear or regret."[17]

Mary Ellen sent a photograph of Harold, which elicited one last letter. "I was delighted to get Harold RIP's photo and he certainly does not look like a boy who would do anything wicked," it read. Then, caustically, Sister Mary continues, "At the same time, there is a weakness round the mouth, which shows that he could easily be led astray. Only God knows the terrible temptations that beset boys and men in times of war, and I think that even if Harold were somewhat guilty of the crime, it was done through weakness and bad companions. Remember he was not alone."[18]

Walter Frederick Glaser was sent back to the United States, where he served out a sentence for desertion. He died in 1994. Bill Holton returned to England and appears to have died in his fifties. As of 1994 Maria Fedele was living out her life in Grimsby, having remarried and raised a daughter. It is unclear what happened to Honess's family. At the beginning of the war, a British military psychiatrist determined that the average soldier might serve two years and after that a breakdown was almost certain. Honess had served twice that, but his record had been worth nothing. As far as the Honess family was concerned, it is fair to say that they might have felt that the Nazis bombed their house and the British took their son.

Tony Basciano returned to Canada, landing at Halifax. He remembers that when the troop ship arrived "there was no one there to greet us, not a soul." He boarded a train back home to Peterborough, but on his way back he stopped in Flinton, intending to see Harold's family. He stayed in Flinton for two days but never made contact. "I went right to the house," he recalled, "but I didn't go in. I didn't have the nerve to see his mother and father."[19] Tony went to barber's college and eventually opened his own shop. He married Pat, raised a family and rarely spoke of the war. Eventually, however, he decided that it "didn't matter" and began to open up.

During one meeting, Tony told me the story of a soldier from the Hasty Ps:

> We were cut off for a while and we were dug down along a road that ran along a long hill. The Support Company was towing a gun that had a lot of ammunition, and it had been hit and there was a lot of smoke everywhere. We couldn't recognize anybody. I was with this guy and we were all being careful of what we saw. Somebody loomed up out of the smoke and he thought it was the enemy and he opened up on him with his Bren gun and killed him on the spot. It turned out to be a Canadian guy, this fellow's best friend from Belleville. This guy just cracked. He wrapped that machine gun around an olive tree with his bare hands. We never, ever spoke of that incident. We didn't want it to get out. But it don't matter now anyway.[20]

The Lane Gang's Gunner Clement Ceccacci escaped from military prison on February 24, 1945. "At 11:00 a guard saw a commotion among a work party of soldiers under sentence and learned that Gunner Ceccacci had escaped over the barbed wire," a report states.[21] Ceccacci made his way to England and then stowed away on a ship to New York City. He spent a week there with a cousin and then went to Boston, where he was once again arrested. Again, he escaped. "He expressed a desire to repair to the latrine," the police report said. "While in the latrine the prisoner used one of the stalls, and realizing that he could watch the prisoner's feet the MP also responded to the call of nature. The guard soon realized that he had been watching the wrong pair of feet and that the prisoner had left."[22]

In early May 1945, Ceccacci turned up in Toronto, where his family held a party to honour his return from war. The celebration lasted only one hour. Ceccacci became paranoid and began attacking his family; his brother, a corporal in the army, called the military police. Clement Ceccacci was examined by a doctor and sent to a military psychiatric hospital in London, Ontario. He had amnesia and could not remember any incidents after his fight in April 1944 with the 349th

American Infantry Regiment at Bologna. His first doctor described him as

> a young withdrawn individual with whom it is difficult to estab-
> lish rapport. He answers questions very slowly and with
> considerable hesitation. Returned from Italy after fours years
> service in the Army and was immediately turned over to Provost
> by his family after violent and peculiar behaviour at a party they
> had arranged to welcome him home. Has fixed delusions, believ-
> ing that everyone is talking about him and calling him yellow.
>
> Young man has tense, vague, mildly confused manner and
> frequently interjects the statement "I want to go home" into con-
> versation. Vague and uncertain about dates and times. "Everyone"
> says he isn't going home. "People" including strangers say he is
> yellow and look at him in a way that indicates they think he is
> yellow. His brother looked at him this way when he arrived home
> and he had a fight with him and they took him to custody bar-
> racks. Can't sleep in the dark. Diagnosis: dementia.[23]

In August, Ceccacci escaped from the hospital and was missing for three weeks. He was captured and brought back to the hospital, where he spent the next two years until his release in 1947. He died in 1978, six years after changing his first name to Orlando.

Hugh Ramsay Park returned to Canada and practised law. His best year, by his estimation, came in 1976, when he tried a case before the Supreme Court of Canada. Park never spoke about Harold Pringle's exe-cution with anyone. Even on the boat ride back to England, it was not discussed; all involved thought it best to leave it behind in Italy. Back in Canada, Park had no contact with any veterans' organizations. He mar-ried a Canadian woman who had served as an air traffic controller in the army during the war. Park never returned to Europe. He tried not to think about Pringle.

In 2000, I appeared in his life, visiting him regularly for almost two years. Initially, Park was "terrified" of my book and what it would reveal, and he was understandably suspicious of my motives. He had grandchildren, he told me, and "it would not be nice for them to learn that their grandfather had killed a man in cold blood."[24] As we began to know each other, however, his misgivings melted away, though he told no one of my visits. I must have seemed like an apparition, a spectre that knew everything about an incident in his past that he had tried to forget almost from the very moment it happened. But Ramsay Park eventually forgave me for telling his story; near the end, he would finish our visits by asking me, "What's our next step?"

Standing by Harold Pringle's grave on a cool November afternoon, I asked myself that question. What was our next step? If there was one belief that most of those that fought and died in the Second World War held, it was that at the end of it all the sacrifice would be worth it. Those who tired but did not falter were buoyed by the notion that some good could come from all the chaos and waste. A private named Craig Heath epitomized this belief in his poem "Sick of It":

> So you're sick of the way the country's run,
> And you're sick of the way the rationing's done,
> And you're sick of the standing around in line.
> You're sick, you say. Well ain't that fine?
> For I am sick of the sun and the heat,
> And I'm sick of the feel of my aching feet,
> And I'm sick of the siren's wailing shriek,
> And I'm sick of the groans of the wounded and weak,
> I'm sick of the slaughter, I'm sick to my soul,
> I'm sick of playing the killer's role,
> And I'm sick of the groans of death and the smell,
> And I'm sick, damned sick, of myself as well.
> But I'm sicker still of the tyrant's rule,
> And conquered lands where the wild beasts drool,
> And I'm cured damned quick when I think of the day
> When all this hell will be out of the way;
> When none of this mess will have been in vain,
> And the lights of the world will blaze again.[25]

Out across the Apennines, a cloud burst and thunder rattled. It was tough to stand before this quiet sepulchral village bearing the news that while the lights were blazing, the mess was far from out of the way. Wars were still being fought, which was a searing form of betrayal, one that might hurt even the dead. If you listened closely to the thunder, you could hear the rumblings of future conflicts starting. Old men were making speeches and young men were listening. There were martyrs in the making.

Then a flash of bright sunlight burst across the cemetery. It was white and startling, and it bleached the marble so that it was almost impossible to see the names etched on the gravestones. It all seemed to become obvious. Atonement. Forgiveness. Penitence. The story of a lost soldier executed by the country he enlisted to serve. I reached down, rubbed the ash between my fingers and touched it to my forehead. Here it was: absolution—in advance, perhaps. Absolution from the generation that passed away in the last Great War for the generations that would inevitably start the next.

Then I stood up, slung my pack across my shoulder and headed back to Rome.

NOTES

CHAPTER 1

1. Harold Pringle to Mary Ellen Pringle, July 5, 1945.
2. *Union Jack*, 8, 3, 1944, Today's Centre Column. Reader's Contribution, cited in Sonia Dougal, *Front-line Story: The Language of Suggestion and Desuggestion on the Front-line in Italy, 1943–1945* (Fribourg, Switzerland: Editions Universitaires Fribourg Suisse, 1996), 111–112.
3. Interview with Don Kernaghan, March 2000.
4. Interview with Marion Jamieson, July 2000.
5. Interview with Tom Jamieson, February 1992.
6. Interview with Marion Jamieson, May 2000.
7. Interview with Matthew Clark, February 1999.
8. Samuel A. Stouffer, Arthur A. Lumsdaine, Marion Harper Lumsdaine, Robin M. Williams, Jr., M. Brewster Smith, Irving L. Janis, Shirley A. Starr and Leonard S. Cottrell, Jr., *The American Soldier: Combat and Its Aftermath*, vol. 3 of *Social Psychology in World War II* (Princeton, NJ: Princeton University Press, 1949–50), 290.
9. Harold Pringle to his family, May 22, 1945.
10. Tom Lenane to Mary Ellen Pringle, August 8, 1945.

CHAPTER 2

1. Interview with Veronica, May 2000.
2. Interview with Teresa, May, 2000.
3. Pat Sullivan, "Still on the Books," *Legion Magazine*, vol. 59 number 12 (May 1985), 14.
4. Interview with Betti Michael, June, 2000.
5. Interview with Betti Michael, June, 2000.
6. Interview with Veronica, July 2000.
7. First World War record of William Pringle, Regimental Number 835142, National Archives of Canada.

8. R. N. Siddle, "Closing the Eyes of the Hun," in *Canada at War*, edited by Michael Benedict (Toronto: Penguin, 1997; article originally published in *Maclean's*, December 1917), 12–25.

9. S. G. Bennett, *The 4th Canadian Mounted Rifles, 1914–1919* (Toronto: Murray Printing, 1926), 69–70.

10. First World War record of William Pringle.

11. Interview with Armand La Barge, October 2000.

12. Interview with Betti Michael, June 2000.

13. Interview with Veronica, July 2000.

14. Interview with Betti Michael, June 2000.

CHAPTER 3

1. Brian Nolan, *King's War: Mackenzie King and the Politics of War, 1939–1945* (Toronto: Random House, 1988), 15.

2. Desmond Morton and J. L. Granatstein, *Marching to Armageddon: Canadians and the Great War 1914–1919* (Toronto: Lester & Orpen Dennys, 1989), 261.

3. Interview with Marion Jamieson, May 2000.

4. Interview with Betti Michael, June 2000.

5. Military Service Record of Harold Joseph Pringle, C-5292, National Archives of Canada. Harold Pringle's service record is the primary source of evidence for his story. It contains all his trial transcripts and all correspondence regarding him and his time in the army.

6. Farley Mowat, *The Regiment* (Toronto: McClelland & Stewart, 1955), 6.

7. "Journals of Major Robert Rogers, 1769." Dublin. Found at users.crols.com/candidus/kings.htm.

8. Michael Calvert, with Peter Young, *A Dictionary of Battles* (New York: Mayflower Books, 1979).

9. Interview with Bill McAndrew, July 2000.

10. No. 1 Canadian Detention Barracks, Headley Downs (renamed No. 3 Canadian Detention Barracks in May 1945), RG 24, National Defence, Series C-3, Volume 16518, Serial: 540, March 1941–December 1943, National Archives of Canada.

11. Mowat, *The Regiment*, p. 39.

12. A. E. Moll, "Neuropsychiatry: Summary of 280 Patients Examined at No. 4 and 5CCs, 12 June–30 Nov. 1942." NA RG24 Vol. 2089.

13. 5th Canadian Infantry Division Reinforcement Unit (formerly 5th Canadian Armoured Division Holding Unit, Armoured Divisions Infantry Reinforcement Unit), RG24, National Defence, Series C-3, Volume 16760, Serial: 599, October 1941–September 1943, National Archives of Canada.

14. Military Service Record of Harold Joseph Pringle.

15. C. P. Stacey and Barbara M. Wilson, *The Half-Million: The Canadians in Britain, 1939–1946* (Toronto: University of Toronto Press, 1987), 135.

16. Stacey and Wilson, *The Half-Million*, 148.

17. Terry Copp and Bill McAndrew, *Battle Exhaustion: Soldiers and Psychiatrists in the Canadian Army, 1939–1945* (Montreal: McGill-Queen's University Press, 1990).

18. In Daniel G. Dancocks, *The D-Day Dodgers. The Canadians in Italy, 1943–1945* (Toronto: McClelland & Stewart, 1991), 140.

19. *The Maple Leaf*, "Rhyme and Reason," Feb. 1945. RG24, National Defence, Series C-2, Volume 16644, National Archives of Canada.

20. Harold Pringle to Mary Ellen Pringle, May 8, 1945.

21. Military Service Record of Harold Joseph Pringle.

22. Military Service Record of Harold Joseph Pringle.

23. Military Service Record of Harold Joseph Pringle.

24. Robert Boyes, *In Glasshouses: A History of the Military Provost Staff Corps* (Colchester, UK: Military Provost Staff Corps Association, 1988), 107–108.

25. Colin McDougall, *Execution* (New York: St. Martin's, 1958).

26. War Diary, No. 1 Canadian Detention Barracks, Headley Downs.

27. War Diary, No. 1 Canadian Detention Barracks, Headley Downs.

28. Military Service Record of William Pringle, Regimental Number 835142, National Archives of Canada.

29. A. E. Moll. "Neuropsychiatry: Summary of 280 Patients Examined at No. 4 and 5CCs, 12 June–30 Nov. 1942." RG 24 Vol. 2089.

30. War Diary, No. 1 Canadian Detention Barracks, Headley Downs.

31. Military Service Record of Harold Joseph Pringle.

32. War Office, Great Britain, *Manual of Military Law, 1929* (London: War Office, 1929), 17–77.

      Militia Act, RSC 1927 c.132 courtesy Department of National Defence.

      The Trail of Discipline: The Historical Roots of Canadian Military Law. 1985 R. A. McDonald LCol. Director of Law/Human Rights and Information. Department of National Defence. P 1–7.

      A perspective on Canada's Code of Service Discipline, "The Development of Canada's Military Justice System to 1950. Judge Advocate General, Department of National Defence Newsletter Vol. IV—1999.

33. "Executed World War I soldiers may get pardons," Scott Edmonds. The Canadian Press. "We Shall Remember Them." Ann McIlroy. *The Guardian*. December 17, 2001.

34. Lt. Col. T. M. Hunter. *Some Aspects of Disciplinary Policy in the Canadian Services, 1914–1946: Historical Section Report 91* (DND, 1960), p. 91.

35. Ibid., p. 91.

36. Interviews with Tony Basciano, Ivan Gunter, October 2000, and Harry Fox, December 2000; Military Service Record of Harold Joseph Pringle.
37. Interview with Hugh Ramsay Park, April 2000.
38. Interview with Hugh Ramsay Park, April 2000.
39. Interview with Hugh Ramsay Park, July 2000.
40. Interview with Hugh Ramsay Park, March 2001.
41. Interview with Hugh Ramsay Park, April 2000.
42. Interview with Hugh Ramsay Park, June 2001.
43. Interview with Bill Stewart, July 2000.
44. In Dancocks, *The D-Day Dodgers*, 62.
45. *The D-Day Dodgers*, 67.
46. Interview with Hugh Ramsay Park, June 2001.

CHAPTER 4

1. Interview with Maj. Robert Bradford, August 2000; interviews with Tony Basciano, September 2000.
2. Interview with Tony Basciano, September 2000.
3. Interview with Patricia Basciano, September 2000.
4. Interview with Tony Basciano and Patrician Basciano, September 2000.
5. Interview with Tony Basciano, October 2000.
6. Interview with Michael Cloney, April 2000.
7. Interview with Bill McAndrew, July 2000.
8. Interview with Tony Basciano, September 2000.
9. Dancocks, *The D-Day Dodgers*, 175.
10. C. Vokes to GOC V Corps, 3 January 1944, DHIST, CMHQ Report 165, appendix, National Archives of Canada.
11. Interview with Harry Fox, December 2000.
12. Battle Experience Questionnaires, RG 24, vol. 10,450, National Archives of Canada.
13. Copp and McAndrew, *Battle Exhaustion*, 64; Chapter Six, "The D-Day Dodgers: Italy 1944" (pp. 63–89), gives a vivid description and explanation of the psychological cost of the prolonged raids made over the Arielli.
14. Copp and McAndrew, *Battle Exhaustion*, 64–65.
15. War Diary, Hastings and Prince Edward Regiment, RG24, National Defence, Series C-3, Volume 15073, National Archives of Canada.
16. Copp and McAndrew, *Battle Exhaustion*, 66.
17. Copp and McAndrew, *Battle Exhaustion*, 66.
18. War Diary, No. 2 Canadian Detention and Field Punishment Camp, RG24, National Defence, Series C-3, Volume 16516, National Archives of Canada.
19. Mowat, *The Regiment*, 161.
20. Mowat, *The Regiment*, 23.

21. Battle Experience Questionnaires, RG24, vol. 10450, National Archives of Canada.
22. Interview with Tony Basciano, September 2000.
23. War Diary, Hastings and Prince Edward Regiment.
24. Interview with veteran, D-Day Dodgers Reunion, May 2000.
25. Harold Pringle to Mary Ellen Pringle, April 11, 1945.
26. War Diary, Hastings and Prince Edward Regiment.
27. Harold Pringle to Mary Ellen Pringle, April 13, 1944.
28. War Diary, Hastings and Prince Edward Regiment.

CHAPTER 5
1. Pages 69–71 are based on the War Diary of the Hastings and Prince Edward Regiment.
2. Raleigh Trevelyan, *Rome '44: The Battle for the Eternal City* (London: Secker & Warburg, 1981), 129. Trevelyan's thoroughly researched book is among the best written about the Battle for Rome.
3. Trevelyan, *Rome '44*, 129–130.
4. David Hapgood and David Richardson, *Monte Cassino* (North Ryde, UK; London: Angus & Robertson, 1984).
5. The Inferno of Dante, trans. Robert Pinsky, (New York: Farrar, Straus and Giroux, 1994), 145.
6. Colin McDougall, Journal, McGill University Rare Books Library.
7. McDougall, Journal, McGill University Rare Books Library.
8. Saul Bellow to Colin McDougall, 1960, McGill University Rare Books Library.
9. McDougall, Notebook, 1955, McGill University Rare Books Library.
10. McDougall, Notebook, McGill University Rare Books Library.
11. McDougall, Journal, 1954, McGill University Rare Books Library.
12. McDougall, Journal, 1953, McGill University Rare Books Library.
13. McDougall, Notebook, 1956, McGill Rare Books Library.
14. McDougall, *Execution*, 54.
15. McDougall, *Execution*, 117.
16. War Diary, Hastings and Prince Edward Regiment.
17. War Diary, Hastings and Prince Edward Regiment.
18. Dancocks, *The D-Day Dodgers*, 243.
19. War Diary, Hastings and Prince Edward Regiment.
20. Dancocks, *The D-Day Dodgers*, 247.
21. Douglas LePan, *Weathering It: Complete Poems 1948–1987* (Toronto: McClelland & Stewart, 1987), 34 from the poem "Campaigning Weather."
22. Pages 97 to 104 are based on information found in Dancocks, *The D-Day Dodgers*; McDougall, *Execution*; and personal interviews with veterans of the battle at the Hitler Line, May 2000, D-Day Dodgers Reunion in Orillia, Ontario.

23. Copp and McAndrew, *Battle Exhaustion*, 79.
24. Interview with veteran May 2000.
25. "Slit-Trench Christianity," *Union Jack*, 3, 3, 1944.
26. Interview with Ramsay Park, July 2001.
27. Peter Stursberg. During the course of my research I spent time listening to CBC Radio broadcasts recorded during the Italian Campaign. I used these reports to help give accuracy to my descriptions of the conflict. All are available at the National Archives of Canada.

    Canadian Infantry, Canadian and British Tanks Storm the Hitler Line, reference number 140554.

    Capture of Pontecorvo, reference number 143698.

    Hitler Line Broken—Tour of Battlefield, reference number 143669

    Cassino and Monastery Hill Captured, reference number 143692

    5th and 8th Armies Building Up to Assault the Hitler Line, reference number 143696.
28. Dancock, *The D-Day Dodgers*, 258.
29. War Diary, Hastings and Prince Edward Regiment.
30. War Diary, Hastings and Prince Edward Regiment.
31. McDougall, *Execution*, 115–119.

CHAPTER 6
1. Trevelyan, *Rome '44*, 193.
2. Trevelyan, *Rome '44*, 299.
3. Manfred Messerschmidt, *Nazi Political Aims and German Military Law in World War II* (Kingston, ON: Royal Military College of Canada, 1981), cited in Copp and McAndrew, *Battle Exhaustion*, 127.
4. Interview with Tony Basciano, September 2000.
5. War Diary, Hastings and Prince Edward Regiment.
6. L. Col. A. M. Doyle, RG24 Vol. 12631 Psychiatric Report. "Morale." National Archives of Canada.
7. Ibid., 16.
8. Farley Mowat, *My Father's Son: Memories of War and Peace* (Toronto: Key Porter, 1992), 108.
9. Nolan, *King's War*, 88.
10. Mowat, *My Father's Son*, 98.
11. Nolan, *King's War*, 127.
12. Interview with veteran, D-Day Dodgers Reunion, May 2000.
13. Nolan, *King's War*, 129.
14. Copp and McAndrew, *Battle Exhaustion*, 66.
15. Cited in Dougal, *Front-line Story*, 8.
16. Interview with Anna Preziuso, November 2000.
17. Copp and McAndrew, *Battle Exhaustion*, 57.

18. Copp and McAndrew, *Battle Exhaustion*, 70.
19. Ibid., 70.
20. Major A. E. Moll, Report from No. 2 Canadian Exhaustion Unit in Italy, RG 24, vol. 12631, National Archives of Canada, 630.
21. Moll, Report from No. 2 Canadian Exhaustion Unit in Italy.
22. Interview with Tony Basciano, September 2000.
23. Interview with Ivan Gunter, October 2000.
24. Doyle, Report of Survey of Canadian Soldiers Under Sentence in the C.M.F. RG 24, Vol. 12631, National Archives.
25. "Operations of British, Indian, and Dominion Forces in Italy." "The Problem of Desertion." Private collection, Bill McAndrew.
26. Military Service Record of Harold Joseph Pringle.
27. McDougall, *Execution*, 179.

CHAPTER 7
1. "The Battle against Venereal Disease," Operations of British, Indian and Dominion Forces in Italy, 3 September 1943 to 2 May 1945, Bill McAndrew's private collection.
2. George Powell, "But the Women!," *The Maple Leaf*, July 1944.
3. Interview with Oreste Schiano di Zenise, November 2000.
4. Trevelyan, *Rome '44*, 62.
5. Trevelyan, *Rome '44*, 218.
6. Trevelyan, *Rome '44*, 217–218.
7. The following documents were found at the Public Records Office, Kew Gardens, UK.

WO 204/2488 "Italy: Allied Military personnel engaged in black market activities." British Merchant seamen ashore: discipline. 1944 April–Nov.

WO 204/2920 "Italy: reports of black market activities involving Allied soldiers or vehicles." 1945 September–October.

WO 204/3279 "Italy: black market operations: reports." 1943 October–1946 January.

WO 204/9765 "Relations between Allied Forces and Italian civilians: assistance to civil power, emergency relief and assistance, incidents involving Allied troops, black market operations, finance etc." 1944 February–July.

WO 204/9766 "Relations between Allied Forces and Italian civilians: assistance to civil power, emergency relief and assistance, incidents involving Allied troops, black market operations, finance etc." 1944 July–September.

WO 204/9766 "Relations between Allied Forces and Italian civilians: assistance to civil power, emergency relief and assistance, incidents

involving Allied troops, black market operations, finance, etc."
1944 September–December.

WO 204/9768 "Relations between Allied Forces and Italian civilians:
assistance to civil power, emergency relief and assistance, incidents involving Allied troops, black market operations, finance
etc." 1944 December–1945 July.

8. Interview with Father Bill Curran, June 2001, Information about Father
Lenane is from his nephew Fr. Bill Curran and from reports from the
Rosminian Chapel in Rome.

9. "The Problem of Desertion," Operations of British, Indian and
Dominion Forces in Italy, 3 September 1943 to 2 May 1945. This
report gives a detailed analysis on the incidence and causes of AWOL
and desertion.

10. "Report of Survey of Canadian Soldiers under Sentence," RG 24 Vol. 12631.

11. "The Problem of Desertion."

12. In Copp and McAndrew, *Battle Exhaustion*, 94.

13. Interview with Betti Michael, June 2000.

14. *The Maple Leaf*, "Rhyme and Reason," February 1945, RG 24 Vol. 16644—
HQ No. 3 Cdn Public Relations.

15. Robert W. Black, *Rangers in World War II* (New York: Ballantine, 1992).
Information on the Rangers in Italy can also found in Trevelyan, *Rome '44.*

16. Trevelyan, *Rome '44*, 76.

CHAPTER 8

1. David, ed. Diaries of Evelyn Waugh, 616, 597 in Fussell, *Wartime:
Understanding Behaviour in the Second World War* (New York: Oxford
University Press, 1989).

2. "The Problem of Desertion."

3. George Powell, "Soldiers Revel in Civvy-Street Atmosphere. Females
Fascinating Feature," *The Maple Leaf*, August 1944.

4. *Union Jack*, 6, 10, 1944 and 5, 12, 1943 in Dougal, *Front-line Story*,
95 and 74.

5. "Rhyme and Reason," *The Maple Leaf*, Feb. 1945.

6. Interview with veteran, May 2000.

7. In Paul Fussell, *Wartime: Understanding and Behavior in the Second World
War*, 125–126.

8. In Fred Cederberg, *The Long Road Home: The Autobiography of a Canadian
Soldier in Italy in World War II* (Toronto: Stoddart, 1984), 70.

9. There are a number of reports dealing with acts against civilians by Allied
soldiers:

From the Public Records office, Kew Gardens, UK.

FO 371/49853 "Events in Italy 1944–1945"

FO 371/49957 "Claims against members of the British Armed Forces." 1945

FO 371/43947 to FO 371/43947 (inclusive) "Reports on conditions in liberated Italy and in enemy-occupied Italy." 1944–1945

FO 371/49869 "Reports on conditions in liberated Italy." 1945.

10. Interview with Ivan Gunter, October 2000.

11. *Union Jack*, 12, 11, 1943, in Dougal, *Front-line Story*, 99.

12. "Italy: black market operations: Reports." 1943 Oct.–1946 Jan. WO 204/3279, Public Records Office, London, UK.

13. "Italy: Allied military personnel engaged in black market activities. British merchant seamen ashore: discipline." WO 204/2488 1944 April–November. Public Records Office, London, UK.

14. "Italy: Allied military personnel engaged in black market activities. British merchant seamen ashore: discipline." WO 204/2488 1944 April–November.

15. Anthony Gardener and Anthony Babington, "For Once in his miserable life," *Daily Mail* (30 April 1994), 28 and 29. This is the only account of Bill Croft's execution.

16. Police statement by Maria Fedele, held in the Military Service Record of Harold Joseph Pringle.

CHAPTER 9

1. Norman Lewis, *Naples '44* (London: Collins, 1978), 147. *Naples '44* is a thoughtful, engaging source for information on life in the city during the Allied occupation.

2. Cpl. Joe Greaves, "This Italy," *The Maple Leaf*, October 1944.

3. All information based on Bill Croft's trial was found at the Public Records Office in his court martial transcript: "Court Martial of Fireman W Croft for murder: sentenced to death: sentence not carried out until confirmed by the Admiralty, report by Sir Bernard Spilsbury on victim," ADM 156/232, 1945, Public Records Office, London, UK. The activities of the Sailor Gang have been reconstructed by using information from the courts martial of all three men; these include testimony from such witnesses as Maria Fedele and Bill Holton.

4. "Court Martial of Fireman W Croft." Lucky spelled his own surname "McGillivary"; court documents and military records spell it "McGillivray"; and the Commonwealth War Graves Commission and the Canadian Virtual War Memorial spell it "MacGillivray."

5. Military Service Record of John Norman McGillivray, Regimental Number F-550044, National Archives of Canada.

6. Military Service Record of John Norman McGillivray.

7. Ibid.

8. Cederberg, *The Long Road Home*, 119.
9. Honess's Statement to SIB, found in Military Service Record of Harold Joseph Pringle.
10. Military Service Record of Harold Joseph Pringle.
11. Interview with Betti Michael, June 2000.
12. WO 204/3279, "Black Market Operation Reports 1943 Oct.–1946 Jan."
13. Copp and McAndrew, *Battle Exhaustion*.

CHAPTER 10

1. War Diary, Hastings and Prince Edward Regiment.
2. War Diary, GHQ 2nd Echelon, Allied Armies in Italy, Canadian Section, National Defence, Series C-3, Volume 13602, National Archives of Canada.
3. The rest of this chapter is taken from Honess, C.H.F. Offence: Murder.
4. Court Martial of Fireman W Croft.

CHAPTER 11

1. "Special Investigations Branches: 76 Section," April to December 1944, WO 170/3598, Public Records Office, London, UK. This was the primary Eighth Army military police unit used in Rome to investigate serious crime. The range and frequency of offences is staggering.
2. "Special Investigations Branches: 76 Section."
3. Mowat, *My Father's Son*, 171.
4. The description of the attack on the Lamone was constructed using information from H+PE War Diary, Dancocks, *The D-Day Dodgers*, 388–97; Mowat, *The Regiment*; and interviews with veterans of the Hastings and Prince Edward Regiment, May 2000.
5. D-Day Dodger's Reunion, May 2000.
6. Interview with Bill Boss, February 2001.
7. War Diary, Canadian Section, GHQ, 1st Echelon, Allied Armies in Italy, National Defence, RG 24 Series C-3, Volume 13579, December 1944–January 1945, National Archives of Canada.
8. Military Service Record of Gunner Clement Ceccacci, B-18135, National Archives of Canada. This document contains a detailed description of the Lane Gang's activities as they related to Allied deserters.
9. Military Service Record of Gunner Clement Ceccacci.
10. Military Service Record of Gunner Clement Ceccacci.
11. War Diary, Canadian Section, GHQ, 1st Echelon, Allied Armies in Italy.
12. "Special Investigations Branches: 76 Section."
13. From the Public Records office, Kew Gardens, UK. FO 371/49853, "Events in Italy 1944–1945"; FO 371/49957 "Claims against members of the British Armed Forces, 1945" ; FO 371/43947 to FO 371/43947 (inclusive) "Reports

on conditions in liberated Italy and in enemy-occupied Italy." 1944–1945; FO 371/49869 "Reports on conditions in liberated Italy, 1945."
14. Service record of Harold Joseph Pringle.
15. War Diary, Canadian Section, GHQ, 1st Echelon, Allied Armies in Italy.
16. Interview with Michael Cloney, April 2000.
17. "Some Aspects of Disciplinary Policy in the Canadian Services," Lt.-Col. T. M. Hunter, 1960, 98.

CHAPTER 12
1. "Court Martial transcript of murder court martial for Private Harold Pringle, C-5292," National Archives of Canada. This provided all the information used to reconstruct Pringle's trial.
2. Lucky spelled his own surname "McGillivary"; see note 4, Chapter 9.
3. "Special Investigations Branches: 76 Section."
4. Clippings file on Doctor Edgar Fielden, Archives of the Ontario College of Physicians and Surgeons, Toronto, Ontario.

CHAPTER 13
1. All information used in recounting Honess's court martial comes from his court martial record: "Honess, C.H.F. Offence: Murder 1945," WO 71/954, Public Records Office, London, UK. Information on the weather etc. taken from "1 Echelon AAI War Diary, RG24 Vol. 13581 NA.

CHAPTER 14
1. Babington and Gardner, "For Once in His Miserable Life." April 30, 1994, *Daily Mail*, 28–29.
2. Ibid.
3. John Horne Burns. *The Gallery* (New York: Harper, 1947), 281.
4. Curzio Malaparte, *The Skin*, translated by David Moore (London, UK: Redman Ltd., 1952), 48.
5. Lewis, *Naples '44*, 171.
6. Malaparte, *The Skin*, 41.
7. Lewis, *Naples '44*, 25–26.
8. Malaparte, *The Skin*, 58.
9. Lewis, *Naples '44*, 115.
10. Malaparte, *The Skin*, 142.
11. "The Battle against Venereal Disease." Operations of British, Indian and Dominion Forces in Italy.
12. Interview with Oreste Schiano, November 2000.
13. Lewis, *Naples '44*, 135.
14. *Union Jack*, 26, 11, 43 in Dougal, *Front-line Story*, 113.
15. Lewis, *Naples '44*, 53.

16. Lewis, *Naples '44*, 53.
17. Military Service Record of Harold Joseph Pringle.
18. Military Service Record of Harold Joseph Pringle.
19. Stacey and Wilson, *The Half-Million*, 117.
20. Babington and Gardner, "For Once in His Miserable Life." My account of Bill Croft's trial is based on his court martial record (ADM 156/232, Public Records Office, London, UK), along with Babington and Gardner, "For Once in His Miserable Life."

CHAPTER 15
1. Military Service Record of Private Harold Joseph Pringle.
2. McDougall, *Execution*, 189.
3. Interviews with veterans, Tony Basciano, September 2000.
4. B. S. Farrell to A. L. Louden, March 29, 1945, Military Service Record of Private Harold Pringle.
5. Harold Pringle to Mary Ellen Pringle, April 6, 1945.
6. "Honess, C.H.F. Offence: Murder 1945."
7. Court Martial of Fireman W Croft.
8. "Honess, C.H.F. Offence: Murder 1945."
9. "Honess, C.H.F. Offence: Murder 1945."
10. Percy Bysshe Shelley, preface to *Adonais*, 1821.
11. "Court Martial of Fireman W Croft."
12. "Court Martial of Fireman W Croft."
13. "Court Martial of Fireman W Croft."
14. Douglas G. Browne and E. V. Tullett, *Bernard Spilsbury, His Life and Cases* (London: Harrap, 1952).
15. "Court Martial of Fireman W Croft."
16. "Court Martial of Fireman W Croft."
17. "Court Martial of Fireman W Croft."
18. Browne and Tullett, *Bernard Spilsbury*, 394–399.
19. Harold Pringle to Mary Ellen Pringle, May 7, 1945.
20. Harold Pringle to Mary Ellen Pringle, May 8, 1945.
21. War Diary, Canadian Section 1 Echelon AFHQ, RG24 Vol. 13581. NAC.
22. Report by Colonel W. A. I. Anglin. This detailed report can be found in Harold Pringle's service record, as can all other JAG reports on the case.
23. Military Service Record of Harold Joseph Pringle.
24. Military Service Record of Harold Joseph Pringle.
25. Military Service Record of Harold Joseph Pringle.
26. Military Service Record of Harold Joseph Pringle.
27. Military Service Record of Harold Joseph Pringle.
28. Military Service Record of Harold Joseph Pringle.
29. Interview with Michael Cloney Nov. 2001.

CHAPTER 16

1. War Diary, Canadian Section, GHQ, 1st Echelon, Allied Armies in Italy (May 1945). RG 24 Vol. 13581. NAC.
2. Interview with Benito Scopa, Nov. 2000.
3. Interview with Teresa Prezzuto, November 2000.
4. Vincenzo Cannaviello, *Avellino e L'Irpinia nella Tragedia del 1943–1944* (Rome: Pergola, 1954), 180–189.
5. Cannaviello, *Avellino*, 180–189.
6. Cannaviello, *Avellino*, 180–189.
7. Interview with Teresa Preziuso, November 2000.
8. Cannaviello, *Avellino*, 180–189.
9. Interview with Andrea Massaro, November 2000.
10. Interview with a resident of Avellino, November 2000.
11. *Echelon Etchings*, in War Diary, Canadian Section, GHQ, 1st Echelon, Allied Armies in Italy (Dec. 1944). RG24 Vol. 13603 NAC.
12. Lewis, *Naples '44*, 173.
13. Interview with Anna Preziuso, November 2000.
14. War Diary, Canadian Section GHQ 1st Echelon Armies in Italy. May 1945.
15. Stanley Scislowski rewrote the article from memory and sent it to me in 2001.
16. McDougall, *Execution*, 179.
17. McDougall, *Execution*, 179–180.
18. Interview with Hugh Ramsay Park, July 2001.
19. Interview with Michael Cloney, March 2000.
20. Interview with Hugh Ramsay Park, July 2001.
21. Babington and Gardner, "For Once in His Miserable Life."
22. Court Martial of Fireman W. Croft.
23. Babington and Gardner, "For Once in His Miserable Life."
24. Interview with Oreste Schiano di Zenise, November 2000.
25. Babington and Gardner, "For Once in His Miserable Life."
26. Babington and Gardner, "For Once in His Miserable Life."
27. Babington and Gardner, "For Once in His Miserable Life."
28. Harold Pringle to Mary Ellen Pringle, May 23, 1945.
29. These dispatches can be found in Pringle's service record.
30. Military Service Record of Harold Joseph Pringle.
31. Interview with Michael Cloney, March 2000.
32. Military Service Record of Harold Joseph Pringle.

CHAPTER 17

1. This chapter is based on information taken from Harold Pringle's service record; his letters home; Father Farrell to HJP, June 1945; Louis-Marie Grignion de Montfort, *True Devotion to the Blessed Virgin Mary*, St. Louis Mary De Montfort, translated from the original French by

Françoise De Castro, adapted by Eddie Doherty (Bay Shore, New York: T.O.P. Montfort Publications, 1955); and interviews with Ramsay Park, April, July 2000 and July, October 2001; Tom Jamieson, March 1993, and Michael Cloney, 2000 and 2001.

2. De Montfort, *True Devotion to the Blessed Virgin Mary*, 32.

3. De Montfort, *True Devotion to the Blessed Virgin Mary*, 35.

4. Canadian Section, GHQ 1st Echelon, 21st Army Group, Appendix 64, RG24, National Defence, Series C-3, Volume 13581, Serial: 1874, March 1945, National Archives of Canada.

5. Office JAG CAO RG24 Vol. 9953 appendix 64 NAC.

6. Harold Pringle to Mary Ellen Pringle, June 1945.

7. War Diary, 1 Echelon Allied Field Headquarters, Canadian Section, National Archives of Canada.

8. Interview with Hugh Ramsay Park, July 2000.

9. Interview with Hugh Ramsay Park, July 2001.

10. Interview with Hugh Ramsay Park, July 2000.

11. Fr. B. S. Farrell to Harold Pringle, June 8, 1945.

12. Harold Pringle to Mary Ellen Pringle, June 11, 1945.

13. Military Service Record of Harold Joseph Pringle.

14. McDougall, Journal, McGill University Rare Books Library.

15. Harold Pringle to Mary Ellen Pringle, June 15, 1945.

16. Military Service Record of Harold Joseph Pringle.

17. Military Service Record of Harold Joseph Pringle.

18. Harold Pringle to Mary Ellen Pringle, June 21, 1945.

CHAPTER 18

1. This chapter is based on information taken from Pringle's service record; his letters home; McDougall, *Execution*; and interviews with Ramsay Park, 2000 and 2001, and Michael Cloney, 2000 and 2001.

2. Nolan, *King's War*.

3. Military Service Record of Harold Joseph Pringle.

4. Military Service Record of Harold Joseph Pringle.

5. Military Service Record of Harold Joseph Pringle.

6. De Montfort, *True Devotion to the Blessed Virgin Mary*, 40.

7. Military Service Record of Harold Joseph Pringle.

8. McDougall, *Execution*, 190.

9. De Montfort, *True Devotion to the Blessed Virgin Mary*, 38.

10. Interview with Hugh Ramsay Park, October 2001.

11. Harold Pringle to Mary Ellen Pringle, July 5, 1945.

12. Interview with Hugh Ramsay Park, July 2001.

13. Interview with Hugh Ramsay Park, July 2001.

14. Interview with Tony Basciano, September 2000.

15. Interview with Michael Cloney, March 2000.
16. Interview with Hugh Ramsay Park, July 2001.
17. Fr. B. S. Farrell to Fr. Kinlin, July 5, 1945.

CHAPTER 19
1. Military Service Record of Harold Joseph Pringle. This chapter is based on information taken from Pringle's service record and interviews with Hugh Ramsay Park, 2000 and 2001, and Michael Cloney, 2000 and 2001.
2. Interview with Teresa, June 2000.
3. Interview with Tony Basciano, September 2000.
4. Copp and McAndrew, *Battle Exhaustion*, 214.
5. William Smith, *What Time the Tempest*, in Copp and McAndrew, *Battle Exhaustion*, 102.
6. Fr. Tom Lenane to Mary Ellen Pringle, August 8, 1945.
7. Fr. B. S. Farrell to Fr. Kinlin, July 5, 1945.
8. "Rhyme and Reason," in *The Maple Leaf*, RG24 Vol. 16644 NAC, February 1945.
9. Interview with Ruth Jamieson, April 2001.
10. Interview with David Bergman, March 2000.
11. Interview with Fr. Bill Curran, April 2001.
12. Military Service Record of Harold Joseph Pringle.
13. Military Service Record of John Norman McGillivray.
14. Military Service Record of John Norman McGillivray.
15. Research trip, November 2000.
16. Sister Mary Anselm to Mary Ellen Pringle, August 8, 1945.
17. Sister Mary Anselm to Mary Ellen Pringle, March 26, 1946.
18. Sister Mary Anselm to Mary Ellen Pringle, April 12, 1947.
19. Interview with Tony Basciano, September 2000.
20. Interview with Tony Basciano, September 2000.
21. Military Service Record of Gunner Clement Ceccacci B-18135.
22. Ibid.
23. Ibid.
24. Interview with Hugh Ramsay Park, April 2000.
25. "Rhyme and Reason," *The Maple Leaf*, RG24 Vol. 16644, February 1945.

BIBLIOGRAPHY

While I consulted many books during the course of doing research, the following were particularly helpful:

Boyes, Robert. *In Glasshouses: A History of the Military Provost Staff Corps.* Colchester, UK: Military Provost Staff Corps Association, 1988.

Browne, Douglas G., and E. V. Tullett. *Bernard Spilsbury, His Life and Cases.* London: Harrap, 1952.

Calvert, Michael, with Peter Young. *A Dictionary of Battles.* New York: Mayflower Books, 1979.

Cannaviello, Vincenzo. *Avellino e L'Irpinia nella Tragedia del 1943–1944.* Rome: Pergola, 1999.

Cederberg, Fred. *The Long Road Home: The Autobiography of a Canadian Soldier in Italy in World War II.* Toronto: Stoddart, 1984.

Copp, Terry, and Bill McAndrew. *Battle Exhaustion: Soldiers and Psychiatrists in the Canadian Army, 1939–1945.* Montreal: McGill-Queens University Press, 1990.

Dancocks, Daniel G. *The D-Day Dodgers: The Canadians in Italy, 1943–1945.* Toronto: McClelland & Stewart, 1991.

Dougal, Sonia. *Front-Line Story: The Language of Suggestion and Desuggestion on the Front-line in Italy, 1943–1945.* Fribourg, Switzerland: Editions Universitaires Fribourg Suisse, 1996.

Fussell, Paul. *Wartime: Understanding and Behavior in the Second World War.* New York: Oxford University Press, 1989.

Hapgood, David, and David Richardson. *Monte Cassino*. North Ryde, UK; London: Angus & Robertson, 1984.

Lewis, Norman. *Naples '44*. London, UK: Collins, 1978.

Malaparte, Curzio. *The Skin*. Translated by David Moore. London: Alvin Redman Ltd., 1952.

McDougall, Colin. *Execution*. Toronto: Macmillan, 1958.

Mowat, Farley. *And No Birds Sang*. Toronto: McClelland & Stewart, 1979.

———. *My Father's Son: Memories of War and Peace*. Toronto: Key Porter, 1992.

———. *The Regiment*. Toronto: McClelland & Stewart, 1955.

Nolan, Brian. *King's War: Mackenzie King and the Politics of War, 1939–1945*. Toronto: Random House, 1988.

Stacey, C. P., and Barbara M. Wilson. *The Half-Million: The Canadians in Britain, 1939–1946*. Toronto: University of Toronto Press, 1987.

Trevelyan, Raleigh. *Rome '44: The Battle for the Eternal City*. London: Secker & Warburg, 1981.

ACKNOWLEDGMENTS

In the course of researching and writing *A Keen Soldier*, I asked for, and received, help and support from friends, colleagues and complete strangers.

I owe a great debt to my editor and friend, Diane Martin, whose patience and skill helped bring *A Keen Soldier* into being. Thanks also to Louise Dennys at Knopf, as well as my copy-editor, Stephanie Fysh.

Thanks to my long-time agent and friend, Dean Cooke, who believed in this book before everyone else and who helped me find the right publisher. Thanks also to David Johnston and Suzanne Brandreth.

Thanks to Harold Pringle's sisters, Teresa and Veronica, for being brave enough to stand up for a brother lost a half century ago.

Thanks to all the veterans, and their families, who shared their stories with me. In particular: H. Ramsay Park, for his candour and courage; Tony and Pat Basciano; Ivan and Irene Gunter; and Justice Michael Cloney. Thanks to war correspondents such as George Powell, Bill Boss, Bill Stewart and Norman Quick for their insights into Canada's war in Italy.

Thanks to Father Bill Curran and Father Simon Giles.

I owe a huge debt of thanks to military historian Bill McAndrew for his expert guidance and advice.

Thanks to Nicoletta Barbarito and Helene Lafortune at the Canadian Embassy in Rome. Also to Rita Melillo, Benito Scopa and

Andrea Massaro in Avellino. Thanks to Oreste Schiano di Zenise in Naples. Thanks to Matthew Kneale and Shannon Russell for a place to stay in Alatri. Also to John Montesano, Aldo di Felice, Agatha Pezzi and Francesco Broccolo at the Telelatino Network. Thanks to my Italian teacher, Antonio Rossini, and to Marco Blefari for help with translation.

Thanks to my family. Thanks to my grandmother Marion Jamieson; my mother, Lynn Jamieson, and her husband, Geoffrey Lester; my brother, Matthew Clark, and his wife, Heidi; my sister, Amy Lester, cousin Alexander Jamieson and my aunts and uncles, Bruce Jamieson, Judy Salley, Nancy Jamieson and Ruth Jamieson, who provided me with their stories. Thanks to my father, C. Scott Clark, his wife, Jocelyn Nadon, and my stepsister, Pamela Matthews. Thanks also to friends such as Kris Begic, David Borenstein, Lisa Wood, Micah Lax, Gordon Stewart and Margaret Corea.

I am enormously grateful to the staff at the National Archives of Canada. In particular, I owe thanks to Larry Richer of the Access to Information and Privacy Division, who adroitly balanced the public's right to know with the individual's right to privacy.

Finally, thanks to my fiancée, Susan Catto, for advice, assistance and for living with me while I lived with this book. Thanks to my young daughter, Ella, who is always an inspiration.

INDEX